Lecture Notes in Computer Science 4922

Commenced Publication in 1973
Founding and Former Series Editors:
Gerhard Goos, Juris Hartmanis, and Jan van Leeuwen

T0223175

Manfred Broy   Ingolf H. Krüger
Michael Meisinger (Eds.)

Model-Driven Development of Reliable Automotive Services

Second Automotive Software Workshop, ASWSD 2006
San Diego, CA, USA, March 15-17, 2006
Revised Selected Papers

 Springer

Volume Editors

Manfred Broy
Technische Universität München, Institut für Informatik
Boltzmannstr. 3, 85748 Garching, Germany
E-mail: broy@in.tum.de

Ingolf H. Krüger
University of California at San Diego, Computer Science and Engineering
9500 Gilman Drive, La Jolla, CA 92093-0404, USA
E-mail: ikrueger@ucsd.edu

Michael Meisinger
University of California at San Diego
California Institute for Telecommunications and Information Technology
9500 Gilman Drive, La Jolla, CA 92093-0436, USA
E-mail: mmeisinger@ucsd.edu

Library of Congress Control Number: Applied for

CR Subject Classification (1998): C.2.4, C.3, C.5.3, D.4, H.3-5, J.7

LNCS Sublibrary: SL 3 – Information Systems and Application, incl. Internet/Web
and HCI

ISSN   0302-9743
ISBN-10   3-540-70929-0 Springer Berlin Heidelberg New York
ISBN-13   978-3-540-70929-9 Springer Berlin Heidelberg New York

Springer is a part of Springer Science+Business Media

springer.com

© Springer-Verlag Berlin Heidelberg 2008
Printed in Germany

Typesetting: Camera-ready by author, data conversion by Scientific Publishing Services, Chennai, India
Printed on acid-free paper   SPIN: 12444144   06/3180   5 4 3 2 1 0

Preface

Software development for the automotive domain has become the enabling technology for almost all safety-critical and comfort functions offered to the customer. Ninety percent of all innovations in automotive systems are directly or indirectly enabled by embedded software. The numbers of serious accidents have declined in recent years, despite constantly increasing traffic; this is correlated with the introduction of advanced, software-enabled functionality for driver assistance, such as electronic stability control. Software contributes significantly to the automotive value chain. By 2010 it is estimated that software will make up 40% of the value creation of automotive electrics/electronics.

However, with the large number of software-enabled functions, their interactions, and the corresponding networking and operating infrastructure, come significant complexities both during the automotive systems engineering process and at runtime. A central challenge for automotive systems development is the scattering of functionality across multiple subsystems, such as electronic control units (ECUs) and the associated networks. As an example, consider the central locking systems (CLS), whose functionality is spread out over up to 19 different ECUs in some luxury cars. Of course, this includes advanced functionality, such as seat positioning and radio tuning according to driver presets upon entry, as well as unlocking in case of a detected impact or accident. However, this example demonstrates that modern automotive systems bridge comfort- and safety-critical functionality. This induces particular demands on safety and security, and, in general, software and systems quality. The resulting challenges and opportunities were discussed, in depth, at the second Automotive Software Workshop San Diego (ASWSD) 2006, on whose results we report here.

Automotive systems are prime examples of the class of *cyber-physical* systems, i.e., systems that combine IT infrastructure and functionality with the control of physical processes. Consequently, the development process for automotive systems has to take into account both the physical environment and its representation in digital systems that get deployed in the vehicle. As an example, cars have a broad spectrum of timing requirements, ranging from hard real-time constraints at the level of motor control to soft real-time constraints at the level of infotainment systems. Automotive systems span the entire spectrum from time- and value-continuous, to mixed continuous and discrete, to discrete systems. The engineering processes used for automotive software have to take these and other domain-specific constraints into account – seamlessly from requirements elicitation to deployment and quality assurance.

Increasingly, industry and academia try to address this challenge by introducing comprehensive requirements and architecture models that capture key domain aspects *and* enable exploitation in terms of code synthesis, simulation and, more generally, verification, and validation. A further goal in adopting a model-based approach to automotive systems engineering is seen in the opportunity to decouple the *logical* from the *deployment* architecture of the vehicle. This decoupling holds the promise for a true product-line approach where conceptualizations of automotive systems structure and behavior are systematically reused across different car models. For instance, CLSs exist in almost all modern cars. Yet, we know that most software functions are developed afresh in the transition from one car model to the next. Furthermore, automotive manufacturers and suppliers hope to have models that help them contain the enormous space of variants and configurations that emerges from the possible combinations of software-enabled functions and their parameterizations.

Of course, due to the traditionally distributed engineering processes between OEMs (original equipment manufacturers, such as car makers) and multiple tiers of suppliers, models are needed that increase the precision and understanding in the communication between OEMs and suppliers. Consequently, to be of value, the models chosen need to be unambiguous to the highest degree possible, yet allow a broad spectrum of properties of structure and behavior to be specified. It is this tradeoff between precision and expressiveness that is a recurring theme through many of the contributions contained in this post-proceedings volume of ASWSD 2006.

Advanced development methods such as tailored development processes, structured systems and software architectures, model-driven development techniques and notations as well as formalized techniques of quality assurance have emerged as an approach to dealing with the mentioned demands and complexities, in particular during the analysis, specification and design phases of the development process. Such advanced development approaches have numerous benefits and advantages, including:

- They provide a basis for traceability from requirements specifications to implementation artifacts. This enables model-based requirements tracing, verification and validation approaches, and addresses systematic changes to models during the development process.
- They hold the promise of reduced turn-around times in iterative and incremental software and systems development. They enable engineers to explore model changes before changing the actual system.
- They support product-line software development by separating different functions for product line alternatives in an otherwise common, integrated model.
- Models, description techniques and associated development processes can be coordinated to provide contiguous, gap-free refinement and transformation steps from requirements to code. Models are connected and integrated to span all abstraction levels. This enables design tools, test and verification tools and code generators to work from the same sets of models to provide improved software quality.

On the infrastructure side, service-oriented architectures and automotive middleware platforms, such as AUTOSAR, are emerging as a means to manage the complex dependencies between vehicular functions, to provide standardized, scalable, and validated infrastructures.

Mastering the complexities of future-generation automotive software development poses a number of important, cross-disciplinary research challenges. The transition from monolithic to flexible, service-oriented solutions requires advances in all aspects of the development process; this includes, in particular, the selection of an adequate service model and corresponding development techniques, together with supporting software infrastructures.

The goal for ASWSD 2006 was to bring together experts from industry and academia who work on highly complex, distributed, reactive software systems related to the automotive domain, and to discuss and further the understanding of the following focus areas:

- Automotive models and model-driven development
- Automotive software and systems architectures
- Automotive domain architectures
- Automotive software services and service-oriented development
- Automotive hardware, middleware, and software platforms
- On- and off-board ad-hoc networking
- Networked automotive services
- Mobile sensor networks
- Reliability, security and privacy for automotive software
- Enabling technologies for telematics applications

The workshop took place March 15–17, 2006 in La Jolla, CA, USA, at the California Institute for Telecommunications and Information Technology (Calit2). It contributed to fostering a deeper understanding of the research challenges and agendas in this area. Potentials for cross-disciplinary research, as well as pertinent curricula and training programs to address these challenges, were identified and discussed.

The workshop program consisted of five keynote presentations, 13 technical paper presentations, a poster session and two panel discussions. The workshop spanned 2 1/2 days and was divided into the following topical sessions: Quality Assurance (QA), Real-Time Control (RT), Services and Components (SC), and Model-Based Development and Tools (MD). The pre-proceedings, consisting of the presentation slide sets, were made available at *http://aswsd.ucsd.edu/2006*.

To foster discussion on cross-cutting and interdisciplinary topics, the organizers decided to have five keynote presentations – three from industry and two from academia, as well as two panel discussions as integral parts of the workshop program. Bruce Emaus (Vector CANtech), Rajesh Gupta (University of California, San Diego), Jeff Greenberg (Ford Motor Company), Thomas Kropf (Robert Bosch GmbH), and Alberto Sangiovanni-Vincentelli (University of California, Berkeley) were recruited as keynote speakers. Professors Frieder Seible (Dean, Jacobs School of Engineering, UCSD) and Larry Smarr (Director, Calit2) delivered opening remarks on the first day of the workshop.

The first keynote presentation, opening the Model-Based Development and Tools session, was given by *Bruce Emaus* (President of Vector CANtech). It was titled "Model-Based Development in the Upcoming Automotive Embedded Software Architecture of AUTOSAR." As automotive product architectures continue to migrate toward higher levels of distribution with increasing system and software complexity, the use of model-driven automotive embedded software development is rapidly changing as the industry pushes forward with a new automotive software architecture called AUTOSAR. This presentation discussed both the essential business case for AUTOSAR and the design challenges of model-based software development in the automotive distributed embedded system domain.

Rajesh Gupta (University of California, San Diego) presented insight into new approaches for hardware design in his talk "Meta Modeling for Component Compositions: A Hardware Guy's View." He stated that novel computational fabrics are approaching intrinsic silicon efficiencies, imposing challenges to ensure programmability and program models. Currently, a methodology evolution occurs from chip design to embedded software design. The availability of programming models, methods and language support for building embedded systems (on chip) will be critical to exploiting the enormous technology capacities. New methods will mature that enable systematic modeling and exploitation of meta-data in design, verification, and synthesis. Gupta showed an approach to developing compositional, verifiable system-on-chip specifications in SystemC. He also hinted at opportunities for marrying service-oriented development techniques increasingly popular in software with a traditional system on chip development.

Jeff Greenberg (Manager of the VIRTTEX driving simulator at Ford Motor Company and Ford's Senior Technical Leader for automotive HMI) explained the challenge of automotive systems engineering from multiple angles. He focused on the necessity to create a simulation platform that not only is able to incorporate the emerging advanced software-enabled automotive systems, but also allows evaluation of the resulting human machine interface (HMI) concerns. The latter becomes increasingly important to ensure that the benefits of driver safety brought about by novel electronic features outweigh the increasing distraction drivers are exposed to (e.g., cell phone use during vehicle operation.)

Thomas Kropf (Vice President for system and software engineering, Driver Assistance Systems, Robert Bosch GmbH) delivered the keynote presentation "Driver Assistance Systems: Challenges for Automotive System and Software Design." He explained recent developments in the domain of driver assistance systems and described the challenges automotive suppliers are facing today in system and software design. He presented examples for new design methods, tools and processes which are used to overcome the current design limitations. Kropf's presentation pointed out the difficulty in applying traditional formal methods in the rich requirements spectrum of automotive systems outlined above.

Alberto Sangiovanni-Vincentelli (University of California, Berkeley) discussed the question "Is Embedded Software for Safety Critical Automotive Systems Really a Software Problem?" in his presentation, delivered by Manfred Broy. He stated that embedded software design is one, albeit critical, aspect of the more general problem of embedded system design, which is about the implementation of a set of functionalities satisfying a number of constraints ranging from performance to cost, emissions, power consumption, and weight. Sangiovanni-Vincentelli's presentation illustrated the main challenges and opportunities of vertical design chain integration. In addition, it presented platform-based design as an important approach to meeting challenges and taking advantage of opportunities in automotive systems development. Platform-based design is a design methodology where reuse and programmability are central. It is an approach that provides unified and harmonious views on embedded software design and hardware architecture, consisting of formal techniques at the abstract level facilitating early verification with the correct set of tools and methods. The Metropolis environment was described as a framework to sustain the methodology.

Two panel discussions complemented the keynote presentations. The first panel discussed "Integrated Automotive System Development – Process, Challenges and Opportunities." Panelists were *Jeff Greenberg* (Ford Motor Company), *Rajesh Gupta* (University of California, San Diego), *Edward Lee* (University of California, Berkeley), and *Wolfgang Pree* (University of Salzburg). The panelists discussed the various phases of the automotive engineering process, into which the software/hardware co-design process is embedded. The malleability of software was discussed as a particular challenge in the seamlessness from early requirements to simulation to implementation and quality assurance. On the technical side, the panelists discussed the absence of adequate programming models that take time (hard- and soft real time) into consideration as a first-class citizen. Consequently, the spectrum from continuous to mixed continuous/discrete to discrete automotive software has yet to be mastered. The panelists formulated this as a challenge for the research community.

The second panel discussed "Model-Based Service Engineering for Automotive – Hype and Substance." Panelists were *Bernhard Schätz* (Technische Universität München, Germany), *Bruce Emaus* (Vector CANtech), *Thomas Kropf* (Robert Bosch GmbH), *Klaus Müller-Glaser* (University of Karlsruhe), and *Daniel Gajski* (University of California, Irvine). The discussion emphasized the increasingly distributed nature of functions realized by automotive software. Signals and information from components are combined in ways that were not intended originally. Service-oriented concepts can effectively help to manage the complexities caused by this heterogeneity. Initial approaches to introducing service-oriented concepts can already be found in industry – sometimes under different names. One of the biggest challenges is the absence of suitable models to describe the functions and their dependencies in a service-oriented way, in addition to existing implementation and hardware-oriented models of automotive controller components.

The discussion also emphasized the importance of approaching automotive system design from a user's view, focusing on the applications that the car as a system provides to its users. Automotive system services should be designed from the perspective of users and applications, not as a combination of pieces of functionality from existing components. The dependency of user-relevant services must be captured in suitable models.

In both panels, it was observed that in automotive system design the black-box controller business model, as a hardware/software unit of specification, integration, maintenance, and contract, is still predominant. This defines the OEM–supplier relationship. Providing pure software solutions to OEMs is currently not a viable business model for suppliers. Here, the industry needs to change and research needs to come up with suitable service-oriented business models and system development models. Automotive systems must open up to facilitate addition of new services – inside and outside of the vehicle. Infotainment systems were cited as likely first candidates to go in this direction.

A poster presentation session provided the opportunity to showcase current research projects for invited presenters from academia and automotive industry.

This volume includes a selection of refereed technical and invited papers presented at the workshop. In the following, we give a brief overview of the selected papers and their contents.

The paper "The Case for Modeling Security, Privacy, Usability, and Reliability (SPUR) in Automotive Software" by *Prasad et al.* emphasizes the importance of the attributes security, privacy, usability, and reliability (SPUR) in creating specifications for embedded in-vehicle automotive software. The paper reviews several real-world use-cases and their functional and non-functional system requirements. From there, the authors derive underlying automotive architectural elements spanning multiple software service domains. In particular, the suggested approach elevates the SPUR requirements from an afterthought to the earliest requirements and architecture design phases.

Neema et al. target the issue of model ambiguities across different tools and methods in their paper "Addressing Cross-Tool Semantic Ambiguities in Behavior Modeling for Vehicle Motion Control." They provide a model and semantics for behavior specifications in the automotive vehicle motion control (VMC) domain, facilitating the exchange of finite state machine models across different tools, and leading towards automated correct interpretation. The authors introduce an extended finite state machine metamodel (eFSM) with semantics definitions based on a mathematical framework. They show how models developed within commercial tool environments are checked for conformance with eFSM-models, promising higher-confidence software engineering for the VMC domain.

The paper "A Software and System Modeling Facility for Vehicle Environment Interactions" by *Nelson and Huang* describes an advanced modeling facility for system and software design, intended to address the growing complexity of automotive embedded software and the resulting issues for vehicle development. Increased complexity will require a broader range of modeling capabilities beyond functional/behavioral modeling. The authors present a more comprehensive modeling process with the capability to model vehicle systems from multiple viewpoints, such as the traditional functional point of view and the viewpoints of software structure, component interactions, and the human-machine interface. All viewpoints are brought together in a common set of models.

Anand et al. describe an approach for "Generating Sound and Resource-Aware Code From Hybrid Systems Models" in their contribution. The authors propose a framework for generating resource-aware code from hybrid systems models with guarantees of no switching discrepancies. They propose an approach to handling faulty transitions and compute execution rates for minimizing missed transitions. The approach is an effort at bridging the semantic gap between the model and the code due to discretization and resource constraints. This work helps to address remaining issues related to ensuring correctness of the implementation with respect to the model in model-based development of real-time embedded systems.

"Towards Verification of Model Transformations via Goal-Directed Certification," a contribution by *Karsai and Narayanan*, investigates a technique called 'goal-directed certification' that provides a pragmatic solution to the problem of verifying the correctness of model transformations within model-based development approaches. Model transformations include generating code from models, transforming design models into analysis models, and transforming a model between variants of a formalism (such as variants of Statecharts). The authors use concepts of bisimulation to verify whether a certain transformation instance preserved certain properties and subsequently extend this idea using weak bisimulation and semantic anchoring to a more general class of transformations.

The paper "An Instrumentation-Based Approach to Controller Model Validation" by *Cleaveland, Smolka and Sims* discusses the concept of instrumentation-based validation (IBV): the use of model instrumentation and coverage-based testing to validate models of embedded control software. Assertions, formalized requirements, are realized through monitors that observe the behavior of executing controller models, which are instrumented with these assertions. The authors describe an implementation within the Reactis tool suite for the automated testing and validation of controller models given in Simulink/Stateflow.

Grossmann et al. describe "TestML – A Test Exchange Language for Model-Based Testing of Embedded Software" in their contribution. TestML supports the exchange of tests between different test notations in a heterogeneous tool environment, for instance, facilitating the reuse of tests between different test levels, such as such as model-in-the-loop (MIL), software-in-the-loop (SIL), and hardware-in-the-loop (HIL) tests. The authors introduce the XML schema of TestML and demonstrate the efficiency of the interchange format by giving examples from the model-based development of electronic control units. Tool support is illustrated by an application with Simulink/Stateflow.

The paper "Towards Integrated Model-Driven Verification and Empirical Validation of Reusable Software Frameworks for Automotive Systems" by *Subramonian and Gill* claims that leveraging reusable software frameworks in the development of automotive systems offers significant potential to reduce engineering costs and cycle times, caused by rapidly increasing complexity and scale. The authors show the relevance of reusable software frameworks, describe an approach to verification and validation of such frameworks based on timed automata models, and present an evaluation of their approach.

Pree and Templ describe in their paper "Modeling with the Timing Definition Language (TDL)" the model-based development process of hard real-time software with the TDL. They explain the modeling and simulation of TDL components in Matlab/Simulink, their mapping to a specific platform, and code generation. The authors claim that benefits of applying a TDL-based development process are significant development and maintenance cost savings, and, for instance, increased flexibility for automakers to change the execution platforms and, if necessary, redefine the OEM-supplier relationship.

"Towards Model-Driven Development of Hard Real-Time Systems—Integrating ASCET-MD and aiT/StackAnalyzer" by *Ferdinand et al.* presents tools, experimental integration, preliminary results, and plans for further tool integration of automatic code generators such as ETAS' ASCET, and static program analysis tools like AbsInt's StackAnalyzer and the timing analyzer aiT. Through an integration of these tools it is, for instance, possible to give ASCET users a direct feedback on the effects of their design decisions on resource usage, allowing them to select more efficient designs and implementation methods, by making aiT/StackAnalyzer analysis results accessible from within ASCET.

Finally, *Giese* introduces "Reusable Services and Semi-Automatic Service Composition for Automotive Software." The author describes a service-oriented approach for the reuse of automotive software functions across models; it exploits a recombination of functions in a restricted manner in order to enable reuse. The author shows how all phases of the development process can benefit from a service-oriented approach and describes how advanced synthesis techniques can be employed to reuse components, patterns, and services and compose them with only minimal manual efforts.

The workshop clearly exhibited the state of the art of model-based automotive software engineering and pointed out various challenges in the area. This is also reflected by the papers selected for this volume.

The organizers were delighted to again observe the extremely positive experience created through the dialog between leading researchers and industry participants from the USA and Europe. During the workshop significant progress was achieved to develop a common understanding of the challenging problems in the automotive domain such as:

– Models and model-transformations for hard and soft real-time systems
– Comprehensive engineering approaches for model-driven hardware/software co-design
– Integrating HMI design and development with automotive systems engineering processes
– Transitioning from component- to service-oriented systems engineering to support product-line development and reuse

The comments we received from participants during and after the workshop were overwhelmingly positive. In particular, the combination of and balance between industrial and academic participation with high-quality contributions from both sides was remarked as a distinguishing positive element of this workshop series.

The organizers and editors extend their profound thanks to all workshop participants, authors, keynote speakers, panelists, poster presenters, reviewers, sponsors, and members of the local organization team for their important contributions to the success of the workshop itself and of this post-proceedings volume.

This material is based on work supported by the National Science Foundation under Grants No. CNS-0413136 and CCF-0702791. Any opinions, findings, and conclusions or recommendations expressed in this material are those of the author(s) and do not necessarily reflect the views of the National Science Foundation.

February 2008   Manfred Broy
                                             Ingolf H. Krüger
                                          Michael Meisinger

AUTOMOTIVE SOFTWARE WORKSHOP SAN DIEGO 2006

Organizers

Manfred Broy
Ingolf H. Krüger
Michael Meisinger

Referees

Sushil Birla
Rance Cleaveland
Mirko Conrad
Werner Damm
Frederic Doucet
Claudiu Farcas
Christian Ferdinand
Christopher Gill
Carlo Ghezzi
Jürgen Grossmann
Stefan Henkler
Gabor Karsai
Hermann Kopetz
Edward Lee
Holger Giese
Thomas J. Giuli
Klaus Müller-Glaser
Sandeep Neema
Edward Nelson
K. Venkatesh Prasad
Wolfgang Pree
Stefan Resmerita
Alberto Sangiovanni-Vincentelli
Bernhard Schätz
Doug Schmidt
Joseph Sifakis
Gerald Stieglbauer
Janos Sztipanovits
Shigeharu Teshima

Local Arrangements

Barbara Haynor
Steve Hopper
Alexandra Hubenko-Baker
Michael Meisinger

Thanks To

David Bareno
Maureen C. Curran
DeAndra Green
Barbara Haynor
David Hutches
Jürgen Schulze

Sponsors

California Institute for Telecommunication and Information Technology (Calit2)
National Science Foundation (NSF)

Table of Contents

Services and Components

The Case for Modeling Security, Privacy, Usability and Reliability (SPUR) in Automotive Software

K. Venkatesh Prasad, Thomas J. Giuli, and David Watson

Ford Motor Company, Dearborn, MI 48121, USA
{kprasad,tgiuli,dwatso80}@ford.com

Abstract. During the past few years, there has been considerable growth in the practice of modeling automotive software requirements. Much of this growth has been centered on software requirements and its value in the context of specific functional areas of an automobile, such as powertrain, chassis, body, safety and infotainment systems. This paper makes a case for modeling four cross-functional attributes of software, namely security, privacy, usability, and reliability, or SPUR. These attributes are becoming increasingly important as automobiles become information conduits. We outline why these SPUR attributes are important in creating specifications for embedded in-vehicle automotive software.

Several real-world use-cases are reviewed to illustrate both consumer needs and system requirements — functional and non-functional system requirements. From these requirements the underlying architectural elements of automotive SPUR are also derived. Broadly speaking these elements span three software service domains: the off-board enterprise software domain, the nomadic (device or service) software domain and the embedded (in-vehicle) software domain, all of which need to work in tandem for the complete lifecycle management of automotive software.

1 Introduction

The nature and terrain of computing in the automobile is in a state of transition. Automotive computing is transforming from being function-oriented to being service oriented, while the terrain (or logical boundaries) of computing *in* an automobile is expanding to include both computing elements in the wireless external infrastructure and the nomadic (or hand held, mobile) infrastructure. This transition is being driven on the one hand by consumers, wanting to keep pace with their changing life styles and, on the other hand, by regulatory agencies placing more stringent demands on the attributes such as safety, emissions, fuel economy. Given the transformation in the nature and terrain of automotive computing, this paper makes the case for modeling security, privacy, usability and reliability (SPUR) — motivated in part by David Patterson's manifesto [1].

M. Broy, I.H. Krüger, and M. Meisinger (Eds.): ASWSD 2006, LNCS 4922, pp. 1–14, 2008.

For nearly a century, the automobile was defined by components with local functionality and differentiated by proprietary systems engineering implementations involving mostly mechanical coupling between components. Over the past three decades, with the advent of microelectronics and local-area networks [2] in the automobile, there has been a steady growth in the use of mechatronics [3] and the practice of allocating functions across multiple components. The applications of systems engineering principles, in turn has been extended to a combination of mechanical, electronic, digital, analog (or discrete-time, continuous-time) sub-systems and components. With the growing maturity of the software ecosystem [4], including operating systems, programming languages, development environments, and engineering tools, the modern automobile is being increasingly defined by software. There is a trend to allocate automobile functions across multiple standardized components (to reduce the number or unique hardware modules) and to use software design, modeling and engineering for function implementation and associated product differentiation [5]. In this context, the automobile is rapidly becoming a distributed computing environment.

Commensurate with the growth in demand for new features, from both consumers and regulatory agencies, is the increase in the complexity of functional allocation across the distributed computing environment in the vehicle. In addition, the computing terrain of the automobile is rapidly changing [6]. With the advent of wireless personal, local, and wide-area technologies, the physical boundary of the automobile is no longer the logical bounding box for functional allocation. Functions may be distributed across on-board computing units [5], off-board (such as roadside) infrastructure units [7] and nomadic devices [8] such as cellular phones.

To manage this growth in the complexity of allocating functions, a higher level of abstraction will likely be required. A service-oriented computing approach [9] is an attractive option. The present day automobile is function-defined — most consumer perceived features are based on the specification of distributed on-board functions; the future automobile will likely be service-defined, with features being specified, modeled and synthesized by aggregating consumer and vehicle related services from both on-board and off-board sources.

The next section (Section 2) of this paper elaborates the case for SPUR in the automotive context and outlines the role of modeling SPUR. Section 3 introduces two broad examples that highlight the new computational terrain of the automobile and the role of modeling SPUR in these contexts: one example shows how the computational terrain logically extends from the the physical boundaries of the automobile into the roadside infrastructure and the second example illustrates how the new automotive computational terrain extends through nomadic devices and services into the wide area communication networks (such as the wireless telephony networks and, in general, the wireless internet). Section 4 shows how SPUR attributes associated with a specific use-case could be modeled. Section 5 lists requirements for tools needed to develop SPUR models. Section 6 discusses related work. Section 7, in conclusion, summarizes the need to model SPUR in the automotive context.

2 SPUR in the Automotive Context

SPUR [1] was advocated on the premise of shifting research efforts in computer science and engineering away from making faster, cheaper systems to making systems that are more secure, privacy-preserving, usable, and reliable. While these attributes can take on many meanings, we are interested in applying them to the experience of the individual people who own and interact with these systems on a daily basis. For example, while security and reliability can be seen as two sides of the same coin from a technology perspective, from a user's perspective they are two very distinct concepts. A system that constantly fails impacts a user very differently from a system that causes her credit card to be stolen. In this context, we believe that the automotive industry is particularly well-suited to understand the value of each aspect of SPUR-oriented design.

Security in the automotive domain has so far emphasized physical security. The first automobiles were produced without any built-in theft deterrents. Gradually they acquired keys to start the engine and door locks to protect property left in the vehicle. Modern vehicles now use sophisticated radio transmission devices with strong cryptography to prevent unauthorized entry.

Network connectivity is being added to vehicles through telematics services (e.g., OnStar,® BMW ASSIST^{TM}) and hands-free telephony, introducing the possibility of remote intrusion into a vehicle's embedded networks. Not only could a remote intrusion compromise the physical security of the vehicle (i.e., unauthorized remote unlock), but it could directly affect the vehicle's drivability. For example, a virus could trigger the vehicle's theft alarm while driving. Clearly, as the automotive industry integrates more digital network technology into vehicles, its impact on both physical and digital security must be assessed.

On the flip-side of the security coin is a concern for privacy. Modern vehicles "know" much more about their drivers and passengers than ever before. Vehicular navigation systems could be used to correlate data and extract potentially private information. For example, correlating driver location data with the locations of points of interest such as stores, places of worship, community centers and other buildings an organization can build an accurate profile of the driver's interests. The privacy concerns of automobile customers must be treated seriously and safeguarded with the introduction of new technologies such as telematics and navigation services.

The usability aspect of SPUR in the automotive context is especially important because of its impact on safety. An automobile's human-machine interface (HMI) must allow the driver to focus on the task of driving while at the same time providing un-occluded access to driver information as well as comfort and convenience features such as climate and radio controls. Complicating the matter are the integration of new technologies such as mobile phone services, voicemail, messaging, and email into the vehicle HMI. A balance must be struck between the complexity of an HMI with many features and safe usability.

Reliability has been a serious concern in the automotive industry and in the consuming public's minds for some time now. Automobiles are increasingly becoming software-driven, not just mechanically driven. Therefore, software reliability will be as important as mechanical reliability in future automobiles.

Table 1 outlines automotive examples that exhibit varying combinations of SPUR attributes. Each row categorizes examples as having or lacking some SPUR attributes. In the text that follows, we describe the reasoning behind the values assigned for each row:

- The Carfax® web service allows anyone to view detailed maintenance and accident histories of any vehicle for a fee. The service must be secure to prevent unauthorized tampering with vehicle records, usable enough for anyone to understand, and reliable to provide correct information. It's important to note that we're considering these attributes from the perspective of an individual user of the system. In this context, these attributes are neither orthogonal or rigorously defined. Instead, these attributes are intended to direct attention to attributes that can be easily overlooked when designing systems that are bigger, better, and faster.
- Safety is the primary concern of anti-lock braking systems (ABS) and so naturally the desire for reliability is high. Along similar reasoning, ABS must be easy and intuitive enough in its function such that untrained drivers can use the system. Security is as much of a concern as for any safety-critical module and should not be vulnerable to remote attack. Privacy is not much of a concern because the ABS does not collect or process any sensitive data to function properly.
- Comparing a standard door key and a valet key, we see that they are similar except in the privacy attribute. Both keys and their associated locking mechanisms must be secure enough to prevent people without keys from entering, both must be highly usable and reliable. However, while a standard door key should grant the holder access to all parts of the vehicle, the valet key is designed to prevent the valet from entering "private" areas, such as gloveboxes or trunks.

Table 1. Examples illustrating SPUR in an automotive context and the relative importance (Low, Medium, High) of each SPUR attribute to each example

Example	S	P	U	R
Carfax® database	H	L	H	H
Anti-lock braking system	M	L	H	H
Door key	H	L	H	H
Valet key	H	H	H	H

The examples shown in Table 1 have software that resides either wholly inside the vehicle, or entirely outside the vehicle. Conversely, software implementing sophisticated telematics services reside not only on-board the vehicle but also off-board, including the IT infrastructure of original equipment manufacturers (OEMs), dealerships, telecommunications operators, and in hand held consumer

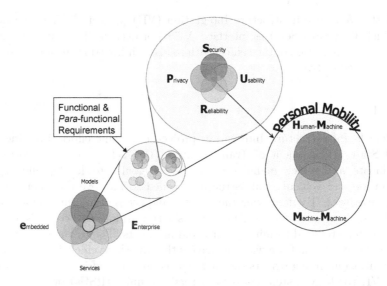

Fig. 1. Diagram of automotive SPUR

devices. Because of the new push of automotive software across module and vehicular boundaries, there is a need to develop models that cross these boundaries as well. Furthermore, because vehicular telematics software relies on dynamic external software, models of telematics systems must change along with deployed systems. A service-oriented approach to implementing automotive software — both in-vehicle software as well as enterprise software — eases the design, implementation and maintenance of systems to ensure that each requirement of SPUR design is present in the system.

Figure 1 illustrates this interesting space. As we stated before, we believe it is important to understand how to model services that cross the embedded and enterprise domains. Within this space are both functional and para-functional (or non-functional) requirements. Functional requirements are more visible, however we believe that the para-functional requirements will be increasingly important. In particular, we are interested in understanding how the mobility inherent in a vehicle impacts this space. Providing functionality to a person driving at highway speeds requires strong attention to SPUR both at the human to machine interface as well as the machine to machine interface. The safety and quality of the driving experience is clearly affected by these attributes. At the same time, designing computer communications systems that support SPUR concerns in these types of mobile applications requires careful attention to system interactions.

3   Examples of Automotive Services

In this section we use two examples to demonstrate the trend towards automotive services extending outside the physical constraints of the vehicle. The first is the Vehicle Infrastructure Integration (VII) project [7]. The second is the Vehicle Consumer Services Interface (VCSI) project [8]. These two examples demonstrate integration of the vehicle with roadside infrastructure and consumer services respectively.

3.1 VII

The Vehicle Infrastructure Integration project is a joint effort involving the United States Department of Transportation (USDOT), state transportation departments, and vehicle manufactures. The VII goal is to develop and deploy the roadside and vehicular infrastructure needed to improve the safety of the nation's roadways. By improving the amount and types of information available from the roadway and by having improved safety warnings and controls, drivers will be better prepared to mitigate or avoid accidents. The features enabled by VII include everything from warning drivers that another vehicle is about to run a red light, to notifying drivers that a given section of road is covered with ice.

The VII roadway system consists of roadside units (RSUs) deployed along highways and onboard units (OBUs) built into vehicles that communicate with each other using the Dedicated Short Range Communications (DSRC) protocol at 5.9GHz. The roadside units are wired to an information services backend that can track traffic conditions as well as log safety problems throughout the system. Vehicles transmit useful sensor data, such as GPS location, velocity, and traction to the roadside units, which in turn process the sensor data and report back to vehicles in the area if any safety issues may be present. For example, if several vehicles report that their traction control and anti-lock brake systems were activated at the same spot on the highway, the roadside unit nearest the problem area can broadcast a warning to oncoming vehicles. Vehicles can also communicate with other vehicles directly, enabling dynamic warnings such as a vehicle notifying the vehicles directly behind it that the driver is braking suddenly.

Table 2 lists the titles assigned to some of the first scenarios being considered. In addition, it highlights how important the SPUR attributes are to each scenario. In general, scenarios that are likely to affect driver behavior or well-being have a high impact from security. For example, an incorrect signal that an emergency vehicle is approaching could cause great headaches to drivers, and potentially disrupt the usage of this signal by true emergency vehicles. Thus, it's important that such a system be secure against malicious manipulation. On the other hand, spurious information about traffic is less likely to significantly impact drivers, hence it is listed as having medium importance relative to security.[1] Privacy is more of a concern when revealing information about specific vehicles, as in the case of intersection warnings. On the other hand, road conditions are likely to be broadcast to everybody, and therefore unlikely to contain a

---

[1] It's important to note that we're talking about a subjective measure of security for illustrative purposes. We strongly believe that all of these attributes are important considerations for any scenario.

Table 2. List of VII use cases and the relative importance (Low, Medium, High) of each SPUR attribute to each use case

Use case	S	P	U	R
Emergency Brake Warning	M	L	H	H
Curve Speed Warning	M	L	H	H
Traffic Signal Violation Warning	H	M	H	H
Stop Sign Violation Warning	H	M	H	H
Emergency Vehicle Approaching	H	L	H	H
In-Vehicle Signage	M	L	M	M
Traffic Information and alt route guidance	M	L	M	H
Electronic payments	H	H	M	H
Roadway Condition Information	M	L	H	H
Traffic Management	H	L	H	H
Emergency Vehicle At Scene	H	L	H	H

significant privacy risk. In general, usability and reliability are significant to all of these scenarios. In some cases, usability is less important, since the consequences are less severe.

3.2 VCSI

The second project, the Vehicle Consumer Services Interface (VCSI), is a project at Ford to provide an interface between consumers, their personal devices, off-board services, and vehicle systems including both networks and devices. VCSI is implemented as a service-oriented architecture, meaning that functions within the vehicle are designed as services to be used by other functions and may reside on one or more hardware modules. This design philosophy has advantages such as code reuse between modules and reduces the impact of the redesign of a module. For a more extensive treatment of VCSI see [8].

To demonstrate this system, we developed a prototype vehicle that contained several specific applications including those shown in Table 3. As with the VII examples above, we've made some attempt to demonstrate the relative importance of each SPUR attribute to each service. Since most of the consumer facing

Table 3. List of VCSI services and the relative importance (Low, Medium, High) of each SPUR attribute to each service

Service	S	P	U	R
Vehicle Personalization	L	H	M	H
Personal Information Management	H	H	M	M
MyHome (Home Automation Services)	H	H	M	M
Bluetooth Technology	H	H	M	M
Real-time navigation	M	L	M	H
Diagnostics	H	M	H	H
In-vehicle media player	M	M	M	M

services provided by VCSI are not safety critical, they have lower requirements on usability and reliability. At the same time, most of these services depend on interfacing with devices that have personal information. In that context, it's important that the privacy of the data contained within those devices be kept secure.

Overall, we think these two projects demonstrate an increasing trend towards increased connectivity with a vehicle, both from consumer devices and from roadside infrastructure. In addition, we believe that modeling provides the means to understand these services provided to the consumer at a system level.

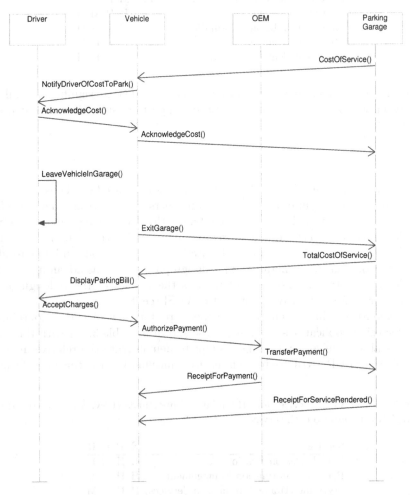

Fig. 2. A sequence diagram showing the interactions between entities in a parking garage with an electronic payment service. In this scenario a driver parks her car in a smart parking garage and electronically pays upon exit.

4   Electronic Payment Use Case

In this section, we present a more in-depth look at the electronic payment use case mentioned in Section 3 and how it relates to SPUR-oriented design. With electronic payments, drivers will have the ability to pay for parking electronically without interacting with a parking meter or a garage attendant. Drivers will no longer have to dig around for spare change and municipalities will no longer have to collect cash from parking meters.

Figure 2 shows a sequence diagram for a vehicle involved in an electronic payment scenario with a parking garage. The main entities in the diagram are the driver of the vehicle, the vehicle's software systems (implemented in a service-oriented architecture, as shown in Figure 3), the vehicle's OEM (or a delegate of the OEM), and the parking garage authority. When the vehicle enters the garage, the garage transmits a list of services and their costs to the vehicle, which in turn presents this information to the driver through the vehicle's HMI.

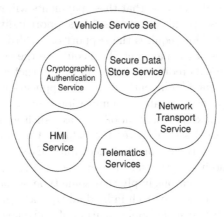

Fig. 3. The vehicle services needed to implement electronic payment in a service-oriented architecture

Assuming that the driver is willing to pay the cost to park, she acknowledges the cost of service, parks the vehicle and leaves. The vehicle sends a signed acknowledgement to the garage. Later, the driver returns and begins driving out of the garage. The garage calculates the amount of money owed and securely transmits a bill to the vehicle. The vehicle notifies the driver of how much is owed through the HMI and requests that the driver consent to pay. Confirmation from the driver causes the vehicle to transmit an encrypted, signed payment authorization message to the OEM. The OEM, acting in the role of an e-payment service, securely credits the funds to the parking garage and returns a signed receipt to the vehicle showing proof of payment. Finally, the garage sends a signed receipt to the vehicle showing that it has received its requested payment.

Thus, at the end of the interaction between the driver and the garage, the driver has proof from both the OEM and the garage that she has paid what she owed. The garage has a signed acknowledgement from the driver stating that she understood the cost to park before she parked her vehicle as well as funds deposited by the OEM to pay for parking. The receipts returned to the driver are necessary to prove that she paid for services in the case of a dispute between the garage and driver. Similarly, the signed acknowledgement agreeing to the cost of parking from the driver is necessary to dissuade a driver from reneging on payment upon exit from the garage.

4.1 Challenges

There are many challenges involving SPUR in the context of such an automotive e-payment system. While many of these challenges are not unique to e-payments in general, the scope of this paper is to understand how these issues are unique in an automotive context.

First are questions of infrastructure. E-payments require a secure, potentially private, system for transferring money from a driver or other occupant in the car to a specific payee. We also assume that these payments will reflect current cash payment characteristics, specifically, we need to support individual transactions of less than one dollar. This requires the support of a third party to aggregate payments on both sides of the payment. This could be the vehicle manufacture, as we've outlined before, a credit card issuer, or an Internet e-payment provider.

Automotive e-payment is inherently a mobile application. Malicious agents are likely to have easy access to all communication that takes place outside the vehicle. In addition, unlike personal mobile devices such as a cell phone, there is inherently less physical security over the vehicle. Cars are often parked in public spaces, and routinely in control of mechanics. Even users sometime have a vested interest in modifying the vehicle software, as evidenced by powertrain modification chips. These reasons imply that some type of end-to-end assurance is needed about the legitimacy of each individual transaction. However, there is an inherent trade-off between the sophistication of a given security system and the risk of compromise. For example, an individual driver is unlikely to notice or care if a individual penny or quarter is missing from his car when she takes it in for service. Similarly, users often trade off convenience for increased risk of monetary loss. For example, many electronic cash cards such as the Octopus card used in Hong Kong [10] require no authentication to use, and the owner assumes that a lost card implies the money associated with that card is also lost. Similarly, in-vehicle e-payment systems need to take into account the unique environment when trading off risk with cost. Mobility also has implications for the reliability of the system. There is no guarantee that a device will always stay in communications range during the period of a transaction.

Providing security and privacy in electronic transactions naturally implies the use of cryptographic protocols. In contrast to general purpose computers, the computational power and upgrade capabilities of embedded devices is severely limited. In addition, unlike the consumer electronics side of the embedded, mobile marketplace, vehicle software has a useful life of over ten years. In this context, how do we ensure that the computational power will be great enough to support key lengths that can't be easily compromised long into the future, without needless expense? At the same time, flaws in cryptographic protocols are not uncommon, so the in-vehicle software should be upgradable, without causing undue burden on the driver.

Second, are questions of authentication. How do we authenticate that the person responsible for the account used in the transaction is authorized to make the payment? We can't always assume that the driver is authorized to make payments with an account associated with the vehicle. Valets or even teenage drivers quickly complicate this assumption. At the same time, we want to authenticate the payee to the driver, making sure that a hacker hasn't set up their own virtual toll booth at the side of the highway, while still making it easy for small businesses to use the system. In some sense, the physical nature of our scenario provides opportunities not usually seen on the Internet. Most drivers require a physical or electronic key in order to enter a vehicle. At the same time, in the scenarios that we described, the payee will be in physical view of the driver. This presents an opportunity to provide out-of-band signaling to facilitate authentication.

Similarly, the physical nature of owning a vehicle presents an opportunity for associating real people with digital identities. In buying or leasing a vehicle, most buyers have little expectation of privacy. Most transactions require some type of financing, necessitating at least a credit check. Even in situations where this isn't the case (e.g. person to person cash transactions), owning a vehicle requires licensing with the state, another transaction which implies a lack of privacy, and a financial interest in correctly identifying the owner.

Finally, the interface between the driver and the vehicle computer system poses several important challenges. Because we are talking about the driver authorizing payments while driving, this interaction needs to require little attention from the driver. At the same time, we need drivers to understand the security implications of the actions they're performing. Studies of web browser security have demonstrated techniques to better inform users of the security implications of the current browser state [11].

5   Modeling Requirements

The electronic payment use case detailed in Section 4 touches on all aspects of SPUR-oriented design. For vehicular electronic payment to be widely accepted, sensitive financial information must be securely exchanged between the vehicle, the OEM, and a service vendor. The privacy of financial dealings must also be preserved. Furthermore, the HMI must clearly present information about the cost of a service and indicate when consent is required. Finally, electronic payment systems must be reliable enough to give drivers the confidence to wholly adopt them.

In order to design an electronic payment system, it's important to model various aspects of the design before building a production system. This modeling would allow designers to understand how the intended system meets these and other important attributes. However, modeling the parking garage use case requires a diverse set of tools and disciplines. The driver must not be distracted while making financial transactions yet the HMI must be involving enough to assure the driver that they are making a secure transaction. The HMI may use a text display, an LCD, voice recognition, or a combination of interface technologies to communicate with the driver. We must be able to realistically model a user interface with all of these qualities.

A significant amount of software of varying complexity is involved in our use case, from less complex programs embedded in the vehicle to highly complex back-end software at the OEM and parking garage vendor. The interactions between the vehicle, the OEM, and the service vendor must be modeled as well. We thus require a software modeling tool that can effectively model heterogeneous software environments with varying levels of complexity.

Each aspect of SPUR is a whole-system attribute. For example, spending resources on creating a security-hardened implementation of the vehicle's embedded programs is useless if the communications between the vehicle and OEM are unencrypted. Similarly, an electronic payment system with a highly reliable embedded program but a buggy OEM back-end interface makes the system as a whole unreliable.

Therefore, to fully evaluate each aspect of SPUR we must be able to study the HMI of the vehicle, its embedded programs, the OEM and parking garage enterprise software as a single system. We require a single tool or suite of tools that can fully inter-operate in order to model the interactions between each of the system's components. The tool must allow us to inject faults or directed attacks and measure the effects both in terms of software metrics (i.e. loss of privacy, reduced reliability) and in terms of customer-facing metrics such as the effect of a fault at the OEM on the in-vehicle HMI.

While many existing tools could be used to realize this goal, there are some important requirements that should be met. First, it's important for a model to accurately reflect the design of the final product. A software system that is modeled in one tool and then completely redesigned and rewritten for production is likely to provide little value in predicting security and reliability concerns. At the same time, a modeling tool needs to allow abstractions that simplify the process of quickly building a model that can be tested before the design is finalized. Another important requirement is a tool that can easily inter-operate with other tools. While a single tool that can model everything from the HMI to the back end database might be simpler, it is unlikely to ever meet all the needs of designers and researchers. Instead such a system is likely to be tested using a suite of tools tied together to meet the unique needs of the team.

Overall, the important attributes for a system for modeling SPUR attributes has less to do with the individual tool features, but more to do with the ability of the tool to adapt to the goals of the modeling project. For example, techniques for compromising the security of a system are constantly evolving. A single tool is unlikely to meet the needs of a system security audit without adapting to new techniques. At the same time, the local resources and techniques available to a design team are likely to be unique. However, we believe that a system level approach to modeling new systems provides a valuable approach to understanding how the SPUR attributes are preserved by a given design.

6 Related Work

While we could not hope to completely cover all relevant works in the individual disciplines of security, privacy, usability and reliability, in this section we present key related work in each of the SPUR attributes related to information systems in the automotive domain.

- *Security* As vehicles become connected to exterior networks, such as through telematics systems, the possibility of malicious hacking of vehicle networks increases. Wolf et al. [12] investigate the vulnerabilities of several common vehicle networking technologies including CAN, FlexRay, and LIN.
- *Privacy* Privacy is a concern in any system where vehicles broadcast their GPS location on a regular basis. A powerful entity, such as a government, could attempt to track the locations of individual vehicles if countermeasures are not taken. Sampigethaya et al. [13] have devised CARAVAN as a way to ensure location privacy in these types of systems. CARAVAN works by, among other techniques, grouping clusters of vehicles together and periodically nominating a new group leader to broadcast probe data while other vehicles remain silent.
- *Usability* Usability is probably the most familiar attribute to the general public. Most people have experienced the frustration of trying to turn on the windshield wipers, for example, in an unfamiliar car. A lot of research has been performed in understanding driver distraction as it relates to the usability of various in-car features. For example, Nowakowski et al. investigate usability problems with in-vehicle navigation systems [14].
- *Reliability* Reliability is also extremely important to the automotive industry and the embedded systems community in general. Unlike a desktop computer, an embedded system, such as an automotive powertrain controller, is expected to work all the time or at least fail in a way that doesn't leave the driver stranded on the side of the road. Tindell et al. look at formal methods for designing safe automotive software [15].

7 Conclusion

Given the transformation that both the nature and terrain of computing in the automobile are undergoing, this paper has outlined the case to model security, privacy, usability and reliability (SPUR) in the context of the software enabled services associated with the automobile. SPUR represents a set of attributes that are not explicitly articulated or demanded by the end customer or consumer and hence, broadly speaking, SPUR represents non-functional, or para-functional, attributes.

Security, privacy, usability and reliability have all been product creation requirements that have been well understood and refined by the automotive industry over the years, but almost exclusively in the mechanical or physical context. With the advent of the information-enabled automobile — connected to the roadside infrastructure and to consumer devices — SPUR takes on a very different interpretation. This paper highlights the importance of SPUR. In addition, we make a case for modeling SPUR, as this would avoid costly and time consuming hardware investments and will likely provide quick insights into how technologies and standards could be adapted to meet automotive SPUR requirements.

References

1. Patterson, D.A.: 20th century vs. 21st century C&C: The SPUR manifesto. Commun. ACM 48(3), 15–16 (2005)
2. Navet, N., Song, Y., Simonot-Lion, F., Wilwert, W.: Trends in automotive communication systems. Proceedings of the IEEE 93(6), 1204–1223 (2005)
3. Bradley, D., Seward, D., Dawson, D., Burge, S.: Mechatronics and the Design of Intelligent Machines and Systems. Stanley Thornes Ltd., London (2000)
4. Messerschmitt, D.G., Szyperski, C.: Software Ecosystem: Understanding an Indispensable Technology and Industry. MIT Press, Cambridge (2003)
5. AUTOSAR GbR: AUTOSAR website (2005), http://www.autosar.org/
6. Jameel, A., Stuempfle, M., Jiang, D., Fuchs, A.: Web on wheels: Toward internet-enabled cars. Computer 31(1), 69–76 (1998)
7. US Department of Transportation: Vehicle infrastructure integration (2006), http://www.its.dot.gov/vii/
8. Nelson, E.C., Prasad, K.V., Rasin, V., Simonds, C.J.: An embedded architectural framework for interaction between automobiles and consumer devices. In: IEEE Real-Time and Embedded Technology and Applications Symposium, pp. 192–199 (2004)
9. Papazoglou, M.P., Georgakopoulos, D.: Service oriented computing. Commun. ACM 46(10), 24–28 (2003)
10. Paynter, J., Law, P.: An arm's length evaluation of Octopus (2006), http://www.code.auckland.ac.nz/e-comWorkshop/work/An/arms/length/evaluation/of/Octopus.pdf
11. Ye, Z(E.), Smith, S., Anthony, D.: Trusted paths for browsers. ACM Trans. Inf. Syst. Secur. 8(2), 153–186 (2005)
12. Wolf, M., Weimerskirch, A., Paar, C.: Secure in-vehicle communication. Embedded Security in Cars: Securing Current and Future Automotive IT Applications (2005)
13. Sampigethaya, K., Huang, L., Li, M., Poovendran, R., Matsuura, K., Sezaki, K.: CARAVAN: Providing location privacy for VANET. In: Embedded Security in Cars (ESCAR) (2005)
14. Nowakowski, C., Green, P., Tsimhoni, O.: Common automotive navigation system usability problems and a standard test protocol to identify them. In: ITS-America 2003 Annual Meeting, Intelligent Transportation Society of America (2003)
15. Tindell, K., Kopetz, H., Wolf, F., Ernst, R.: Safe automotive software development. In: DATE 2003: Proceedings of the conference on Design, Automation and Test in Europe, Washington, DC, USA, pp. 616–621. IEEE Computer Society Press, Los Alamitos (2003)

Addressing Cross-Tool Semantic Ambiguities in Behavior Modeling for Vehicle Motion Control

Sandeep Neema[2], Sushil Birla[1], Shige Wang[1],
and Tripti Saxena[2]

[1] General Motors Corporation, Warren, MI 48090
[2] Vanderbilt University, Nashville, TN 37203

Abstract. Emerging model-based development methods in the Automotive Vehicle Motion Control (VMC) domain are using different tools at various stages of the engineering process. Behavioral models created in various forms of finite state machines have to be exchanged across these tools, but semantic unknowns in modeling environments and semantic variations across tools preclude automated correct interpretation. This research presents an approach to address this issue through an unambiguous, math-based, tool-neutral extended finite state machine metamodel (eFSM) for behavior specifications in the automotive VMC domain. The semantics of the metamodel are anchored to formal specifications in a mathematical framework. Our approach requires modeling with commercial tool environments conforming to the eFSM. The conformance is enforced by exporting the tool native models into eFSM-conformant models and checking them against the well-formed rules encoded as OCL constraints in the eFSM. We have performed "proof of concept" exercises with two commercial tools in transforming their native models into eFSM-conformant forms, and have been able to show that certain ambiguities in both tools can be prevented through the eFSM, promising higher confidence software engineering for the VMC domain.

1   Introduction

High integrity functions in Automotive Vehicle Motion Control (VMC) software are becoming increasingly complex as more functions are being realized in software. Factors contributing to the rising complexity include increasing number of interactions, distribution across many electronic control units (ECU-s) and buses, number of different suppliers, and number of engineering stages spread across different disciplines and different tool environments. To add to the complexity, VMC functions are tightly constrained in timing interrelationships, combining discrete and continuous control in ways that are difficult to analyze. The size and complexity of VMC systems have grown beyond the ability to assure their correctness through exhaustive testing and simulation. These difficulties motivate the need for VMC systems engineering processes that prevent errors from the earliest stage and provide work products that are correct by construction [1].

M. Broy, I.H. Krüger, and M. Meisinger (Eds.): ASWSD 2006, LNCS 4922, pp. 15–33, 2008.

In order to improve engineering quality, industry has been shifting effort from program code level activity towards model based control and software engineering [2,3]. However, it is not possible to transfer model data unambiguously from the tool of one engineering stage to that of another. In other words, different tools are not able to interpret the model with the same meaning. Although tools popular in the VMC engineering process, such as MathWorks Stateflow, I-Logix Rhapsody, and ETAS ASCET, support modeling in the finite state machine (FSM) paradigm, there are semantic unknowns and variations in their FSM-s. Therefore, model data has to be manually interpreted, manipulated and transferred from one engineering stage to the next, imposing penalties in integrity, quality, cost, and time.

Many research and industrial endeavors have addressed cross-tool model exchange issues. Industrial efforts include various standardization activities. ISO 10303 AP 233 [4] extends STEP, the international standard for exchange of product data, to support exchange of behavioral models of various kinds, including the FSM. The Object Management Group (OMG) SysML [5] is developing a standardized system modeling language, as a profile of UML 2.0 [6]. However, UML 2.0 does not have a strong mathematical foundation, e.g., it does not specify constraints on relationships such as generalization-specialization. Thus UML 2.0 does not support unambiguous model transformation and exchange. SAE Analysis Architecture Description Language (AADL) [7] is a modeling language to model system architecture for analysis. AADL focuses on structure and parafunctional properties, and is not suitable for systems engineering activities such as requirement specifications. EAST-ADL [8] was developed as a modeling language for electronic architecture with similar objectives, but does not provide unambiguous semantic support for behavior specification. EAST-ADL relied on external tools and languages for behavioral specifications. In parallel, researchers have endeavored to formally specify the semantics of commercial tools. For example, the formal operational semantics for Stateflow by Hamon and Rushby [9] and the operation semantics of Stateflow in BSpec notation by Kestrel Technologies [10] are two of a dozen published Stateflow semantics. However, the formal semantics defined by these research activities are "reverse engineered", without support from the tool vendors, based on the behaviors observed over a set of examples. Conformance to vendor-implemented semantics is demonstrated in most cases by comparing traces with a few tests. It does not provide adequate confidence for the VMC domain.

While the international standards and commercial tools seek breadth of application to enlarge their market, we seek disambiguation of model data for a narrowly defined domain of applications, VMC, where integrity is paramount. The scope is limited to statically configured systems with statically defined deterministic behaviors. The typical behavior of a VMC application can be described in a finite state machine with the continuous closed loop control functions embedded in its action elements. The scope of data exchanges includes VMC systems engineering processes such as requirement specification, functional design, analysis of various types, specification of the distributed platform, allocation of application functions and interactions to platform elements, code generation, integration, verification at every step, and overall validation. Behaviors of this kind can be metamodeled as an extended finite state machine (eFSM). In this paper, we propose an eFSM, with unambiguous semantics anchored in a mathematical foundation, as a well-suited medium for interchange across different stages of the engineering process mentioned above. The proposed approach requires modeling constraints, which are VMC domain-specific to enable a correct-by-construction process.

The rest of this paper is organized as follows. Section 2 explains the language requirements for unambiguous model exchange in the context of the systems engineering process for future VMC development. Section 3 presents the math-based eFSM and its support for unambiguous model exchange. Section 4 describes model export exercises with two commercial tools, using the eFSM, and the lessons learned from these exercises. The concluding Section 5 recapitulates the approach, in the context of planned future work.

2   Disambiguation Needs in a High Integrity Process

Elimination of errors in interpreting model data transferred across engineering process stages is the primary objective of this research. The eFSM is required as an enabler for the process framework shown in Fig. 1 and Fig. 2. The objectives of the process framework are to provide correct by construction products at the minimum feasible life cycle cost, time-to-market, and execution complexity. Vehicle-specific construction, verification and certification constitute a significant part of vehicle cost and time to market. Other supporting requirements are discussed during the following overview of the process framework.

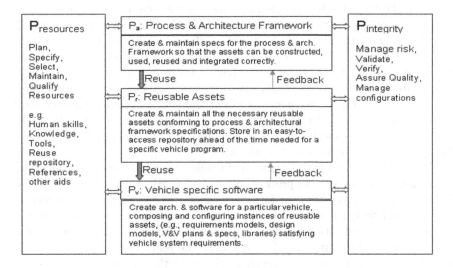

Fig. 1. Systems engineering process framework for vehicle motion control development

The process framework shown in Fig. 1 is based on principles of domain engineering [11] and product line engineering [12]. It has five major groups of processes or sub-frameworks, designated and related as follows. P_v are processes specific to a vehicle and are based on reusing assets created and maintained through processes, P_r, which in turn, follow the process and architectural framework specifications created in the processes, P_a. The eFSM is a part of P_a. $P_{integrity}$, the processes of risk management, configuration management (CM), quality assurance (QA), and V&V are applied to processes, P_v, P_r, and P_a. $P_{resources}$, the processes to plan, specify, select, maintain and qualify resources (e.g. human skills, knowledge, tools, reuse repository, and other aids), are also applied to processes, P_v, P_r, and P_a. $P_{resources}$ also include processes for upgrade, growth, and adaptation. Thus, VMC systems are specified and created with the reuse of proven elements and in ways proven to "plug & play" (compose) correctly. In other words, P_v should be a correct-by-construction process that guarantees the resultant models satisfy the specified system requirements. This process imposes a requirement that the asset be reusable correctly in future VMC applications yet unknown, thus requiring unambiguous semantics. As in the systems engineering process framework, the software development processes include the resource-related processes, $P_{resource}$, the development processes, P_a, P_r, and P_v, and the integrity processes, $P_{integrity}$.

With formal reuse of a full complement of assets from a library or repository, system conceptualization becomes a composition process rather than the traditional decomposition process. Formal reuse begins with formal fine-grained requirements models (in the form of extended finite state machines or automata) from which vehicle-specific requirements are composed, following pre-defined composition rules, applied to the requirements space (see layer 2 in Fig. 2). The process requires that incorrect compositions, including unwanted interactions, be prevented.

While the formal external behavioral models will endure over time, it is expected that the concrete realizations, for example layer 3 and greater in Fig. 2, will change as implementation technologies change. Referring to P_v in Fig. 1, the system conceptual architecture evolves bottom-up from the fine-grained requirements models by searching for matching design & implementation (D & I) entities in the reusable assets library in P_r. Search and matching criteria include not only the functional requirements model, but also associated parafunctional requirements and D & I constraints. When the best match is determined, the requirements are "allocated" to the matching "D & I" entities. The process is iterated until all requirements are allocated.

For provably correct transformation of requirements into concrete realizations or implementations, certain process and architectural constraints are imposed. Referring to the layer 2-3 transformation, shown as $^2T_3$ in Fig. 2, the process of functional design is constrained to be an elaboration (or refinement) of the requirements specification automata. More than one requirement automaton may be allocated to a functional design unit. The refinement constraint assures that the functional design inherently conforms to the specification. When the

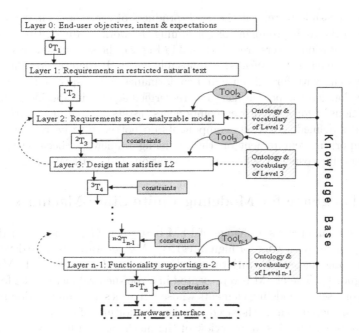

Fig. 2. Multi-stage model transformation in the systems engineering process

engineering process progresses to the stage of identifying a component, for example in layer 3-4 transformation — $^3T_4$, the external interface of the functional design (which is the same as the requirements specification) maps on to the component, and becomes a part of the components external interface (through its service access points). Thus the component is also a composable automaton. More than one functional design unit may be allocated to a component.

The framework provides for a number of stages or layers of transformation, $^{i-1}T_i$, (beyond layer 3 in Fig. 2), depending on the complexity of the system, in order to localize and isolate the effects of implementation decisions. Each transformation stage uses previously proven transformation rules, mappings, metamodels and ontologies defining the language of each stage, collectively shown as the knowledge base. It is a combination of work products from processes P_a and P_r. The language of each layer defines the universe of services available from that layer, specified as composable automata.

As engineering, denoted as P_v in Fig. 1, progresses beyond the $^3T_4$ transformation (Fig. 2), the modeling frameworks on both sides of the transformation, $^{i-1}T_i$, must be compatible, i.e., the semantics of elements in layers (i-1) and i be unambiguous, the transformed elements have a defined correspondence from layer (i-1) to layer i, and the process, $^{i-1}T_i$, be semantic-preserving. Each transformation, $^{i-1}T_i$, requires a combination of tool automation for the rule-driven part and human effort for the creative part of the work. It should be possible to use the best-in-class tool for each $^{i-1}T_i$. The reusable assets and work products of P_v should be protected from obsolescence due to changes in the tools. It should be possible to reposit the work products of every stage in a form independent of the tools producing or consuming the work products. Upon a change in implementation (layers greater than 3 in Fig. 2), the systems engineering process is reapplied to the affected composable entity. If there is no other change in the system, with formal reuse and conformance to the specified architecture, only the changed component has to be re-verified against its specification. When compositions of formally proven components (assets created in P_r) are created, using rules defined in P_a, the components do not have to be re-verified. This is an important requirement on the modeling framework, because it reduces vehicle-specific costs of verification, rectification, and certification.

3   A Language for Modeling Finite State Machines

To enable unambiguous exchange of FSM-based behavioral models in the conceptual process framework for high integrity VMC software, we have developed a modeling language, eFSM, with rules and constraints, for describing FSM models unambiguously. The eFSM is represented in a tool-neutral metamodel form and consists of a set of modeling elements whose semantics and composition rules are formally anchored to a math-based specification for unambiguous interpretation and processing. Fig. 3 is an overview of the mathematical framework for defining and interpreting the eFSM. The basic elements of a FSM, such as states, events, transitions, and actions, and their relationships are defined in the eFSM and are linked to additional mathematical specifications (ontologies) which may be expressed in other mathematical languages and processed by their respective mathematical engines to reason about the model. The semantics of eFSM have been developed as a composition of multiple semantic domains using ASML. A detailed description of eFSM language, examples, and semantics are presented in [13]. Multiple mathematical languages are accommodated by means of language transformation, based on their respective metamodels and cross-language transformation rules.

Adopted from the Mealy machine definition [14], the transition in the eFSM, F, is a mathematical function defined as follows:

$$F : S \times \Sigma \to S \times \Gamma \tag{1}$$

where S is a finite, non-empty set of states. Σ is the input alphabet for a finite, non-empty set of symbols, and Γ is the output alphabet for a finite, non-empty set of symbols. We choose to formalize transition as function which precludes non-determinism, owing to the high-integrity needs of the VMC domain. The tradition formalization of transition as a relation allows for non-determinism, which is not suitable for the VMC domain. The arrow labeled T_{ij} in Fig. 3 shows an example transition from state S_i to state S_j.

The elements in the input alphabet and output alphabet are called events (e_{in} and e_{out} in Fig. 3). The FSM function uses "saturated" expressions for input and output events [15]. Events may have associated parameters when needed for input to the function performed during a transition or for the output

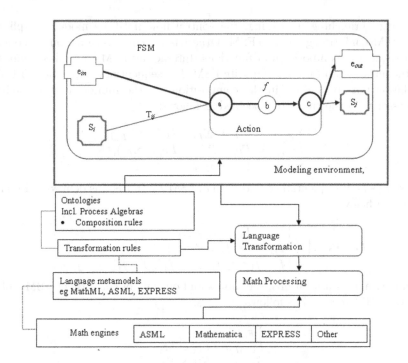

Fig. 3. eFSM for unambiguous cross-tool model exchange

generated by the function during the transition. The function performed during a transition, called an action, is defined mathematically as follows:

$$f : \sigma \rightarrow \gamma$$

where f is an action function (b in Fig. 3) with σ being a set of inputs related to the parameters associated with an input event (a in Fig. 3) in Σ and γ being a set of outputs related to the parameters associated with an output event (c in Fig. 3) in Γ. The guard condition, modeled as a function with a Boolean output, can also be associated with an input event, the truth-value of which is interpreted as presence or absence of the event. With this definition, a FSM can itself be treated as a mathematical function that maps an input alphabet into an output alphabet. In the eFSM, a FSM is a specialization of a mathematical function where each transition is also a function, whose input alphabet is a combination of event, guard, and state, and output alphabet, a combination of event and state.

3.1 Composition Rules

Compositions of FSM-s, transitions, and actions in eFSM are all constrained to mathematical function composition with one-to-one or many-to-one mapping from input to output. Complex functions in a model are composed from primitive functions or less complex functions. If a composite function involves control flow, e.g., branching or forking, the control flow must be modeled explicitly in a FSM conforming to the eFSM. Otherwise, a composite action is modeled as a sequential composition of functions. Interacting FSM-s are also composed mathematically to form a composite FSM. For sequential composition of FSM-s, the outputs of a FSM in the composition are the inputs of its immediate successor with the rules [16] specified as follows:

$$
\begin{aligned}
\Sigma_{F_1 * F_2} &= \Sigma_{F_1} \cup \Sigma_{F_2} - (\Gamma_{F_1} \cap \Sigma_{F_2}), \\
\Gamma_{F_1 * F_2} &= \Gamma_{F_1} \cup \Gamma_{F_2} - (\Gamma_{F_1} \cap \Sigma_{F_2}), \\
S_{F_1 * F_2} &= S_{F_1} \cup S_{F_2},
\end{aligned}
\tag{2}
$$

where $F_1 * F_2$ is sequential composition of FSM F_1 and F_2 (as defined in Eq.(1)), as shown below:

$$
F_1 * F_2 = \bigcup \begin{array}{l} \{f | f \in F_1, f(\gamma) \notin \Sigma_{F_2}\} \\ \{f | f \in F_2, f(\sigma) \notin \Gamma_{F_1}\} \\ \{f = f_1 * f_2 | f_1 \in F_1, f_2 \in F_2, f_1(\gamma) = f_2(\sigma)\} \end{array}
\tag{3}
$$

For parallel compositions, the inputs and outputs of constituent FSM-s obey the rules [17] specified as follows:

$$
\begin{aligned}
\Sigma_{F_1 || F_2} &= \Sigma_{F_1} \cup \Sigma_{F_2}, \\
\Gamma_{F_1 || F_2} &= \Gamma_{F_1} \cup \Gamma_{F_2}, \\
S_{F_1 || F_2} &= S_{F_1} \times S_{F_2}
\end{aligned}
\tag{4}
$$

where $F_1 || F_2$ is the parallel composition of FSM F_1 and F_2, as shown below:

$$
F_1 || F_2 = \bigcup \begin{array}{l} \{f | f \in F_1, f(\sigma) \notin \Sigma_{F_2}\} \\ \{f | f \in F_2, f(\sigma) \notin \Sigma_{F_1}\} \\ \{f = f_1 || f_2 | f_1 \in F_1, f_2 \in F_2, f_1(\sigma) = f_2(\sigma), f(\gamma) = \{f_1(\gamma)\} \cup \{f_2(\gamma)\}\} \end{array}
\tag{5}
$$

3.2   Constrained Generalization-Specialization Relationship

The eFSM supports extensions through a generalization-specialization relationship. It utilizes the generalization-specialization relationship from the object-oriented modeling paradigm as a technique to unify related concepts and thereby support integration and reuse. The eFSM constrains specialization to be performed by restriction and extension only, in order to eliminate ambiguity and to reduce computational complexity. Specialization by restriction may be performed by restricting the type of at least one element used in the more general model type to a specialization (e. g., subtype) of the corresponding element in the more general model. Restriction of the type of an element representing some value may also be performed by limiting the range of eligible values (i.e. the domain of a function), often expressed with an addition of constraint clauses. Extension of a model type is performed through addition of elements. For example, a FSM model type may be specialized to derive another FSM model type through the addition of a state or a transition.

A model type can also be specialized through a composition of elements from multiple more general model types, if the elements in these general types are mutually exclusive. An element in the specialized model type can be either of the same type as the element in its corresponding more general model type or a specialization of the element in the more general model type. The object-oriented analogy of this type of specialization would be a class C composed of class A and class B, is specialized to a class C' that is composed of A' and B where A' is a specialization of A.

Multiple levels of specialization are possible to form a generalization-specialization chain. With multi-level specialization, the eFSM can support the creation of reusable assets (types) through recursively-chaining type instances. At the first level of reusability are the types defined in the metamodeling environment, which include the FSM, State, Event, Transition, etc. as mentioned earlier. These elements in effect constitute the modeling constructs for the first level. When creating a FSM model, i.e., an instance of a FSM model type, as many instances of these modeling elements are created and assigned values as required to model the intended behavior. The behavior specification thus created in a FSM model can also be made a "type" (say level-2 type), and a collection of level-2 types constitutes the "type library" for the second level of reuse. At the second level, instances of level-2 types are created for a particular vehicle (or a vehicle product family). The level-2 types could also be specialized and placed in the type library, and then instantiated for a particular vehicle. A third, or in general n^{th}, level of reuse will include in its "type library" elements created in the $(n-1)^{th}$ level.

3.3 Ontology

The ontologies used in the eFSM are based on mathematical languages. The fundamental modeling elements in the eFSM have a one-to-one correspondence with mathematical concepts in the externally-defined mathematical specifications. Common elements include the mathematical function, its domain (including co-domain hereafter), and set. Domains include numbers with quantities extensible to physical quantities. The language elements for specifying constraints in the metamodeling environment map into first order logic (FOL). Structures of modeling elements, constructed in the modeling environment, can also be represented in FOL. To achieve semantics-preserving, unambiguous model transformation, we adopt a rule-based model transformation method with a set of formally-defined, isomorphic transformation rules. The mathematical reasoning can then be performed by established mathematical engines external to the modeling tool. Examples of such math-processing engines include Abstract State Machine Language (ASML), Mathematica, and ISO 10303-11, EXPRESS.

As an example of domain-specific specialization, definitions of Action related elements in the eFSM utilize an ontology which defines the basic knowledge of rigid body motion in VMC, related to displacement, time, velocity, acceleration, and jerk, and includes units of measurement, their dimensions, and unit balancing rules. When this ontology is specified as a constraint-set on functions relating these physical quantities in a composition, $f_1(f_2(x))$, the codomain of f_2, must match the domain of f_1, i.e., be the same set of physical quantities. Thus, this constraint-set is used to assure that the specification is unambiguous and consistent with the physics of the controlled process. This check on the specification prevents errors from propagating and multiplying in the D&I stages of the engineering process.

3.4   Language Transformation

In the systems engineering process, commercial tools are commonly used as the engineering interface for creation of work products at each stage. The work products, typically in the form of models, must have unambiguous semantics for (re)use across the stages. As the modeling languages adopted by different commercial tools are different, unambiguous semantics of models across tools and engineering stages cannot be achieved by directly using the tool native modeling languages. The models created in the tools must then be transformed to the eFSM-conformant models for exchanges with unambiguous interpretation and processing. This implies the semantic domain of a commercial tool must be mapped to the semantic domain of the eFSM. Such mapping is the metamodel-level transformation of modeling languages, and it requires the modeling constructs in the tool native modeling language have semantically equivalent modeling constructs in the eFSM. This can be achieved through constraining tool native modeling language followed by mapping of allowed tool native modeling language constructs to the eFSM modeling constructs unambiguously. The feasibility of such a mapping is assured if the semantic domain of the eFSM is wider than that of the tool's restricted native modeling language, though we do not provide a formal proof. To meet this condition and avoid introducing the ambiguity when modeling using a tool, only those modeling elements of the tool-specific modeling language, whose semantics can be unambiguously mapped to those of the eFSM elements, are allowed to be used in modeling. This requires applying domain-specific constraints to the tool native modeling languages. The modeling elements with tool-specific, implicit semantics, such as priorities of transitions captured in graphical layout, must be explicated before they can be used for modeling. To ensure the resultant model in a tool is eFSM-conformant, the constraints must be checked inside the tool, if the tool-APIs support user-specified constraints, or during exportation of the model. Models satisfying the constraints are eFSM-conformant.

The constrained tool-specific modeling elements can be transformed into semantic equivalent eFSM modeling elements (simple or composite) through a one-to-one mapping. The semantic, one-to-one mapping between the constrained tool-specific modeling elements and the eFSM modeling elements can be defined as transformation rules. Some tool-specific semantics defined unambiguously within a tool, which may be ambiguous across tools, such as data retention during event processing, can also be captured in the transformation rules. Additional semantic well-formedness rules, such as the presence of required elements and matches of their types, can also be defined as rules incorporated in the eFSM. The transformation of a model created natively in a tool to an eFSM-conformant model is then realized by applying transformation rules. The rules are encoded and operationalized using techniques such as a graph rewriting and transformation engine [18], and are applied to the tool-native models to obtain the eFSM-conformant models. When the transformation encounters elements for which a mapping rule is not defined, it flags a violation of the elements, thereby testing conformance of the eFSM. Rules for mapping from the "canonical form to the tool are part of future work.

3.5 Execution Semantics

Given the basic modeling elements, composition rules, constrained relationship and ontology, and parafunctional [1] specification support, the eFSM is further constrained to achieve the following execution semantics. The FSM processes only one event in each computation cycle. A computation cycle, modeled using a parafunctional element, starts from an arrival of an triggering event and ends with the production of the output. The next computation cycle begins only after the completion of the preceding computation cycle. All parts of the input are available before the computation cycle starts and are stable during the cycle. Discretized continuous control behavior is modeled as an action, triggered by a periodic event occurring at the fixed time period, required by the executing control algorithm. A simple unit of continuous control behavior can then be modeled as a function, $f(x)$. Its domain and co-domain are limited to a specified topological vector space. Multiple functions, f_1, f_2, and f_3, which are limited to the same topological vector space, may be composed sequentially as $f_1(f_2(f_3(x)))$ to create a complex behavior. These semantics assume the completion of the action before the start of next computation cycle.

The assumption on the action completion is specified as a rule and must be verified in order to ensure correct operation. To allow the verification, the eFSM is extended to associate some normalized equivalent of its worst case execution time (WCET).

4   Proof of Concept Exercises

Our proof-of-concept exercises is to examine the mapping from the semantic domains of two selected commercial tools, Rhapsody [19] from I-Logix and Stateflow [20] from Mathworks, to the eFSM semantic domain for unambiguous interpretation and processing. The exercises follow the transformation principles in Section 3.4. Since neither Stateflow nor Rhapsody provides API-s for specifying and checking user-specified constraints, the constraints and transformation rules were checked during and after transformation.

---

[1] Parafunctional refers to properties of software that are considered beyond the functional requirements, and is equivalent to Quality of Service (QoS) properties.

Table 1. Transformation rules from Rhapsody Statechart to eFSM ($r2e()$ is a injective mapping from a Rhapsody element to an eFSM element)

Rhapsody element	eFSM element	Mapping rules
basic states S_R	states S_F	$s_r \in S_R \Rightarrow (s_f = r2e(s_r))$ $\wedge(S_F = S_F \cup s_f)$
termination states S_R^t	final states S_F^t	$s_r \in S_R^t \Rightarrow (s_f = r2e(s_r))$ $\wedge(S_F^t = S_F^t \cup s_f)$
actions A_R	actions A_F	$a_r \in A_R \Rightarrow (a_f = r2e(a_r))$ $\wedge(A_F = A_F \cup a_f)$
triggers E_R	events E_F	$e_r \in E_R \Rightarrow (e_f = r2e(e_r))$ $\wedge(E_F = E_F \cup e_f)$
guards G_R	guards G_F	$g_r \in G_R \Rightarrow (g_f = r2e(g_r))$ $\wedge(G_F = G_F \cup g_f)$
transitions T_R	transitions T_F	$t_r \in T_R \Rightarrow (t_f.event = r2e(t_r.trigger))$ $\wedge(t_f.guard = r2e(t_r.guard))$ $\wedge(t_f.action = r2e(t_r.action))$ $\wedge(T_F = T_F \cup t_f)$
termination connectors C_R^t	final states S_F^t	$c_r \in C_R^t \Rightarrow (s_f = r2e(c_r))$ $\wedge(S_F^t = S_F^t \cup s_f)$
junction connectors C_R^j	transitions T_F	$(j_r \in C_R^j) \wedge (t_r^1 \ldots t_r^i, t_r^j \in T_R)$ $\wedge(\{t_r^1, ..., t_r^i\} \to j \to t_r^j)$ $\Rightarrow (t_f^1.event = r2e(t_r^1.trigger))$ $\wedge(t_f^1.guard = r2e(t_r^1.guard))$ $\wedge(t_f^1.action = r2e(t_r^1.action + t_r^j.action))$ $\ldots$ $\wedge(t_f^i.event = r2e(t_r^i.trigger))$ $\wedge(t_f^i.guard = r2e(t_r^i.guard))$ $\wedge(t_f^i.action = r2e(t_r^i.action + t_r^j.action))$ $\wedge(T_F = T_F \cup \{t_f^1, ..., t_f^i\})$
condition connectors C_R^c	states S	$(c_r \in C_R^c) \wedge (t_r^c, t_r^1 \ldots t_r^i \in T_R)$ $\wedge(t_r^c \to c_r \to \{t_r^1, ..., t_r^i\})$ $\Rightarrow (t_f^1.event = r2e(t_r^c.trigger))$ $\wedge(t_f^1.guard = r2e(t_r^c.guard + t_r^1.guard))$ $\wedge(t_f^1.action = r2e(t_r^c.action + t_r^1.action))$ $\ldots$ $\wedge(t_f^i.event = r2e(t_r^c.trigger))$ $\wedge(t_f^i.guard = r2e(t_r^c.guard + t_r^1.guard))$ $\wedge(t_f^i.action = r2e(t_r^c.action + t_r^i.action))$ $\wedge(T_F = T_F \cup \{t_f^1, ..., t_f^i\})$
action_on_entry $a_r^i \in s_r$	action a_f	$a_r^i \in s_r \Rightarrow (t_f.tostate = r2e(s_r))$ $\wedge(a_f = r2e(a_r^i))$ $\wedge(t_f.action = t_f.action + a_f)$ $\wedge(T_F = T_F \cup t_f)$
action_on_exit $a_r^o \in s_r$	action a_f	$a_r^o \in s_r \Rightarrow (t_f \in T_F) \wedge (t_f.fromstate = r2e(s_r))$ $\wedge(a_f = r2e(a_r^o))$ $\wedge(t_f.action = a_f + t_f.action)$ $\wedge(T_F = T_F \cup t_f)$
reaction_in_state $a_r^r \in s_r$	transition t_f	$a_r^r \in s_r \Rightarrow (t_f.fromstate = s_r)$ $\wedge(t_f.tostate = r2e(s_r))$ $\wedge(t_f.event = r2e(a_r^r.trigger))$ $\wedge(t_f.guard = r2e(a_r^r.guard))$ $\wedge(t_f.action = r2e(a_r^r.action))$ $\wedge(T_F = T_F \cup t_f)$

4.1   Rhapsody

Rhapsody 6.0 employs Statecharts for state-based behavior modeling. In Rhapsody Statecharts, a *State* can be a basic state, or a termination state, or an or-state, or an and-state. Each state can have *action_on_entry*, *action_on_exit*, and *reaction_in_state* defined. A connector can be *Condition*, or *History*, or *Termination*, or *Junction*, or *Diagram*, or *Sync-Join*, or *Sync-Fork*. A transition has *Trigger*, *Guard*, and *Actions*. To support unambiguous model exchange, we mapped a defined subset of the Statechart to our eFSM with the rules, as shown in Table 1, according to the behavioral semantics of the modeling constructs. The transformation rules shown in Table 1 show the mathematical mapping of syntactic constructs of Rhapsody into eFSM, and are operationalize with a rule-based transformation engine [21] that matches the appropriate syntactic construct in Rhapsody and performs the mapping actions as shown in the table. For example, a junction connector j_r with a set of transitions $\{t_r^1 \ldots t_r^i, t_r^j\}$ in Rhapsody indicates that $t_r^1 \ldots t_r^i$ sharing some common actions in t_r^j. Consequently, the mapping rule for j_r transforms the junction connector with its transitions $\{t_r^1 \ldots t_r^i, t_r^j\}$ into a set of eFSM transitions $\{t_f^1 \ldots t_f^i\}$ with the event and guard of $t_f^k (1 \leq k \leq i)$ being the trigger and guard of t_r^k and the actions of t_f^k being the actions of t_r^k followed by the actions of t_r^j. Since the eFSM does not yet incorporate State hierarchies, composite states and state hierarchy were outside the defined subset. Similarly, since the eFSM execution semantics allows only one event to be processed each computation cycle, History is outside the defined subset.

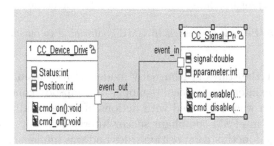

(a) Sensor interface and signal processor

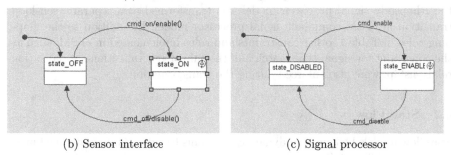

(b) Sensor interface   (c) Signal processor

Fig. 4. Behavioral models in Rhapsody

With the above defined transformation rules, we translated a part of a behavioral model for a cruise control defined using elements within the defined subset of Rhapsody Statecharts, to eFSM realized in the Generic Modeling Environment (GME) [22]. Fig. 4 and 5 show the sensor interface and signal processing portion of the whole model in Rhapsody and in eFSM in GME, respectively. After the transformation, we performed checks of the rules and constraints defined in the eFSM, and detected errors such as signal mismatches in value ranges or units, which were not detectable in the Rhapsody model.

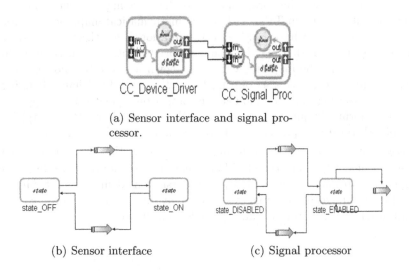

(a) Sensor interface and signal processor.

(b) Sensor interface   (c) Signal processor

Fig. 5. Behavioral models in GME conforming to our eFSM

As can be seen, the states in Rhapsody models were transformed to states in eFSM. The sensor interface Statechart model in Rhapsody contained entry and exit actions, which were combined with actions of corresponding transitions as composite actions in eFSM-compliant sensor interface transitions. The composition followed the function composition rules and was implemented as mapping rules in Table 1. Similarly, the *reaction_in_state* action in *state_Enable* state in the Rhapsody signal processor model was transformed to a separate, self-loop transition in eFSM-compliant signal processor model. In addition to the mapping rules in Table 1, other constraints and rules implemented in eFSM, such as the constraint for signal type match and the rule of generalization-specialization relationship, were also enforced during the transformation.

4.2   StateFlow

Stateflow models behaviors of dynamical systems based on finite state machines, and uses a different Statechart formalism with additional semantic elements, notably junction structures, and flow charts. Also, the Stateflow action language

Table 2. Transformation rules from Stateflow to eFSM ($s2e()$ is a injective mapping from a Stateflow element to an eFSM element)

Stateflow element	eFSM element	Mapping rules
leaf states S_S	states S_F	$s_s \in S_S \Rightarrow (name(s_f) = s2e(s_s))$ $\wedge(S_F = S_F \cup s_f)$
actions A_S	actions A_F	$a_s \in A_S \Rightarrow (a_f = s2e(a_s))$ $\wedge(A_F = A_F \cup a_f)$
condition actions C_{A_S}	actions A_F	$c_{a_s} \in A_S \Rightarrow (a_f = s2e(c_{a_s}))$ $\wedge(g_f = s2e(c))$ $\wedge(A_F = A_F \cup a_f)$ $\wedge(G_F = G_F \cup g_f)$
triggers E_S	events E_F	$e_s \in E_S \Rightarrow (e_f = s2e(e_s))$ $\wedge(E_F = E_F \cup e_f)$
guards G_S	guards G_F	$g_s \in G_S \Rightarrow (g_f = s2e(g_s))$ $\wedge(G_F = G_F \cup g_f)$
transitions T_S	transitions T_F	$t_s \in T_S \Rightarrow (t_f.event = s2e(t_s.trigger))$ $\wedge(t_f.guard = s2e(t_s.guard))$ $\wedge(t_f.action = s2e(t_s.conditionaction))$ $\cup(s2e(t_s.action))$ $\wedge(T_F = T_F \cup t_f)$
entry_action $a_s^i \in s_s$	action a_f	$a_s^i \in s_s \Rightarrow (t_f.tostate = s2e(s_s))$ $\wedge(a_f = s2e(a_s^i))$ $\wedge t_f.action = t_f.action \cup a_f)$ $\wedge T_F = T_F \cup t_f$
exit_action $a_s^o \in s_s$	action a_f	$a_s^o \in s_s \Rightarrow (t_f.fromstate = s2e(s_s))$ $\Rightarrow (a_f = s2e(a_s^o))$ $\wedge(t_f.action = a_f \cup t_f.action)$ $\wedge(T_F = T_F \cup t_f)$
during_action $a_s^d \in s_s$	transition t_f	$a_s^d \in s_s \Rightarrow (t_f.fromstate = s2e(s_s))$ $\wedge(t_f.tostate = s2e(s_s))$ $\wedge(t_f.event = s2e(E_S - \{e_s | t_s.fromstate = s_s\}))$ $\wedge(t_f.action = s2e(a_s^d))$ $\wedge(T_F = T_F \cup t_f)$

differs from Statecharts, and has been extended to reference Matlab functions, and Matlab workspace variables.

As in the Rhapsody case, we restricted Stateflow modeling elements to a defined subset, disallowing Junctions, History, State hierarchies, and Function States [20] to avoid ambiguity. Table 2 summarizes the transformation rules for mapping the defined Stateflow subset into eFSM. Similarly, the mapping rules are based on the behavioral semantics of the modeling constructs in Stateflow and eFSM. For example, the entry actions a_s of a state s in Stateflow is transformed into the last actions of each incoming transition t_f of the s_s in the eFSM model. According to the rule, $t_f.tostate = s2e(s_s)$ identifies all transitions t_f in the eFMS, whose destination state is s_s. The Stateflow action a_s is then transformed into the eFSM action a_f and is added to the transition's action set with $t_f.action = t_f.action \cup a_f$. Due to different graphical representations, the transformed eFSM model in Fig. 5 has the trigger events and the transition actions as embedded elements in the blockarrows instead of representing as textual labels as in the Rhapsody model. One major advatage of using embedded type elements over textual labels is that the type elements support better type checking.

In addition to the above rules, while parsing and mapping actions, we checked that (i) the arguments of the actions are from the set of inputs and/or outputs to the Stateflow model, similar to what the Stateflow compiler does, and (ii) the functions are contained in a pre-defined set of mathematically well-formed functions. According to the Stateflow semantics, *Data* variables are persistent and retain their their values over multiple computation cycles, while *Events* are transient and consumed in a single computation cycle. These implicit semantics results in creation of unintentional state variables. In the transformation rules specified here these are transformed to explicit definition in eFSM as parameterized *Events* carrying *Data* of sampled signals. This results in elimination of the implicitly defined state variables in the original Stateflow model.

As in the Rhapsody case, we have been able to map Stateflow models created within the eFSM-imposed constraints, into eFSM models in GME. We are currently investigating techniques for natively enforcing the eFSM restrictions within the Stateflow environment using the Stateflow provided API-s.

4.3   Lessons Learned

Through the proof-of-concept exercises, we gathered some valuable lessons on modeling language support for high integrity VMC control software. Modeling language support for strong type and modeling constraints are essential for unambiguous model exchange. For example, while the signals in both Rhapsody and Stateflow can be strongly typed with a specified unit, these tools do not incorporate any automated check for type compatibility prior to simulation or code generation. Some of the typing errors related to programming data-types are occasionally caught by a compiler; however, the more serious ones related to units and dimensionality are never caught since programming languages do not offer any abstractions for capturing physical quantities. In such a modeling environment, integration of discrete and continuous control behaviors in a unified, unambiguous model is not possible. Large amounts of effort have been spent on reducing model ambiguity through restrictions using some ad hoc approach such as a style guide for Stateflow. However, these approaches have not enabled unambiguous exchange of models across different tools.

As the behavioral models for VMC have complex interactions, ad hoc transformation is infeasible. The mathematical foundation of the eFSM allows creation of rules and constraints formally so that they can be interpreted and executed by machines automatically. Our experiences indicate that domain-specific rules and constraints are the key to support correct-by-construction modeling and unambiguous model exchange. Such domain-specific rules allow unambiguous semantic model transformation, thus preventing errors in the model and enabling a correct-by-construction process. For example, a constraint that any transition involving physical devices must be explicit and deterministic with all exceptions and interruptions captured as events will be implemented as a rule in eFSM.

Many semantic mistakes made by the designer during modeling, which cannot be captured otherwise, can be captured with such domain-specific rules.

5   Conclusions and Future Work

Semantics-preserving cross-tool model exchange is a key requirement to support a correct and efficient systems engineering process. In this paper, we have presented a math-based eFSM to enable software engineering of high integrity systems, e.g. drive-by-wire vehicles, with higher confidence and lower effort than current techniques. The eFSM contains modeling elements with explicitly-defined generalization-specialization relationship, mathematical composition rules and constraints, and domain-specific ontology. It also enables mathematical reasoning, transformation, and checking for the satisfaction of system requirements from early stages of the engineering life cycle. Models conforming to the eFSM can be unambiguously exchanged across different tools. The developed eFSM enables better "process efficacy" in the systems engineering processes, mostly in the requirements specification and verification and validation aspects.

It should be noted that our approach involves overlaying a restricted semantic domain (eFSM semantics) on the wider semantic domains of COTS tools such as Stateflow and Rhapsody. Enforcing this common semantic domain across multiple tools enables semantic preserving transformation and reduces the problem of verifying transformation correctness from establishing behavioral equivalence to structural equivalence.

One of the consequential challenge of this approach lies in imposing restrictions on the engineers using the Stateflow and Rhapsody tools. This is both a technological and an educational challenge. The availability of certain features in a tool, despite their semantic ambiguity, makes it attractive for the users. Automatic overlays, and online constraint checkers embedded within tools may make it technologically feasible to impose the restrictions, by automatically ensuring conformance to the high confidence high integrity design subset. Educational aids must also be created to assist the developers in understanding the cause and impact of the ambiguity in the use of certain abstractions. Some degree of restrictions are already in use by way of adherence to "best practice" and "safety guidelines" developed by Automotive Manufacturers, and other bodies such as Mathworks Automotive Advisory Board (MAAB).

The restrictions also impose challenge on the overall scalability of our approach, since the restrictions while improve the semantic preciseness of the models, also increase the effort in representing some behaviors. For example history driven behaviors can be conveniently represented with history junctions in Stateflow, and have to be otherwise represented with larger number of states. The transformations as described earlier are polynomial complexity and are not subject to scalability concern.

The eFSM represents early work on building the foundations for correct-by-construction process for VMC domain. However, much work remains to be done in the area of transformation and verification. We will continue this research to extend and evaluate the eFSM through constructing challenge problem model sets of representative VMC applications and platforms, and exercising the full systems engineering process with tool-assisted modeling and transformation. The extensions will include additional domain-specific rules for VMC modeling and transformation. The evaluations will include examining the breadth of the eFSM applicability, i.e., the scope of the domains over which various rule-sets hold, proving semantic mapability between tool native modeling elements and the eFSM modeling elements in both directions, and studying the effect on software correctness, process efficacy, system complexity reduction, and overall scalability of eFSM.

References

1. Birla, S.: Challenge problems for model-based integration of embedded systems (MoBIES. DTIC AFRL-IF-WP-TR-2004-1523 (2004)
2. Torngren, M., Larses, O.: Characterization of model based development of embedded control systems from a mechatronic perspective: drivers, processes, technology and their maturity. Technical Report TRITA-MMK 2004:23, Mechatronics Lab, Department of Machine Design, Royal Institute of Technoglogy, KTH, Stockholm, Sweden (2004)
3. Mellor, S.J., Clark, A.N., Futagami, T.: Model-driven development. IEEE Software 20(5), 14–18 (2003)
4. Price, D.: Ap233 state machine support (2005), http://www.ap233.org/ModuleSets/Behavior/AP233_State_Machine_2005-09-15_update.zip/view
5. Object Management Group: Uml for systems engineering, request for proposal (2003), http://www.sysml.org/artifacts/refs/UML-for-SE-RFP.pdf
6. Object Management Group: Unified modeling language: Superstructure, version 2.0 (2005), http://www.omg.org/docs/formal/05-07-04.pdf
7. International Society for Automotive Engineers (SAE) AADL Team: Architecture analysis & design language (AADL) standard (2004), http://www.aadl.info
8. EAST-EEA Partners: East-eea architecture description language, version 1.0.2 (2004), http://www.east-eea.net/start.asp
9. Hamon, G., Rushby, J.: An Operational Semantics for Stateflow. In: Wermelinger, M., Margaria-Steffen, T. (eds.) FASE 2004. LNCS, vol. 2984, pp. 229–243. Springer, Heidelberg (2004)
10. Anton, J., da Costa, P., Errington, L.: Formal synthesis of generators for embedded systems. Technical report, Kestrel Technology, Palo Alto, CA (2005)
11. Arango, G.: Domain Analysis. In: Marciniak, J. (ed.) Encyclopedia of Software Engineering, vol. 1, pp. 424–434. Wiley, Chichester (1994)
12. The Software Engineering Institute (SEI): A framework for software product line practice version 4.2 (2005), http://www.sei.cmu.edu/productlines/framework.html
13. Chen, K., Sztipanovits, J., Neema, S.: A case study on semantic unit composition. In: MISE 2007: Proceedings of the International Workshop on Modeling in Software Engineering, Washington, DC, USA, p. 3. IEEE Computer Society Press, Los Alamitos (2007)
14. Villa, T., Kam, T., Brayton, R.K., Sangiovanni-Vincentelli, A.L.: Synthesis of Finite State Machines: logic Optimization. Kluwer Academic Publishers, Dordrecht (1997)

15. Girault, A., Lee, B., Lee, E.A.: Hierarchical finite state machines with multiple concurrency models. IEEE Transactions on Computer-Aided Design of Integrated Circuits and Systems 18(6), 742–760 (1999)
16. Lee, E.A., Varaiya, P.: Structure and Interpretation of Signals and Systems. Addison-Wesley, Reading (2003)
17. Broy, M.: Algebraic specification of reactive systems. In: Nivat, M., Wirsing, M. (eds.) Proceedings of the 5th International Conference on Algebraic Methodology and Software Technology, Lecture Notes in Computer Science, p. 487. Springer, Heidelberg (1996)
18. Agrawal, A., Karsai, G., Shi, F.: Graph transformations on domain-specific models. Technical Report ISIS-03-403, Institute for Software Integrated Systems, Vanderbilt University, Nashville, TN (2003)
19. I-Logix Inc.: Rhapsody user guide (2005)
20. The MathWorks: Stateflow and stateflow coder, user's guide version 6 (2005), http://www.mathworks.com/access/helpdesk/help/pdf_doc/stateflow/sf_ug.pdf
21. Karsai, G., Agarwal, A., Shi, F., Sprinkle, J.: On the use of graph transformation in the formal specification of model interpreters. Journal of Universal Computer Science 9(11), 19–27 (2003)
22. Institute for Software Integrated Systems: The generic modeling environment (2005), http://www.isis.vanderbilt.edu/Projects/gme

A Software and System Modeling Facility for Vehicle Environment Interactions

Edward Nelson and Henry Huang

Research and Advanced Engineering, Ford Motor Company,
enelson7@ford.com, hhuang@ford.com

Abstract. This paper describes an advanced modeling facility for system and software design that is being constructed at the Ford Research and Innovation Center. This facility is intended to address the growing complexity of automotive embedded software and the resulting issues for vehicle development. Software complexity is expected to grow at a significantly higher rate in the near future as vehicle systems begin to interact with external software based systems to provide significant new capabilities in both the infotainment and the safety areas. Increased complexity will require a broader range of modeling capabilities than just functional/behavioral modeling. Our recent experience with the latter has shown substantial benefits for the product development process, and we expect that the more comprehensive modeling process described here will bring even greater benefits.

1 Introduction

Automotive electronics systems have traditionally been self-contained in the sense that they did not depend on systems outside of the vehicle. The primary form of interaction was to transfer information from the vehicle to an external system as with diagnostics, or to import information in an unmodified form, as in entertainment systems, such as the radio or CD player. This is changing somewhat with the advent of telematics systems, but it still has not reached the point where the off board system and the vehicle system can be described as co-operating processes. This is likely to change in the near future for two reasons. First, there is a trend towards integrating mobile consumer devices with the vehicle such that the consumer device functionality can be accessed using the vehicle human machine interface (HMI). This requires a more complex integration between the consumer device and the vehicle entertainment system. Second, there is a major effort, led by the United States Department of Transportation to create a nationwide wireless communication infrastructure that would allow communication between vehicles and the roadside in order to prevent accidents and reduce congestion. The primary purpose of the resulting network would be to improve safety, but driver information and commercial services using this mechanism are envisioned as well. These developments raise new concerns of security and privacy that are not present when the vehicle electronics forms a

M. Broy, I.H. Krüger, and M. Meisinger (Eds.): ASWSD 2006, LNCS 4922, pp. 34–47, 2008.
© Springer-Verlag Berlin Heidelberg 2008

self-contained system. They also make the job of validating the correct functioning of the vehicle more complex because interactions with external systems must be taken into account as well as interactions between on-board components. Since these interactions with external systems are primarily implemented through software, the net result is to raise new concerns about the correctness of embedded vehicle software. In addition to the complexity brought about by interactions with external systems, vehicle software complexity is also rising due to the fact that traditional vehicle features are increasingly being implemented through software, and new features are being created by software implementations, many of them based on interactions of vehicle subsystems that previously did not interact. Perhaps the canonical example of the latter is adaptive audio volume, which adjusts the radio volume depending on the vehicle speed.

In order to address these concerns, as well as the related issues of vehicle embedded software quality, we are constructing a facility for model based embedded software design and engineering at the Ford Research and Innovation center. This facility will have the capability to model vehicle systems from multiple viewpoints, both the traditional functional point of view and the viewpoints of software structure, component interactions and the human machine interface. In order to enable this multi-view modeling we are connecting models built with a number of very different tools. The tools themselves are not novel and are used individually by different groups within the company. What is unique in our effort is the attempt to bring these separate viewpoints together in a common set of models.

The remainder of this paper will discuss the issues that we are trying to solve with this facility, the reasons that we feel that a multi-tool approach to modeling is essential to address these issues, the reasons behind our specific choice of tools and the detailed steps that we are taking to approach the problem. At this point we do not have specific results from this facility, but it builds on previous results that we have done.

2   Motivations for Modeling Vehicle Software

2.1   Validation of Embedded Software Implementation

Current vehicles contain a number of Electronic Control Units (ECUs) for control of body electronics functions, such as door locks, interior and exterior lights, power seats and windows, climate control, driver information systems, electrical load distribution and so forth. These are in addition to ECUs that control powertrain (engine, transmission and emission systems) function, and those that control vehicle motion (brakes, traction control, cruise control, etc.). Powertrain and vehicle dynamics generally require a combination of discrete and continuous control. Modeling tools based on Simulink and Stateflow are now widely used in the design and development of software where discrete and continuous controls coexist [1]. Body electronics functions, on the other hand, are almost exclusively limited to discrete control. The functionality of body ECUs can normally be described as an interacting set of state machines of limited to moderate complexity.

For example, Fig. 1 shows the state machine for the courtesy lights battery saver function. Because of the relative simplicity of body functions, modeling has not previously been used in the development of body control software to the same extent that it has for powertrain and chassis control software. Increasingly, however, features are being added to the vehicle that depend on the interaction between two or more distinct functions, such as turning on the interior lights when the doors are unlocked. The state machine shown in Fig. 1 is typical in that it has a small number of states with relatively complex transition conditions due to interactions with other subsystems. As more and more of these features are added to body electronics systems, dependencies are being created between different features that lead to interactions between ECUs that are increasingly complex and often unintended. Currently, 60% of all new features are distributed functions. The number of interactions have increased to the point where even a simple system such as the central locking system, for example, may interact with eighteen other subsystems in the vehicle.

The effect of this development has been to increase the number of issues that are first found at vehicle integration time, when all of the ECUs have been designed and built at least as prototypes. However, problems that occur late in the development process are expensive to correct and raise the risk of delays in the overall vehicle program. Our experience at Ford has been that there has been a large increase in the number of issues related to embedded body module software in recent years, These range from issues that affect a single module, to issues that only occur as the result of the interaction of multiple modules. An example of the former might be the failure to initialize a filter in software that displays the outside air temperature, resulting in grossly inaccurate temperatures being displayed for a significant period of time after the vehicle is turned on. Many examples of module interaction issues are related to the sleep/wakeup protocol where modules go into low power mode when certain conditions are satisfied. For example, a module may go to sleep but fail to send a message on the CAN bus indicating that it has gone to sleep. This would cause a second module that depended on a periodic value output to the bus by the first module to assume that there was an error condition and to use an incorrect default value in place of the last value output by the first module. Or a module might not monitor the network for changes that occur between the time that it decided to go to sleep and the time that the entire CAN network shut down. This could result, for example, in the courtesy lights not working because the module that controls them did not see the key out of ignition message before it went to sleep.

Because of this increased complexity modeling tools are increasingly being used in the development of body control software in addition to their use in the powertrain and vehicle dynamics domains. As a result of its use in the latter domains, the Simulink/Stateflow toolset from MathWorks is being used in this domain as well. In a recent project involving the development of a new ECU that integrated the functionality of a number of modules in earlier vehicles, the use of models combined with hardware in the loop testing based on systems from dSPACE led to over 60 issues being uncovered that would otherwise not have

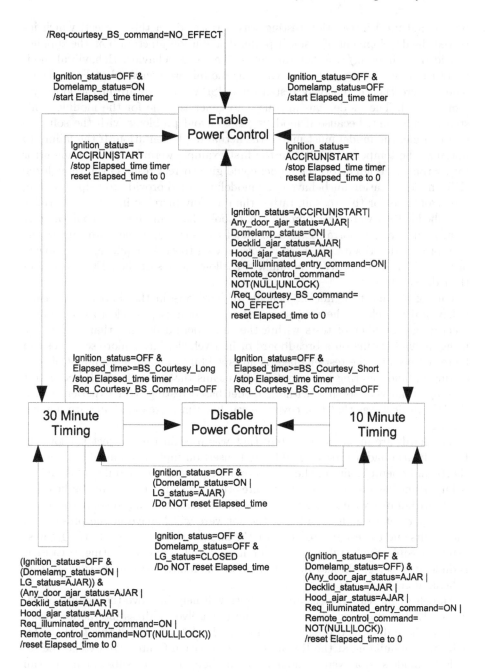

Fig. 1. State diagram of the power management feature for the vehicle courtesy lights

been found until integration testing was performed. In this project, which involved the development of a smart power distribution junction box, the supplier provided a Simulink/Stateflow model of the ECU behavior. Behavioral models of the modules that interact with this module were created at Ford. These models were then extensively tested on a dSPACE hardware in the loop system at Ford. The model was also used to generate code for the module. This step is important, because if modeling is to avoid problems with the software in a module, the model must match the actual implementation. If the failure to initialize the temperature filter in the first example were due to a coding error rather than a design error, the model could give correct results even though the ECU implementation misbehaved and modeling would provide no help in finding the error. It is for this reason, rather than for any increase in the productivity of embedded software development, that tools that can generate code directly from models are important. As a result of the success of the hardware in the loop project described here, Ford is now moving towards requiring all suppliers of body modules to provide Simulink/Stateflow models of their ECU as one of their deliverables.

One of the most significant benefits of hardware in the loop testing using behavioral models of the vehicle systems is that it is possible to carry out a much larger number of tests within the same period of time than is possible using manual testing on a breadboard or in a vehicle. Many more scenarios can be tested because the test engineer is not spending a significant amount of time setting up and entering test inputs. This means that there is much better test coverage than was possible without model based testing. Our experience with the HIL project was that test coverage was five times greater than with manual testing.

The hardware in the loop system that was used in this project is shown in Fig. 2. It also had a programmable fault insertion unit that was able to create shorts and open circuits in the inputs and outputs of the module. This facility is important because most of the failures that occur in vehicles in the field are hardware failures, with wiring harness problems being the largest source of issues. It is important to understand how the software will behave in the presence of such faults and to design it to mitigate the impact of such failures to the greatest extent possible. Such fault testing is often neglected in manual testing, because it is difficult to set up the hardware to exhibit the fault, particularly when testing is being done in a vehicle.

Models of individual electronic modules will help improve the quality of delivered ECUs. However, they will not, by themselves address interaction issues such as those described in the second example. To accomplish this goal the facility we are building at the Research and Innovation Center will extend the set of ECU models to a system model. For the body modules subsystem this can be accomplished by integrating state machine models with models of the CAN network over which they communicate. To this end we have added a network modeling tool to the set of tools that will be a part of the modeling lab. Another important extension to the HIL modeling process that we are investigating is the

Fig. 2. body electronics hardware in the loop facility

automatic generation of test cases from Stateflow models of a feature or an ECU using a tool such as Reactis [2]. Such tools have the potential to extend the test coverage of a module significantly beyond the improvement that is obtained just by testing with a hardware in the loop system. However additional investigation is required to determine whether the tools can generate complete coverage of the ECU behavior without generating a large number of redundant tests. The process that we envision for this application of behavior modeling is illustrated in Fig. 3.

2.2 New and Emerging Software Mediated Functionality; the Connection to the External World

The applications discussed thus far relate to the development of existing or well defined technology. An even more important use of modeling, however, lies in the exploration of new concepts. The emerging trends toward increasing interaction between vehicle systems and off-board systems referred to above fall into this category. It is in this area that the most interesting challenges for software modeling lie, and it is in this area that the need for types of modeling beyond functional modeling, such as modeling of the HMI design, arises. The process that we envision for new concept development is illustrated in Fig. 4. The challenges in this area can be divided into two categories: challenges in enabling consumer devices that are brought into the vehicle to work with vehicle systems, and challenges relating to the upcoming enablement of vehicle-to-vehicle and vehicle-to-roadside wireless communication.

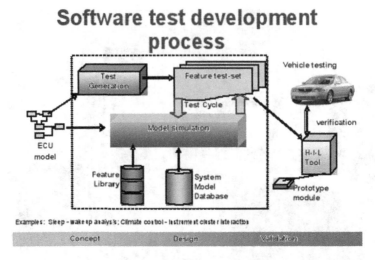

Fig. 3. Software validation process

The fourth domain of vehicle electronics software is the infotainment system. This domain includes traditional entertainment devices, such as the radio and CD player, as well as systems whose primary purpose is providing information, such as navigation and telematics systems, or communication systems such as in-vehicle cell phones. Systems in this domain have been more self-contained and less "vehicle related" than electronics in the other domains. A radio, for example, has been more or less self contained with respect to other modules in the vehicle. However two major trends are changing this.

Consumer Devices. One is the trend to provide a closer connection between consumer devices that are brought into the vehicle by the occupants and the vehicle electronics systems. A major example of this is the provision of allowing occupants to use their personal cell phone through the vehicle's audio system to make hands free phone calls. Many vehicles will have Bluetooth interfaces to support this capability. Vehicle based voice recognition systems will also become common to support the same capability. Just as with other vehicle systems, there are a number of additional features that can be offered to the user by integrating the functions of infotainment systems. Navigation system data bases, for example, often have phone numbers associated with points of interest, and it would be useful if the navigation system could offer the option to dial such a phone number on the user's cell phone.

The opportunities provided by combining functionality provided by consumer devices with that provided by vehicle electronics has led to a trend towards the implementation of service oriented architectures in the vehicle. Groups such as AMI-C have designed vehicle multimedia standards that incorporate a service oriented architecture [3] and a number of vehicle manufacturers are producing or considering systems that are based on the OSGi platform [4]. Service oriented architectures are more dynamic than traditional embedded software architectures and require different techniques to model them properly [5].

New feature analysis process

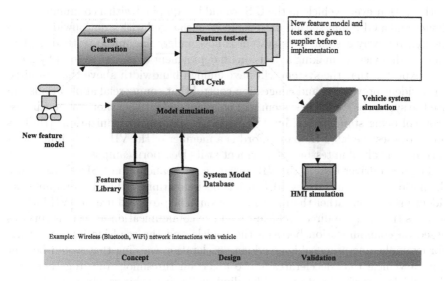

Fig. 4. The new concept development process

The infotainment domain also differs from the other domains in that the human machine interface is more complex for many of these features and less well known to the user than interfaces to traditional vehicle functions such as braking and acceleration. Thus it becomes more important to model the human machine interface in this area, both for usability and to ensure that it does not contribute to driver distraction. Other consumer devices that users might like to access through vehicle HMI systems include mp3 players, such as the Ipod, PDAs, hand held navigation devices and hand held gaming devices. Additionally, existing devices are offering more services in addition to the ones they were originally designed for. Cell phones, for example, not only maintain a contact list, but in many cases allow the user to play games. There are few standards for interfacing to these devices and services. Bluetooth profiles provide standards for some services, but these are a minority of all the possibilities. For the others, the variety of devices and manufacturers makes it completely infeasible to delay testing the interfaces until the hardware becomes available in a prototype vehicle.

In each of these cases it is important to model not only the functionality of the device or service as presented over the vehicle HMI, but also the usability and aesthetic acceptability as well. Since we have no control over the consumer devices in question, it is important to model how they will behave with a proposed vehicle HMI at the stage that the latter is being designed.

The Vehicle and Infrastructure Integration Initiative. The second major trend that will affect vehicle infotainment systems is the Vehicle and Infrastructure Integration (VII) initiative of the US Department of Transportation [6]. This initiative is aimed at providing crash prevention and congestion relief through vehicle-to-vehicle and vehicle-to-roadside communication. The vision of this initiative is that every vehicle in the U.S. would be equipped with a communications device and a GPS unit so that data could be exchanged with a nationwide instrumented roadway system. This system is now undergoing initial testbed deployment with a view to making a decision on deployment of the full system by 2007. It is expected that the system will have enough bandwidth above that required for accident prevention and congestion control that commercial applications can use the system as well.The system will be based on DSRC, a short range wireless protocol being standardized by ASTM, IEEE and other organizations [7]. This protocol uses the 5.9 GHz band. Ford is a member of the VII consortium and is currently involved in testbed deployment at its Dearborn campus.

The main driver behind the VII initiative is a mandate on USDOT to reduce the national accident rate by 50%. It has been determined that This requires accident prevention rather than just mitigation. The proposed uses for VII include services that require direct vehicle to vehicle communication as well as services based on communication between the vehicle and the roadside infrastructure. For example, one proposal is a sudden deceleration warning that would be sent from a vehicle that decelerates above a certain threshhold rate together with the vehicle's precise location and heading. Following vehicles which would then provide a warning to their drivers that a vehicle ahead is decelerating rapidly. This would help to reduce the number of rear end collisions, particularly in conditions of poor visibility. However, for this technique to work correctly, without giving false warnings that could in themselves be dangerous, the algorithm in the receiving vehicle that decides whether to warn the driver based on the deceleration message must be carefully designed. This is an example of a problem that our facility is designed to address since we have the capability to model the wireless communication link, the software in the controller and the vehicle HMI and their interactions in this situation.

Opening vehicle safety systems to outside communications both from other vehicles and from a national roadside infrastructure also raises serious security and privacy concerns that must be addressed. Possibilities such as spoofing critical sources and inserting malicious information into vehicle systems did not exist previously, and we have little experience with them. Security expert Bruce Schneier has raised the possibility of a scenario where a virus from a Bluetooth device in a passing car could enter your vehicle's Bluetooth gateway module and cause the navigation system to suddenly stop working [8]. Prevention of scenarios such as this while maintaining the connectivity desired by consumers will require extensive modeling of these new vehicle systems, including threat modeling.

3   The Modeling Facility

In order to address these concerns we have put together a modeling facility that consists of a number of tools. This lab is intended to address software and system design in the infotainment and body electronics domains rather than the vehicle dynamics or powertrain domains. Our primary goal is to extend the modeling that has proven successful for body electronics ECUs to the system level and to the infotainment domain, and particularly to the requirements for wireless connectivity that are emerging in that domain.

This lab has five major modeling tools and two hardware in the loop systems. These tools provide different views on the software of a vehicle system and when combined allow the modeling of different aspects of the system from multiple viewpoints. The relation between these tools is shown in Fig 5. In addition to the components shown in the figure there is one other major component; a repository with version control for holding the models. This repository will hold two types of models. The first are feature models that describe the intended functionality of a vehicle feature or service and that will serve as a detailed specification for the implementation of that feature or service. The second are ECU models that describe the behavior of a vehicle electronic module, including all of the services and features that are implemented by that module. In a production development environment, the first type of model will be created by Ford engineers and given to module suppliers to guide their implementation of the desired vehicle functionality, while the second will be produced by the module supplier and given to Ford for validation against the vehicle system level model.

In order to cover the wireless communications area, we have added to the MathWorks / dSPACE behavioral modeling tools an RTlab hardware in the loop system designed by OpalRT and based on National Instruments equipment. This equipment includes RF analyzer and generator boards that can be used to analyze and produce a number of RF protocols, such as Bluetooth, 802.11 and DSRC through the use of appropriate software to drive the boards. The boards are also capable of handling automotive specific RF protocols, such as the remote keyfob protocol and the tire pressure monitor protocol. Both the dSPACE and the RTlab HIL systems can be connected to a CAN bus to allow communication with other modules, or with a CANoe network modeling tool [9]. The RTlab HIL system also includes a fault insertion unit to allow simulation of hardware failures. The other components shown in figure 5 are workstations running tools for network modeling (CANoe), HMI development and modeling (Altia), software modeling (Rhapsody) and requirements capture and analysis.

These tools allow actual consumer devices to be tested against a model of the vehicle interface prior to its implementation in a vehicle. For example, the designer of a Bluetooth phone module might implement the Bluetooth Handsfree profile in terms of a certain set of CAN messages. by modeling this module plus the audio system and testing it against actual Bluetooth enabled phones one can ensure that both the vehicle module designer and the implementor of the cell phone have the same understanding of the Hands-free profile.

In the simpler world of device control it suffices to model an algorithm that provides the required functionality and then to generate code from this model without being concerned about the structure of the resulting software or the resources that it uses. In the more complex world that is presented by infotainment functions however, the software is much more dynamic and its structure becomes

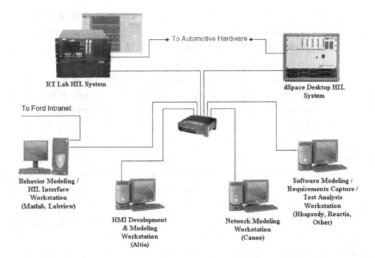

To Automotive Hardware

RT Lab HIL System

dSpace Desktop HIL System

To Ford Intranet

Behavior Modeling / HIL Interface Workstation (Matlab, Labview)

HMI Development & Modeling Workstation (Altia)

Network Modeling Workstation (Canoe)

Software Modeling / Requirements Capture / Test Analysis Workstation (Rhapsody, Reactis, Other)

Fig. 5. Modeling facility toolset

important. For this reason we thought it important to have a tool that could model other aspects of the software than its functionality. The most widely used tool in this area is the Unified Modeling Language, UML [10]. UML is already being used by Ford in Europe as well as Jaguar and Volvo for entertainment systems software design.Models already exist therefore for the software architectures used by those groups. We chose Rhapsody from Ilogix as a UML modeling tool because it is heavily oriented towards embedded software and supports the new UML 2.0 standard from the Object Management Group, as well as SYSML, a variant of UML designed for system modeling. A significant advantage of UML 2.0 is that there is a standard vendor independent representation of models based on XMI and the diagram interchange standard using SVG. This is important because we expect that eventually software models will be shared between various groups within Ford and our global supplier base, and we cannot expect all of these groups to use tools from a single vendor. The fact that the models have a standard vendor independent representation also makes it easier to apply new tools that may be developed in the future to implement improved methodologies.

Software oriented modeling is particularly important when dealing with service oriented software architectures. Behavioral modeling techniques, such as state machines, are inadequate by themselves to analyze processes such as service discovery and their associated data structures, such as registries. This makes it important to model the middleware layer that implements service based architectures with a comprehensive tool. UML sequence diagrams provide an important technique for analyzing the interactions between servers and their clients that define services. They can be used for example to lay out the interactions that must occur between a consumer device and the vehicle components that are providing HMI services to it and the resulting scenarios can be tested against behavioral (state machine) models of those components to ensure that the implementation is adequate.

The UML model can communicate with a CANoe model over a TCP/IP network using the COM interface of CANoe. One simply creates a class in the model representing the CAN driver software that is implemented to talk over TCP/IP instead. For Simulink/Stateflow, CANoe has a built-in interface. Thus UML models and stateflow models can talk to each other using CANoe as an intermediary, and we can execute a detailed software model of the code in a particular ECU against behavioral models of the rest of the ECUs in the system and of the network.

The final tool that is required is a tool to model the human machine interface in a realistic way. The tool that was chosen for this purpose is Altia Design from Altia [11]. This tool, like the others, is already in use within Ford by the ergonomics group. They use the tool to model and evaluate layouts of the vehicle HMI that have been proposed by designers before hardware prototypes are built. The limitation of the process that they are using is that the models, although exact in terms of appearance, cannot be made functional unless the functionality is hand coded in C. This requires a significant amount of effort, and even if it is done there is no guarantee that the resulting model behaves in the same way as the ECU that controls the HMI in the vehicle will behave. To address this issue we are connecting the Altia tool to the other modeling tools by writing adapters between the modeling tools and the Altia interface. These adapters exist for Labview and Simulink/Stateflow, end we have written them for Rhapsody and CANoe. Tying the HMI modeling to functional models provides an important opportunity to improve the communication between the ergonomics and engineering activities that should result in improved vehicle interiors.

The HMI modeling provided by the Altia tool can provide important information on the usability of an HMI design, but there are important issues related to driver distraction that arise when consumer devices are brought into the vehicle. Ultimately these questions require studying human reactions in a more realistic environment than a lab based modeling tool. Ford has such an environment in its Virttex driving simulator [12, 13]. In the longer term we hope to be able to connect the system and software modeling tools to the Virttex simulator to study the driver distraction issues that are raised by consumer devices and novel multimedia systems in the vehicle and to use these studies to eliminate driver distraction from those sources.

4   Conclusion

A number of issues remain to be resolved before the facility described here is fully functional. A major one that was not discussed here is the issue of model configuration management. As a significant amount of effort is involved in creating an accurate model of a vehicle system or feature, it is important to be able to reuse the models that have been created and thus to be able to configure them readily to represent different combinations of systems that are implemented in different vehicles. Moreover, as a software enabled feature moves through different stages of its lifecycle, from concept to validation of the implementation in the final product, it will be modeled from different viewpoints. The same feature will thus be represented by a number of different models, which need to be linked to each other to maintain traceability throughout the development process. This requires model management tools that understand the relationship between different types of models and that fit into the broader product development process as well.

Another issue that must be resolved to support model reusability is the development of guidelines for constructing models with each of the tools that can ensure that the models developed by different groups are compatible. This has already been done for Simulink/Stateflow models in the powertrain area. It will be particularly important for UML modeling, because UML is a very large language that is designed to support many very different uses. Some restriction of the UML constructs that are used will certainly be necessary. Our current usage is primarily limited to class diagrams, sequence diagrams and state diagrams, but it remains to be seen which of the other diagram types will be useful as well.

We are addressing these and other issues in our current work with the modeling lab. Based on our experience with the use of modeling and hardware in the loop testing on a single body module, we expect that the extension of this modeling to the vehicle systems level will result in substantial productivity increases in the development of embedded software. The work that we are doing this year will confirm or deny this expectation.

Acknowledgement

Henry Huang was principally responsible for the HIL modeling project on the power distribution box described in this paper. He provided most of the information reported here on the results of that project. David Watson and T. J. Giuli are carrying out the new concepts modeling projects and are responsible for much of the methodology of connecting the various modeling tools. Craig Simonds was instrumental in planning for and procuring the various components of the lab and in interfacing with the Ford IT activities. Venkatesh Prasad has provided valuable advice on the strategy and direction for the lab and on the set of problems that will be initially addressed by the facility. The authors also wish to thank the reviewers for numerous useful comments and suggestions.

References

1. Sun, J., Kolmanovsky, J.C.I., Buckland, J.: Modeling and control of automotive powertrain systems: A tutorial, Portland, OR (2005)
2. Reactive Systems Inc.: Model based testing and validation with reactis, http://www.reactive-systems.com
3. Automotive Multimedia Interface Collaboration: Ami-c release 2 architectural overview (2003), http://www.ami-c.org/publicspecrelease.asp?filename=1003.zip
4. OSGi Alliance: OSGi Service Platform Release 3. IOS Press, Amsterdam, The Netherlands (2003)

5. Krüger, I.H., Nelson, E., Prasad, K.V.: Service-based software development for automotive applications, Warrendale, PA. Society of Automotive Engineers, Inc. (2004)
6. United States Department of Transportation, http://www.its.dot.gov/vii/
7. Armstrong, L.: Dedicated short range communications (DSRC) at 5.9 GHz, http://www.leearmstrong.com/DSRCHome/StandardsPrograms/NorthAmerican/DSRCSummary.ppt
8. Hutson, S.: Ten emerging technologies: Cell phone viruses (2005), http://www.technologyreview.com/articles/05/05/issue
9. VECTOR CANtech Inc.: CANoe and DENoe 5.2, http://www.vector-cantech.com/products/canoe-features.html
10. Object Management Group Inc.: UML superstructure specification, v2.0. (2003), http://www.omg.org/cgi-bin/doc?formal/05-07-04
11. Altia Incorporated: Altia design, http://www.altia.com/products_design.php
12. Greenberg, J., Tijerina, L., Curry, R., Artz, B., Cathey, L., Kochhar, D., Kozak, K., Blommer, M., Grant, P.: Driver distraction: Evaluation with event detection paradigm. Transportation Research Record 1843, 1–9 (2003)
13. Grant, P.R., Artz, B.E., Greenberg, J.A., Cathey, L.W.: Motion characteristics of the virttex motion system. In: Proc., 1st Human Centered Transportation Simulation Conference, CD-ROM(ISSN 1538-3288) (2001)

Generating Sound and Resource-Aware Code from Hybrid Systems Models*

Madhukar Anand, Sebastian Fischmeister, Jesung Kim,
and Insup Lee

Department of Computer and Information Science
School of Engineering and Applied Sciences
University of Pennsylvania
{anandm,jesung,lee}@cis.upenn.edu, sfischme@seas.upenn.edu

Abstract. Modern real-time embedded systems are complex, distributed, feature-rich applications. Model-based development of real-time embedded systems promises to simplify and accelerate the implementation process. Although there are appropriate models to design such systems and some tools that support automatic code generation from such models, several issues related to ensuring correctness of the implementation with respect to the model remain to be addressed.

In this work, we investigate how to derive sampling rates for distributed real-time systems generated from a hybrid systems model such that there are no switching discrepancies and the resources spent in achieving this are a minimum. Of particular interest are the resulting mode switching semantics and we propose an approach to handle faulty transitions and compute execution rates for minimizing missed transitions.

1 Introduction

Modern real-time embedded systems are complex, distributed, feature-rich applications. For example a car incorporates thirty to sixty micro-controller units [1] and desired functionality includes automatic parking, automatic car coordination, and automatic collision avoidance. The development of such functionality is time-consuming and difficult, since faults in the temporal or value domain may lead to system failures, which in turn can lead to catastrophes with possibly human losses. Model-based development of real-time embedded systems promises to simplify and accelerate the implementation process. This is because of its promises such as formal guarantees and code generation. Several mathematical models such as Timed Automata [2], Hybrid Systems [3], State-charts [4] have been successfully applied to real-time embedded systems. For embedded control software, hybrid systems are an appropriate modeling paradigm because it

---

* This research was supported in part by NSF CNS-0509143, NSF CNS-0720703, NSF CNS-0720518, FA9550-07-1-0216, OEAW APART-11059 and ARO W911NF-05-1-0182.

M. Broy, I.H. Krüger, and M. Meisinger (Eds.): ASWSD 2006, LNCS 4922, pp. 48–66, 2008.
© Springer-Verlag Berlin Heidelberg 2008

can be used to specify continuous change of the system state as well as discrete transition of states [5, 6].

Although modeling and analysis play an important part in development of applications, it is also essential to establish the same guarantees in the implementation of the model. In particular, it is imperative that the correspondence between the model and the code is precisely understood. In keeping with this objective, our efforts are directed towards automatic and faithful code generation from hybrid systems models.

Introduction to CHARON. CHARON [7], is a tool for modular specification of interacting hybrid systems based on the notions of agent and mode. For hierarchical description of the system architecture, CHARON provides the operations of instantiation, hiding, and parallel composition on agents, which can be used to build a complex agent from other agents. The discrete and continuous behaviors of an agent are described using modes. For hierarchical description of the behavior of an agent, CHARON supports the operations of instantiation and nesting of modes. Furthermore, features such as weak preemption, history retention, and externally defined Java functions, facilitate the description of complex discrete behavior. Continuous behavior can be specified using differential as well as algebraic constraints, and invariants restricting the flow spaces, all of which can be declared at various levels of the hierarchy. The modular structure of the language is not merely syntactic, but also reflected in the semantics so that it can be exploited during analysis.

Code generation from hybrid system models. A problem for code generation from verified models is to understand the relationship between the model and the code. The model's verification and analysis are only useful, if the generated code has the same properties as the model. Several code generators can derive code from a model, however, the relationship between model and the code using continuous time is not their primary concern (c.f., [4, 8] or commercial tools like Real-Time Workshop or TargetLink). On the other hand, some academic code generators ensure that the model and the code have the same properties (c.f., [9]), but the issue remains challenging.

Code generation from hybrid systems models eventually involves assigning a *rate* by which the continuous state evolves. In such a *discretized* hybrid systems model, the state changes in a discrete manner according to the rate typically assigned by the model designer. Further, the concurrency of the model is broken in distributed implementations where delays in updates can result in semantic differences. Realizing a faithful implementation of the model, therefore, involves addressing all of these issues.

Dynamic elements in the model aggravate the problem of faithful implementation. Such dynamic elements are, for instance, battery power output, sensor quality, actuator precision, which change over time and with respect to the changing environment. Current models rely on a steady environment and resource set. Our research is motivated by the need to provide formal semantics and guarantees in dynamic environments.

1.1 Related Work and Problem Statement

Model-based automatic code generation has been an extensive research initiative in recent years, in the industry as well as academia. Commercial modeling tools such as RationalRose [10], TargetLink [11], and SIMULINK [12] also support code generation and address the effect of errors in the code. However, their concerns are largely limited to numerical errors occurring each step during simulation, and the effect of such errors on to discrete behavior is not addressed rigorously. Synchronous languages for reactive systems, such as STATECHARTS [4], ESTEREL [13], and LUSTRE [14], also support code generation. However, they do not support hybrid systems modeling. SHIFT [15] is a language for hybrid automata that also also supports code generation, but the focus is on dynamic networks. A complementary project is the time-triggered language Giotto that allows describing switching among task sets so that timing deadlines can be specified in a platform independent manner separately from the control code [16]. This concern is orthogonal, and in fact, CHARON can be compiled into Giotto.

Model-based development of embedded systems is also promoted by other projects with orthogonal concerns: Ptolemy supports integration of heterogeneous models of computation [8] and GME supports meta-modeling for development of domain-specific modeling languages [17]. Girard et al [18] also consider hybrid systems modeling of embedded applications, however, their focus is on verification of safety properties and not code generation. There also exist other efforts towards model-driven development of embedded software from models other than hybrid systems(c.f., [19]). In a closely related work, Stauner [20] discusses at length, the discrete refinement of hybrid automata, considering implementation effects such as sampling errors and its impact on verification.

There are several modeling tools for hybrid systems such as CHARON [7], PTOLEMY [8], SHIFT [15], the Matlab/Simulink Hybrid Toolbox [21], HYTECH [22], and d/dt [23]. However, most of them are only modeling tools and do not support automatic-code generation. A listing of many tools and their description is available at [24].

Code generation from hybrid models was introduced with focus on single-thread execution in [3]. This was extended to multi-threaded models accounting for faulty transitions in [25]. and distributed systems in [26,27]. All these previous works however, are not aware of the resources available on the implementation platform and therefore need manual parameter assignment in the code.

Contributions. In this paper, we extend previous, related work to consider the problem of calculating sampling rates based on the platform resource model. Specifically, we investigate how to derive criteria to preserve the model's switching semantics based on the platform resource model to ensure that there are no faulty or missed transitions. Our ideas are demonstrated in the context of the modeling language CHARON, where we propose an additional step in the code generation module. This additional step involves (1) specifying a platform resource model for the available hardware and its properties and (2) using this model to compute the optimal sampling rates so that switching semantics are preserved while expending the least amount of resources in the process.

2   Basic Model and Assumptions

A hybrid model consists of a real vector x denoting the continuous state, a finite set of discrete states P that associates x with a differential equation $\dot{x} = f_p(x)$. For each $p \in P$, and a set of transitions $E \subseteq P \times P$. The continuous state x evolves according to the differential equation $\dot{x} = f_p(x)$ when the current discrete state is p. When the current discrete state is changed from p to p', x is optionally reset to a new value $R(x, p, p')$ defined by a map $R : \mathbb{R}^n \times P \times P \to \mathbb{R}^n$, and continues evolution in accordance with a new differential equation $\dot{x} = f_{p'}(x)$ associated with p'. To control the discrete behavior, discrete transitions can be guarded by predicates over x and externally updated variables. That is, a set $G((p, p')) \subseteq \mathbb{R}^n$ for each $(p, p') \in E$ specifies the necessary condition on the continuous state that the transition (p, p') can be taken. Note that a discrete transition is not necessarily taken immediately even if the guard is true. To enforce a transition, an invariant set $I(p) \subseteq \mathbb{R}^n$ is associated for each $p \in P$ to specify the condition that the discrete state can stay in p (that is, the condition that x will follow $\dot{x} = f_p(x)$). An outgoing transition should be taken before the continuous state goes out of the invariant set.

In this paper, we assume that there is a network of hybrid automata (called *agents*) communicating via a set of shared variables. We will denote a single agent by $\mathcal{A} = (A, SV)$ where A is the hybrid model of the agent, and SV is the set of shared variables. A system of communicating hybrid agents is represented by the tuple $\mathcal{C} = \langle (A, SV)_1, \dots, (A, SV)_n \rangle$. We assume that every $s \in SV$ is updated by a unique agent, and it follows dynamics such that $\dot{s} \in [\mathcal{L}_1, \mathcal{L}_2], \mathcal{L}_1, \mathcal{L}_2 \in \mathbb{Q} \setminus \{0\}$. Such linear automata are of practical significance, as hybrid systems with very general dynamics can be locally approximated arbitrarily closely using rectangular dynamics [28]. The transition guards at a location are assumed to be such that at most one of them is enabled at a time.

Example 1. Consider the example of vehicle coordination where we assume that there are two vehicles. The first vehicle is the leader and follows the dynamics depicted as agent A_1 in Figure 1. x_1 denotes the distance of the leader from the baseline, v_1, its velocity. The leader's dynamics are determined by the control function u. The second vehicle trails the leader and maintains a safe distance from it. The dynamics of this vehicle is described as the agent A_2. Its distance from the baseline is given by x_2, and velocity by v_2. If it is closer than d_{min} from the leader, it slows with a rate $\dot{v}_2 = -1$ and if it is farther than d_{max}, it accelerates with a rate $\dot{v}_2 = 1$. The invariant in the state q_1 is $x_1 - x_2 \in [d_{min} - \eta, d_{max} + \eta]$, in q_2 is $x_1 - x_2 \geq d_{min} - \eta$, and in q_3 is $x_1 - x_2 \leq d_{max} + \eta$, where η is the tolerance parameter. It is assumed that, there is an infrastructure for communicating variables between the vehicles and that, the transmission delay is bounded and known.   □

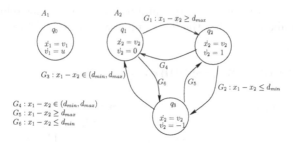

Fig. 1. A system with two agents

We now formally define the resource model and the platform on which the code will be implemented. Implementation of the continuous model involves assigning a suitable sampling rate to every agent. Such a discretization of the continuous model can be defined as,

Definition 1. *(DCHA) Given a system of communicating hybrid agents $\mathcal{C}$, and a relative period of update of variables ρ, $\rho \in \mathbb{Z}^+$, the discretized system of communicating agents (DCHA) is given by $\mathcal{D} = \langle (A, SV, \rho)_1, \ldots, (A, SV, \rho)_n \rangle$, such that $\gcd(\rho_1, \ldots, \rho_n) = 1$[1,2].* □

In our notation, we denote the maximum difference between the sampling rates of agents as *skew*[3].

Note that the DCHA is the model implemented on actual platforms. We will therefore, give guarantees of execution with reference to this model. For a rigorous definition of system of communicating agents and their semantics, we refer the reader to [25].When the discretized model is mapped to a real time task in the code-generation environment, each agent is assigned a period of execution. These periods of execution are assigned taking into consideration correctness guarantees and the resources available at each node. The exact procedure for assigning periods is elaborated in Sections 4.

Our objective in incorporating the resource model (i.e., model of memory, energy, CPU,etc) in addition to the hybrid model is that, we can generate a minimal sampling frequency that can be supported on the platform. This optimum is calculated by ensuring the model semantics and conserving the resources available. Therefore, we define a resource as consisting of a utilization function and a specification of energy utilization for every operation.

Definition 2. *(Resource) A resource R is defined by the tuple $\langle id, U, \mathcal{E} \rangle$, where, $id \in \mathbb{Z}^+$ is a unique identifier of the resource, U is the maximum amount of utilization, and an optional field $\mathcal{E}$ which indicates the amount of energy consumed per unit of utilization. A node N is defined as a set of interacting resources.* □

---

[1] Greatest common divisor.

[2] This assumption is not necessary but introduced to keep the discussion simple.

[3] We acknowledge that our definition here differs from the standard definition of skew. However, our use of the term is motivated by similar considerations.

The definition of platform consists of a mapping between the model and the node that executes the code corresponding to that model, the communication delay involved, and finally a quantum of execution supported at each node. The quantum is defined by how often a computation can be performed on any node.

Definition 3. *(Platform) A platform $\mathcal{P}$ is defined as the tuple $\langle \mathcal{N}, \mathcal{M}, \phi, \nu \rangle$ where $\mathcal{N}$ is a system of nodes, $\mathcal{M} : \mathcal{A} \to \mathcal{N}$ is a function that maps an agent to a node on which it is to be executed, ϕ is a map that takes as input the agent ids and returns the bound on communication delay between two agents in $\mathcal{A}$, and ν is the baseline period, i.e., the quanta of the period of execution of any agent.*

Note that we assume a underlying reliable communication mechanism The abstractions for platform and code consider only the basic of all the actual implementation effects and make several simplifying assumptions. For instance, jitter, clock drift, message loss, and other errors in the system, which are often observed in real systems, have not been considered here. These effects can potentially weaken some of the results presented in this work. The aim of this work however, is to establish a sound theory as a first attempt at categorizing some of the implementation effects. More artifacts of the implementation can be incorporated into the model at the cost of more involved analysis.

Example 2. Consider the vehicle coordination system with two agents as shown in Figure 1. For the trailing vehicle (V_2), the resources could be a battery, the CPU and the sensor for tracking the leader(V_1). The resource model for the vehicle V_2 can thus be represented as,

V_2	id	U_{max}	$\mathcal{E}$
	$Batt_1$	1000mAh	-
	CPU	5Mhz	0.001J/op
	$Sensor_1$	1kHz	0.2J/sample

The target platform here consists of two nodes, the leader and the trailing vehicle, and if we assume no communication delays, it is described as $\langle \{V_1, V_2\}, \mathcal{M}, \phi(V_1, V_2) \rangle$, where $\mathcal{M} = \{A_1 \to V_1, A_2 \to V_2\}$, and $\phi(A_i, A_j) = 0$. The baseline period (quantum of execution) is the smallest sampling period that could be supported. For example, we could have ν to be 0.01. □

3   Code Generation from Hybrid System Models

This section gives a brief overview of the procedure of code generation from hybrid models. We first present translation of continuous behavior specified by differential equations and algebraic equations, and then explain translation of discrete actions specified by guarded transitions. Later in this section, we discuss the issue of discrepancy between the model and the generated code, real-time resource concerns and choice of correctness criteria. For more details on code generation, we refer the reader to [3, 25].

3.1   Code Generation Procedure

A differential equation of the form of $\dot{x} = f(x)$ specifies continuous change of variable x at the rate specified as the first derivative $f(x)$ of x with respect to time (i.e., $dx/dt = f(x)$). Continuous change of a variable can be simulated by stepwise update of the variable based on a numerical method that computes an approximate value of the variable after a discrete time step (e.g., Runge-Kutta method [29]). The simplest numerical method is the one known as Euler's method, which projects the value of the variable at the next time step through linear extrapolation. For example, a differential equation $\dot{x} = 2$ is translated into an assignment statement $x := x + 2 \times h$, where h is the step size. In fact, no more sophisticated method is necessary if the right-hand side of the differential equation is a constant.

Once the differential equations are solved, algebraic equations are evaluated to reflect the change due to differential equations. The general form of algebraic equations is $y = g(x)$. An algebraic equation can be implemented by an assignment statement of the same form. That is, an algebraic equation $y = g(x)$ is simply translated into an assignment of the form $y := g(x)$.

Discrete actions of hybrid automata specify instantaneous switching of system dynamics and optional reset of variables. Discrete actions are specified by transitions between positions, where each position defines different dynamics. The transition has a guard that specifies the necessary condition for the transition to be taken, and may have optional assignments to variables that are performed at the moment when the transition is taken. When a transition is taken, differential equations and algebraic equations defined in the source position become no longer active, and those defined in the destination position take effect immediately.

The guard in the hybrid system model enables or disables a transition, rather than immediately triggers a transition in hybrid systems models. This means that enabled transitions may be taken delayed as long as the invariant is satisfied. Conceptually, transitions are non-deterministic in the model, and the implementation determines exactly when a transition is taken. An obvious policy is an *urgent* transition policy where a transition is taken as soon as the guard evaluates true. We have proposed a transition policy what we call *instrumentation* [25] that enforces transitions to be taken some time Δ after the transition is enabled but no later than Δ before the transition is disabled. The value of Δ is chosen such that all faulty transition possibilities are eliminated (Section 4.1). Yet another possibility is to enforce a transition once it *evaluated* to be enabled. We call such a policy an *eager* transition policy. Surely, the urgent transition policy is an eager transition policy. The instrumented transition policy is an eager transition policy if the instrumented guard set is a non-empty set. We only consider an eager transition policy in this paper.

3.2   Switching Discrepancies in the Code

There are a number of issues, such as ensuring the switching semantics and faithful translation of continuous dynamics, that need to be addressed to provide guarantees in the generated code. Here, we focus on preventing switching discrepancies. The continuous semantics of the model are implemented in the code with the help of numerical methods which introduce an error due to discretization in addition to the roundoff and truncation errors on target platforms. These errors along with the order of scheduling of the reads may cause a transition to be falsely enabled. If such a faulty transition is taken, the dynamics of the system may be completely different from the intended model. The example below highlights such a possibility.

Example 3. (Faulty Transition) Consider the vehicle coordination system in Example 1. Let us say that the relative period of update for agents A_1 and A_2 be $(5, 3)$ and the actual periods of updates be $0.1s$ and $0.06s$, respectively. Also, let $u = 2$, $d_{min} = 0.1$, $d_{max} = 0.5$, and initial positions of vehicles be $x_1^0 = 0.3072$ and $x_2^0 = 0.2$, from the baseline, initial velocities $v_1^0 = 0$, $v_2^0 = 0$, the communication delay $\phi(A_1, A_2) = 0.03$, and the current states of agents be q_0 and q_2. Then, a possible run of the system is,

t	$x_1(A_1)$	$x_1(A_2)$	$x_2(A_2)$
0.06	0.3072	0.3072	0.2018
0.10	0.3172	0.3072	0.2018
0.12	0.3172	0.3072	0.2072
...			

where $x_i(A_j)$ denotes the value of variable x_i on agent A_j. Notice that at time 0.12, the difference between vehicles is $0.3172 - 0.2072 = 0.11 (> 0.1)$, but the estimated distance at A_2 is $0.3072 - 0.2072 = 0.0956 < 0.1$ and the system makes a faulty transition to q_3.   □

Although the above example indicates a faulty transition, since the transition is made to q_3 in which the trailing vehicle decelerates, it is not critical to ensuring safety. However, in some cases, if the system makes a faulty transition to an accelerating state q_2, then, the trailing vehicles accelerates. This is critical to safety as the gap between the vehicles decreases in this case. The example below illustrates this.

Example 4. (Faulty Transition) Now consider that the relative period of update for agents A_1 and A_2 be $(2, 1)$ and the actual periods of updates be $0.2s$ and $0.1s$, respectively. Also, let $d_{min} = 0.1$, $d_{max} = 0.2$, and initial positions of vehicles be $x_1^0 = 0.19$ and $x_2^0 = 0.1$ from the baseline, initial velocities $v_1^0 = 0.1$, $v_2^0 = 0.2$, the communication delay $\phi(A_1, A_2) = 0.01$, and the current states of agents be q_0 and q_3. The first vehicle reverses its direction at $\dot{v}_2 = -1$ at time $0.1s$. Then, a possible run of the system is,

t	$x_1(A_1)$	$x_1(A_2)$	$x_2(A_2)$
0	0.19	0.19	0.1
0.1	0.21	0.19	0.1
0.2	0.20	0.21	0.11
...			

At time 0.2, the difference between vehicles is $0.20 - 0.11 = 0.09(< d_{max})$, but the estimated distance at A_2 is $0.21 - 0.11 = 0.1(= d_{max})$ and the system could a faulty transition to q_2. Since q_2 is an accelerating state, this transition reduces the distance between vehicles, potentially causing a collision.   □

Yet another possibility for switching errors is that of missed transitions. Insufficient sampling rates, choice of scheduling of reads, etc., may cause a transition to be missed. Missing some transitions may cause the system to end up in an erroneous state. We illustrate this with an example below.

Example 5. (Missed Transition) Consider the system in Example 1. Let the relative periods of execution be $(5, 3)$, the actual periods of update $(0.25s, 0.15s)$, $d_{min} = 0.25$, $d_{max} = 0.5$, the control parameter $u = 0$. $x_1 = 0.48$, $v_1 = 5$, $v_2 = 4.5$ at $t = 0.15$, and the current state of A_2 be q_2. Further, let $d = x_1 - x_2$, $\dot{d} = \dot{x}_1 - \dot{x}_2 \in [0.45, 0.5]$. The guard G_4 is then the condition $d \in (0.25, 0.5)$ which on instrumentation will become $d \in (0.25 + 0.1 \times 0.5, 0.5 - 0.1 \times 0.5) = (0.3, 0.45)$ as the maximum skew is 0.1, and $\mathcal{L}_2 = 0.5$. We would then have a run of the system as,

t	$x_1(A_1)$	$x_2(A_2)$
0.15	0.48	0.0
0.25	0.98	0.0
0.30	0.98	0.6862
...		

We see that the transition from q_2 to q_1 is missed here, and at time $t = 0.3s$, the system transits to q_3.   □

Switching can also be affected by resource constraints and its dynamic nature. For example, as the battery wears off, it may not yield the same output causing a deadline miss of some task. If the tasks scheduled to run do not meet the deadlines, it may affect the dynamics which in turn could induce faulty transitions. To counter this, in our proposed approach, we start with an assignment of relative periods to different agents. From these relative periods, and the current estimates of resources, the actual periods of execution are synthesized. We choose these actual periods so that these correspond to the least amount of energy used while retaining the guarantees of switching behavior.

3.3   Correctness Criteria

The generated code and the model can be termed equivalent if the code exhibits a trace that is also a trace in the model. However, to account for delays in communication and skew due to different rates of execution in the code, we relax this requirement and define a relative faithful implementation. Under this relaxed form of correctness, the code exhibits a trace of the model, but the state of the model is entered at a later time. This can be captured formally as,

Definition 4. *(Relative Faithful Implementation) Let VC be the set of all variables and α_x be the maximum bound on the error of a variable x. Given a trace*

of states of the code $\mathcal{K}$ for an agent A_j, $\langle q_0, q_1, \ldots \rangle$, at physical timestamps $\langle clk_0, clk_1, \ldots \rangle$, if, $\forall clk$,

1. *$\forall x \in VC$, $|x_\mathcal{D}(lt) - x_\mathcal{K}(lt)| < \alpha_x$, where $x_\mathcal{K}$ and $x_\mathcal{D}$ represent the value of variable in the code and the model respectively, and lt, the logical time in the code.*
2. *$\forall j$, $\exists q_\mathcal{D}, q_\mathcal{K} = q_\mathcal{D}$, $(lt_\mathcal{D} - lt_\mathcal{K}) < \phi_j(lt_\mathcal{K}) + \varphi(lt_\mathcal{K})$ where $q_\mathcal{K}$ is the state of the code of logical time $lt_\mathcal{K}$, at physical time clk, $q_\mathcal{D}$ is the projection of the state of the model onto the code for A_j at logical time $lt_\mathcal{D}$, $\phi_j = \max_i \phi(i, j)$ and φ is the maximum skew due to different rates of updates at logical time $lt_\mathcal{K}$.*

then, code for A_j is a relative faithful implementation. If $\forall j$, A_j is a relative faithful implementation, then $\mathcal{K}$ is a relative faithful implementation of $\mathcal{D}$.   □

Informally, a relative faithful implementation says that (1) the error in continuous variables is bounded , and (2) the difference between the state of the model and the implementation can be off by at most the sum total of worst case communication delay and skew in update of variables. Under this relaxed scheme of things, the implementation can enter the state of the model after updates are received (which can arrive at worst $\phi_j(lt_\mathcal{K}) + \varphi(lt_\mathcal{K})$ late). We now present the framework that would help ensure that the implementation is relative faithful to the model.

4   Proposed Implementation Framework

In this section, we propose a framework for code generation with an emphasis to avoid switching discrepancies (faulty and missed transitions) and conserve resources while giving these guarantees. The Figure 2 provides an overview of how the model-driven development process in our framework with CHARON: first, the developer creates the application-specific hybrid systems model by programming agents, modes, and mode changes and by defining relative update periods. Then he specifies the platform resource model, which includes, for instance, an agent-to-node assignment, each node's hardware properties, power levels, communication delays, and agent's worst-case execution times. This resource model is then fed into a constraint solver, which computes the optimal agent's sampling rates to prevent faulty and missed transitions as described in the following sections. Note that we do assume that the base period of updates of variables in an agent (ρ) are provided beforehand, and we compute the actual period of updates (which is a multiple of base periods) depending on available resources.

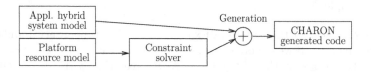

Fig. 2. Resource-aware Code-generation Framework

Before we elaborate on computing the optimal rates of sampling of agents, we highlight the solution to avoiding faulty and missed transitions.

4.1   Preventing Faulty Transitions

A faulty transition is a violation of equivalence of discrete states in a faithful implementation. It may occur due to the following reasons : 1) errors in the variables cause the guard to be evaluated true that should otherwise be false, or 2) variables are updated at different times due to scheduling and/or different update frequencies, causing the guard to be evaluated to be true. To prevent this from occurring, we have proposed a technique what we call instrumentation. The essence of that technique is to refine the model by tightening transition conditions according to the maximum errors due to numerical and different sampling rates. The approach enforces that the transitions in the code are consistent with the model.

Errors in variables could be due to roundoff, truncation or be timing-induced due to the different rates of execution of the agents. Roundoff and truncation errors are assumed to be given, the communication delay is obtained by monitoring and the maximum *skew*, denoted by φ due to dissimilar periods can be computed by, $\varphi(A_i, A_j)_{max} = \max_{n \in [1..N]} \left(nh_j - \left\lfloor \frac{nh_j - \phi(A_i, A_j)}{h_i} \right\rfloor h_i \right)$ where $N = \frac{LCM(h_i, h_j)}{h_j} 4$, h_i and h_j are the step sizes in the sampling of Agent A_i and A_j, respectively.

Definition 5. *(Instrumentation) Let p be a state of agent A_j with $E_{A_j}(p)$ being the set of discrete transitions, and the interval under consideration be $[lt, lt + \Delta]$. If the guard set $g \in G_{A_j}(e)$, $e \in E_{A_j}$ is of the form, $g = \bigwedge_i x_i \in [l_{x_i}, u_{x_i}]$, the invariant $I_{A_j}(p) = \bigwedge_i x_i \in [l'_{x_i}, u'_{x_i}]$, φ and $\phi(A_i, A_j)$ compute the skew and delay between the agents, then, the instrumented guards and invariants are given by,*

$$g^{inst} = \bigwedge_i x_i \in \left[l_{x_i} + \gamma_{p,x_i} + \mathcal{L}_{2_{x_i}} \delta_{x_i}, \quad u_{x_i} - \gamma_{p,x_i} - \mathcal{L}_{2_{x_i}} \delta_{x_i} \right] \tag{1}$$

$$I^{inst} = \bigwedge_i x_i \in \left[l'_{x_i} + \gamma_{p,x_i} + \mathcal{L}_{2_{x_i}} \delta_{x_i}, \quad u'_{x_i} - \gamma_{p,x_i} - \mathcal{L}_{2_{x_i}} \delta_{x_i} \right] \tag{2}$$

where $\delta_{x_i} = \varphi(A_i, A_j) + \phi(A_i, A_j)$, x_i is updated by agent A_i, with $\dot{x}_i \in [\mathcal{L}_{1_{x_i}}, \mathcal{L}_{2_{x_i}}]$, and γ_{p,x_i} is the roundoff and truncation error in x_i in the state p. □

We now illustrate how instrumentation prevents faulty transitions with the following example.

Example 6. Consider the system in Example 3 and the time interval under consideration be [0,1]. If we denote $d = x_1 - x_2$, then, $\dot{d} = \dot{x}_1 - \dot{x}_2 = 2t - t = t$. Since $t \in [0.05, 1]$, we can say that $\dot{d} \in [0.05, 1]$. Now, given that $\phi(A_1, A_2) = 0.03$, and

---

[4] Least common multiple.

the skew at $t = 0.12$ is 0.02, and assuming the bound on roundoff and trunca-tion errors is 0.001, the transition guard, $x_1 - x_2 \leq 0.1$ upon instrumentation becomes $x_1 - x_2 \leq (0.1 - 0.001 - 1 \cdot (0.02 + 0.03)) = x_1 - x_2 \leq 0.049$. Therefore, the faulty transition at $t = 0.12$ can be prevented.   □

The theorem below formally states that instrumentation prevents faulty transi-tions. For a sketch of the proof, we refer the reader to [25].

Theorem 1. *Let the code $\mathcal{K}$ of the model $\mathcal{D}$ be implemented on a distributed platform. Let for every agent A_j, p be the current state with $I_{A_j}(p)$ the set of invariants in that state, and $G_{A_j}(e)$ the set of guards. If every guard (in $G_{A_j}(e)$) that evaluates to true is instrumented as given in Definition (5) then there will be no faulty transitions.*   □

Notice that in Example 6, the instrumentation reduces the guard interval sub-stantially. In general, it is possible that with the shrinking of the guard set, the transition is missed completely. In the next section, we will analyze and derive a condition to check for missed transitions and possibly avoid them by sampling at a higher rate.

As a final note in this section, we add that while instrumentation reduces the guard set, it does not affect switching in any other way. In particular, if the original interval was such that only one transition was enabled from the location at any time, the property remains valid with instrumented guards as well as it is a subset of the original interval.

4.2   Preventing Missed Transitions

Missed transitions are transitions that are enabled in the model but not taken in the code. They occur either because the guard is not evaluated sufficiently or scheduling affected the order of evaluation. In general, a transition will not be missed, if it stays enabled long enough to be detected. The theorem below gives a sufficient condition to prevent missed transitions.

Theorem 2. *Let the code $\mathcal{K}$ of the model $\mathcal{D}$ be implemented on a distributed platform, h_j be the period of sampling in agent A_j. Let I be an instrumented invariant in a state and $g = \bigwedge_i x_i \in [l_{x_i}, u_{x_i}], g \subseteq I$ represent the instrumented guard of a transition in that state. If lt represents the current logical time at A_j, $x_i(lt)$ the current estimate of x_i at A_j, and T_{x_i} are defined as,*

$$T_{x_i}(k) = \begin{cases} \left[lt + \frac{l_{x_i} - x_i(lt)}{\mathcal{L}_{k_{x_i}}} + \delta_{max}, \; lt + \frac{u_{x_i} - x_i(lt)}{\mathcal{L}_{k_{x_i}}} + \delta_{min} \right] & \text{if } (x_i(lt) < l_{x_i}), \dot{x}_i > 0 \\ \left[lt + \frac{u_{x_i} - x_i(lt)}{\mathcal{L}_{k_{x_i}}} + \delta_{max}, \; lt + \frac{l_{x_i} - x_i(lt)}{\mathcal{L}_{k_{x_i}}} + \delta_{min} \right] & \text{if } (x_i(lt) > u_{x_i}), \dot{x}_i < 0 \end{cases}$$

$k = 1, 2$, *then, the transition will not be missed if,*

$$\left\| \bigcap_i \left(\bigcap_{k=1,2} T_{x_i}(k) \right) \right\| \geq 2 h_j \tag{3}$$

where $\delta_{min} = \varphi_{min} + \phi(A_i, A_j)$, $\delta_{max} = \varphi_{max} + \phi(A_i, A_j)$ *between agents* A_i *and* A_j, *and* $\dot{x}_i \in [\mathcal{L}_{1_{x_i}}, \mathcal{L}_{2_{x_i}}]$, *then, the transition will be detected and will not be missed if they are taken as soon as enabled.*

Proof. (sketch) We proceed to sketch the proof of the theorem in two parts. First, we will derive a condition on the overlap of guard and invariant that will allow us to detect the enabling of the transition. Then, given that the guard is of the form $g = \bigwedge_i x_i \in [l_{x_i}, u_{x_i}]$, we will derive a sufficient condition to meet this overlap, based on the periods of execution of agents.

To prove the first statement, assume that we are given a task-period set $\Omega = \{(\tau_i, h_i)\} 1 \leq i \leq n$. Each task τ_i will be treated as a periodic task with period h_i executing in a distributed environment. Let the execution time of τ_i be η_i and this is scheduled to run every h_i time units. Note that η_i here includes both execution time and also perhaps communication delay associated. Also, we speak of time in the reference frame at the processor executing task τ_i. Therefore, in the worst case, τ_i might be scheduled at time jh_i and a guard might be enabled (in the code, perhaps on a different processor) immediately after that, i.e., at time $jh_i + \epsilon, \epsilon > 0$ and be detected only when τ_i is next scheduled to run which may be as late as $(j+2)h_i - \eta_i$. Since we assume eager switching, this transition will be taken at $(j+2)h_i - \eta_i$. Thus, if a guard is not enabled at $(j+2)h_i - \eta_i$, it will go undetected and this will result in a missed transition. Hence, the guard should stay enabled for at least $((j+2)h_i - \eta_i) - (kh_i + \epsilon) = 2h_i - \eta_i - \epsilon$ time units. Since ϵ is arbitrary, to be safe, we can claim that it should stay enabled in the code for $2h_i$ time units so that the transition is not missed. This is illustrated in Figure 3. Now, consider the guard set $g = \bigwedge_i x_i \in [l_{x_i}, u_{x_i}]$. Let the current

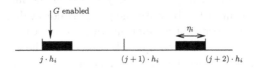

Fig. 3. Worst case scenario

logical time be lt and current values of variables at agent A_j given by $x_i(lt)$. We will consider the case where $x_i(lt) < l_{x_i}$ and $x_i(lt) > 0$, the argument for the case where $x_i(lt) > u_{x_i}$ and $x_i(lt) < 0$ is similar. Since $\dot{x}_i \in [\mathcal{L}_{1_{x_i}}, \mathcal{L}_{2_{x_i}}]$, $\dot{x}_i$ can utmost grow as $\mathcal{L}_{2_{x_i}}$. The guard on x_i, $([l_{x_i}, u_{x_i}])$ will then be enabled for the time interval $T_2 = [lt + \frac{l_{x_i} - x_i(lt)}{\mathcal{L}_{2_{x_i}}} + \delta_{max}, lt + \frac{u_{x_i} - x_i(lt)}{\mathcal{L}_{2_{x_i}}} + \delta_{min}]$, assuming that in the worst case, the notification for enabling of the guard gets to A_j in time δ_{max} and the notification for exiting comes at δ_{min}. This is true because x_i is continuous and the guards are assumed to be disjoint in time, otherwise there could be resets and the dynamics of x_i would be different. Similarly, if $\dot{x}_i$ grows as slow as $\mathcal{L}_{1_{x_i}}]$, then, it will be enabled for the time interval of $T_1 = [lt + \frac{l_{x_i} - x_i(lt)}{\mathcal{L}_{1_{x_i}}} + \delta_{max}, lt + \frac{u_{x_i} - x_i(lt)}{\mathcal{L}_{1_{x_i}}} + \delta_{min}]$. Therefore, if $T_1 \cap T_2 \neq \emptyset$, then it represents the time interval for which guard on x_i will be enabled. Hence considering the time interval for each of the x_i's, we can find the time interval when the guard will definitely be true.

From the above arguments, we can conclude that a Condition (3) gives a *sufficient condition* for preventing missed transitions, if the transitions are taken as soon as they are detected. □

The example below illustrates a case where a transition is missed and the sufficient condition is not met.

Example 7. Consider the case of Example 5. As a quick check, we find that if the system evolves as fast as 0.5, then $T_2 = (\frac{0.48-0.45}{0.5} + 0.1, \frac{0.48-0.3}{0.5} + 0.05) = (0.16, 0.41)$. Similarly, $T_1 = (\frac{0.48-0.45}{0.45} + 0.1, \frac{0.48-0.3}{0.45} + 0.05) = (0.167, 0.45)$. We find that $\|T_1 \cap T_2\| = 0.243 \not\geq 2(0.15)$ does not satisfy the sufficient condition for preventing missed transitions. However, if we choose the period of execution to be 0.12, we can see that the transition will not be missed. □

With the Theorems 1 and 2, we have a sufficient condition to ensure a relative faithful implementation that we record in the following corollary.

Corollary 1. *Let the code $\mathcal{K}$ of the model $\mathcal{D}$ be implemented on a distributed platform. If the code for every agent A_i every $G \in G_{A_j}$ is dynamically instrumented so that G and corresponding invariant I satisfy the condition of overlap in Theorem 2, and all variables in $\mathcal{K}$ have bounded error, then, $\mathcal{K}$ is a relative faithful implementation of $\mathcal{D}$.* □

4.3 Minimal Periods of Execution

In this section, we describe an algorithm to choose minimal periods of execution to avoid missing a transition and meeting the resource constraints. The main idea of the approach described as Algorithm 1 is to scale the relative periods of execution so that they meet the supported level of utilization. Specifically, as we are interested in finding the minimal periods of execution, we start with the smallest possible assignment and keep incrementing the periods till the supported level of utilization is met. Note that our algorithm needs to be run every time the available resource changes. We assume that the run time is instrumented to take this into consideration and call the procedure appropriately.

This is implemented in the function *SMALLEST-K*. Here we consider schedulability under EDF and Rate Monotonic (RM) algorithms. The function takes as input α, that is the level of utilization permissible with the supported levels of energy, and returns the smallest multiple of the base period of update k for which all the agents mapped onto a particular node (N) can be scheduled. We assume that voltage scaling techniques (c.f., [30]) can be used to fix a level of utilization of the CPU. In addition to checking schedulability, we assume that a function *RESOURCE-CHECK* is implemented that checks to see if agents are scheduled with a particular period and other resource constraints. For example, the function could check to see, if the frequency of reading of sensor data is less than the maximum permissible sampling frequency of the sensor. If an energy budget is associated, then it can be used to check whether the budget is met. If a particular k does not satisfy schedulability or resource constraints, it is incremented and then tested again. Note that increased k results in longer periods of execution. In the algorithm, W_j and ρ_j denote the maximum execution requirement and the sampling rate of Agent A_j which we assume are fixed.

Algorithm 1. Algorithm to find periods of execution of agents.

SMALLEST-K (α, N):
1: $k \leftarrow 1$
2: CASE-EDF:
3: **while** $\left(\left(\sum_{\mathcal{M}(j)=N} \frac{W_j}{k \cdot \rho_j} \not\leq \alpha \right) \vee (\text{RESOURCE-CHECK(N)} \neq \text{true}) \right)$ **do**
4:   $k \leftarrow k + 1$
5: **end while**
6: CASE-RM:
7: $J = \{j_1, \ldots j_n | \mathcal{M}(j_i) = N\}$
8: **while** $\left(\left(\forall j \in J, \sum_j \lceil \frac{\rho_j}{\rho_1} \rceil \cdot W_j \not\leq \alpha \cdot k \cdot \rho_j \right) \vee (\text{RESOURCE-CHK(N)} \neq \text{true}) \right)$ **do**
9:   $k \leftarrow k + 1$
10: **end while**
11: return k

SELECT-PERIODS-NODE (N):
1: $k_{N_{max}} \leftarrow \text{SMALLEST-K}(\alpha_{min})$
2: $k_{N_{min}} \leftarrow \text{SMALLEST-K}(\alpha_{max})$
3: return $(k_{N_{min}}, k_{N_{max}})$

SELECT-PERIODS $(\langle p_1, \ldots, p_n \rangle)$:
1: $(k_{min}, k_{max}) \leftarrow (0, 0)$
2: **for** $N \in \mathcal{N}$ **do**
3:   $(k_1, k_2) \leftarrow \text{SELECT-PERIODS-NODE}(N)$
4:   $(k_{min}, k_{max}) \leftarrow (\max(k_{min}, k_1), \max(k_{max}, k_2))$
5: **end for**
6: $k \leftarrow k_{max}$
7: **while** $k \geq k_{min}$ **do**
8:   **if** $(\text{CHECK-MISSED}(\langle p_1, \ldots, p_n \rangle, k))$ **then**
9:     return k
10:   **end if**
11:   $k \leftarrow k - 1$
12: **end while**

The function *SELECT-PERIODS-NODE* returns the maximum and minimum possible utilization and returns the range of scaling factor k possible on that node. The $K_{N_{min}}$ corresponds to the smallest periods possible on the node N with the supported amount of resources on node N. The *SELECT-PERIODS* function takes as input the present set of states $\langle p_1, \ldots, p_n \rangle$ and computes the possible values of k for every node and computes the range of k's possible for all the nodes. This range is represented by (k_{min}, k_{max}). To find the minimal value of k, we start iterating from k_{max} since it represents the least utilization level. At each iteration, we check to see whether choosing that value of k would result in a missed transition. The function *CHECK-MISSED* implements this check. Thus, at the end of the while loop (Steps 7-12), we would have found a k which can be supported on all nodes while being guaranteed for no missed transitions. Once we have found the value of k, we can supply the parameters to the code.

Example 8. (Room Heater) Our example for illustrating the algorithm is adapted from the heater benchmark for hybrid systems verification [31]. The benchmarks considers the case of a set of rooms being heated by limited number of heaters that are shared by the rooms. The number of heaters is strictly less than the number of rooms. In our example, we consider two rooms and one heater. The model of this system, described in Figure 4 consists of two thermostats and a heater. The temperature in a room is assumed to vary as, $\dot{x}_i = c_i h_i + b_i(u - x_i), i = 1, 2$ where h_i is 1 if the heater is in the room, otherwise 0, u is the outside temperature, and c_i, and b_i are constants. The heater model is a pure switched system. If $(x_i \leq get_i) \wedge (x_j - x_i \geq dif_i)$, then the heater is moved from room j to room i, where $i = 1, 2; j = 2/i$.

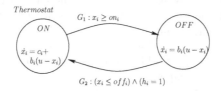

Fig. 4. The hybrid system model of the thermostat

The system is implemented on two nodes. There are two agents, one to check whether the heater has to be moved (A_1), and the other for switching on or switching off the heaters(A_2). The controller in the room with the heater runs both of them, and the controller in the other room runs only the second agent.

Let us assume that the relative periods of the two agents are $(3, 1)$ and the relative worst case execution times be $(2, 1)$. Let us also assume that the levels of utilization are 0.25 and 0.5. In the room with the heater (say room 1), the controller has to schedule both the agents so, we have $k_{1_{min}}$ is such that $\frac{1}{k_{1_{max}}}(\frac{2}{3} + \frac{1}{1}) \leq 0.5$ which yields $k_{1_{min}} = 4$. Similarly with utilization 0.25, we can get $k_{1_{max}} = 7$. In room 2, since there is only one agent to be scheduled, we have, $k_{2_{min}}$ is such that $\frac{1}{k_{1_{max}}}(\frac{1}{1}) \leq 0.5$ which yields $k_{2_{min}} = 2$. Similarly with utilization 0.25, we can get $k_{2_{max}} = 4$. Therefore, after taking the maximum over both nodes, we get $(k_{min}, k_{max}) = (4, 7)$. The agent A_2 in room 1 is waiting on transition G_1 and in room 2 is waiting on transition G_2. It can be seen that $k = 7$ that corresponds to utilization 0.25, indeed satisfies the sufficient condition for no missed transitions.   □

5   Conclusions and Future Work

We have proposed a framework for generating resource-aware code from hybrid systems models with guarantees of no switching discrepancies. Our approach is an effort to bridge the semantic gap between the model and the code due to discretization and resource constraints. We accomplish this by incorporating a resource model of the target platform in addition to the application model and generating parameterized code from this model. The parameters are supplied at runtime by monitoring the state of the resources and checking for missed transitions.

There are potentially many directions of future work. We hope to complete the implementation of the framework. In the paper, we have largely focused on power and CPU as the main resources. We would like to extend it to more comprehensive set of resources. Also, in the present scheme of things, a change in resource levels or transition on any agent can trigger a recalculation of the periods of all the agents. This is so because of the assumption that all the agents have relative periods of execution. An alternative, would be to start with constraints on periods, such as $\rho_1 \le 2\rho_2$. This way, we would only need to recompute the periods whenever the constraints are about to be violated. Another possible extension to the framework, would be to mask faults and failures or consider graceful degradation by viewing it as an extreme case of resource dynamism. Finally, we hope to use ideas from runtime monitoring [32] to monitor and steer the system towards desirable behavior.

Acknowledgments. We would like to thank anonymous referees for their suggestions in improving this paper.

References

1. Martin, N.: Lock who's talking: Motorola's c.d. team. LockSmart Online Article (1998)
2. Alur, R., Dill, D.L.: A Theory of Timed Automata. Theoretical Computer Scienc 126, 183–235 (1994)
3. Alur, R., Ivančić, F., Kim, J., Lee, I., Sokolsky, O.: Generating embedded software-from hierarchial hybrid models. In: Proceedings of LCTES (2003)
4. Harel, D.: Statecharts: A visual formalism for complex systems. Science of ComputerProgramming 8, 231–274 (1987)
5. Alur, R., Courcoubetis, C., Halbwachs, N., Henzinger, T., Ho, P., Nicollin, X., Olivero, A., Sifakis, J., Yovine, S.: The algorithmic analysis of hybrid systems. Theoretical Comp. Science 138, 3–34 (1995)
6. Maler, O., Manna, Z., Pnueli, A.: From timed to hybrid systems. In: Real-Time:Theory in Practice, REX Workshop. LNCS, vol. 600, Springer-Verlag, Heidelberg (1991)
7. Alur, R., Grosu, R., Hur, Y., Kumar, V., Lee, I.: Modular specification of hybridsystems in CHARON. In: HSCC, pp. 6–19 (2000)
8. Eker, J., Janneck, J., Lee, E., Liu, J., Liu, X., Luvig, J., Neuendorffer, S., Sachs, S., Xiong, Y.: Taming heterogeneity–the Ptolemy approach. Proceedings of the IEEE 91, 127–144 (2003)

9. Alur, R., Grosu, R., Hur, Y., Kumar, V., Lee, I.: Charon: a language for modular specification of multi-agent hybrid systems. Technical Report MS-CIS-00-01, Dept. of Computer and Information Science, University of Pennsylvania (2000)

10. RationalRose, http://www-306.ibm.com/software/awdtools/developer/rose/

11. TargetLink,   http://www.dspaceinc.com/ww/en/inc/home/products/sw/pcgs/targetli.cfm

12. Simulink, http://www.mathworks.com/products/simulink/

13. Berry, G., Gonthier, G.: The synchronous programming language esterel: design,semantics, implementation. Technical Report 842, INRIA (1988)

14. Halbwachs, N., Caspi, P., Raymond, P., Pilaud, D.: The synchronous dataflow programming language Lustre. Proceedings of the IEEE 79, 1305–1320 (1991)

15. Deshpande, A., Göllu, A., Varaiya, P.: SHIFT: a formalism and a programming language for dynamic networks of hybrid automata. In: HS 1997. LNCS, vol. 1567, Springer, Heidelberg (1996)

16. Henzinger, T., Kirsch, C., Sanvido, M., Pree, W.: From control models to real-time code using Giotto. IEEE Control Systems Magazine (2003)

17. Karsai, G., Sztipanovits, J., Ledeczi, A., Bapty, T.: Model-integrated development of embedded software. In: Proceedings of the IEEE, vol. 91, pp. 145–164 (2003)

18. Model-Driven Hybrid and Embedded Software for Automotive Applications. In: 2nd RTAS Workshop on Model-Driven Embedded Systems (MoDES 2004) (2004)

19. Shah, B., Dennison, R., Gray, J.: A model-driven approach for generating embeddedrobot navigation control software. In: ACM-SE 42: Proceedings of the 42nd annual Southeast regional conference, pp. 332–335. ACM Press, New York (2004)

20. Stauner, T.: Discrete-Time Refinement of Hybrid Automata. In: Tomlin, C.J., Greenstreet, M.R. (eds.) HSCC 2002. LNCS, vol. 2289, pp. 407–420. Springer, Heidelberg (2002)

21. Hybrid Toolbox - Hybrid Systems, Control, Optimization, http://www.dii.unisi.it/hybrid/toolbox

22. Henzinger, T.A., Ho, P.H., Wong-Toi, H.: HYTECH: A model checker for hybridsystems. International Journal on Software Tools for Technology Transfer 1, 110–122 (1997)

23. Asarin, E., Dang, T., Maler, O.: The d/dt Tool for Verification of Hybrid Systems. In: Brinksma, E., Larsen, K.G. (eds.) CAV 2002. LNCS, vol. 2404, pp. 365–370. Springer, Heidelberg (2002)

24. Tools, H.S.: http://wiki.grasp.upenn.edu/graspdoc/hst/

25. Hur, Y., Kim, J., Lee, I., Choi, J.Y.: Sound Code Generation from Communicating Hybrid Models. In: Alur, R., Pappas, G.J. (eds.) HSCC 2004. LNCS, vol. 2993, pp. 432–447. Springer, Heidelberg (2004)

26. Anand, M., Kim, J., Lee, I.: Code generation from hybrid systems models for distributed embedded systems. In: Proceedings of the IEEE ISORC, pp. 166–173 (2005)

27. Anand, M., Fischmeister, S., Kim, J., Lee, I.: Distributed-code generation from hybrid systems models for time-delayed multirate systems. In: EMSOFT 2005: Proceedings of the 5th ACM international conference on Embedded software, pp. 210–213. ACM Press, New York (2005)

28. Henzinger, T.A., Ho, P.H.: Algorithmic analysis of nonlinear hybrid systems. In: Wolper, P. (ed.) Proceedings of the 7th International Conference On Computer Aided Verification, Liege, Belgium, vol. 939, pp. 225–238. Springer, Heidelberg (1995)

29. Press, W.H., Teukolsky, S.A., Vetterling, W.T., Flannery, B.P.: Numerical Recipes in C: the Art of Scientific Computing, 2nd edn. Cambridge University Press, Cambridge (1999)
30. Pillai, P., Shin, K.: Real-time dynamic voltage scaling for low-power embedded operating systems. In: Proceedings of the 18th Symposium on Operating Systems Principles SOSP 2001 (2001)
31. Fehnker, A., Ivancic, F.: Benchmarks for Hybrid Systems Verification. In: Alur, R., Pappas, G.J. (eds.) HSCC 2004. LNCS, vol. 2993, pp. 326–341. Springer, Heidelberg (2004)
32. Tan, L., Kim, J., Lee, I.: Testing and Monitoring Model-based Generated Program. In: Proceeding of Runtime Verification Workshop (RV 2003), Boulder, Colorado (2003)

Towards Verification of Model Transformations Via Goal-Directed Certification

Gabor Karsai and Anantha Narayanan

Institute for Software Integrated Systems,
Vanderbilt University, P.O. Box 1829 Sta. B.
Nashville, TN 37235, USA
gabor.karsai@vanderbilt.edu, ananth@isis.vanderbilt.edu

Abstract. Embedded software is widely used in automotive applications, often in critical situations where reliability of the system is extremely important. Such systems often use model based development approaches. Model transformation is an important step in such scenarios. This includes generating code from models, transforming design models into analysis models, or transforming a model between variants of a formalism (such as variants of Statecharts). It becomes important to verify that the transformation was correct, and the transformed model or code preserved the semantics of the design model. In this paper, we will look at a technique called "goal-directed certification" that provides a pragmatic solution to the verification problem. We will see how we can use concepts of bisimulation to verify whether a certain transformation instance preserved certain properties. We will then extend this idea using weak bisimulation and semantic anchoring, to a more general class of transformations.

Keywords: Behavior Preservation, Bisimulation, Weak Bisimulation, Semantic Anchoring.

1 Introduction

Model-driven development of embedded systems relies on the use of model transformations that translate and establish linkage between different modeling formalisms, design artifacts produced during the development process, and possibly executable code. The validity of these transformations is crucial for the correct functioning of the system. To prove that the system will work as predicted, we must be able to assure that the model transformations preserved the semantics of the models. For instance, the control logic of an automotive application (say, an Anti-lock Braking System) may be developed using a model-based approach (say, using Stateflow). We may transform this model to verify its control logic (say, using NuSMV), or generate code from it (say, using Mathworks' Real-time Workshop). In a high-consequence application (like the ABS) it is essential that the results of the verification hold true for the generated code. The question at the heart of any model-based development process is: for applications where

M. Broy, I.H. Krüger, and M. Meisinger (Eds.): ASWSD 2006, LNCS 4922, pp. 67–83, 2008.

safety is essential, do the transformations on the models provide verifiable assurances for the preservation of properties across the transformation?

Observe that the problem is similar to the verification of compilers for high-level languages. Compiler verification, in general, is currently not solved: we don't have a full formal "proof" of a production-quality compiler. The pragmatic approach is to use a "certification process" which validates the behavior of a compiler using a large set of test examples and observing the results of the compilation (often through execution). Unfortunately, this approach may not be feasible for model transformations, as model transformations often do not produce executable code. It may not be economical to develop a large set of test examples for certifying a highly specialized transformation tool, and the correctness of the transformations' results is difficult to establish only via reading.

2   Background

2.1   Goal-Directed Certification

If the requirement for total verification can be relaxed, some verification problems could be solved using techniques from program synthesis tools. NASA ARC [8] has recently developed an approach to generating assurances for code produced by automatic program synthesis tools. Their approach is based on

1. adding annotations to the generated code that capture certain pre-conditions and post-conditions on each statement,
2. capturing safety properties that need to be verified in some logic notation,
3. translating the conditions from (1) and the safety properties from (2) into a set of verification conditions that are simplified,
4. using a symbolic (and automatic) theorem prover to generate a formal proof that the selected safety conditions hold for the generated code, and
5. using a proof checker to check that the proof is valid.

The result of this process is a "certificate": a formal proof that the generated code does satisfy the desired safety properties.

This approach does not solve the verification problem in general. It answers the question for a specific generated code, and for a selected set of safety properties. This simplifies the process greatly, and makes it technically feasible. We will call this approach "goal-directed certification".

Note that this approach removes the need for *trust* in the generator, as the certificate is evaluated after the generation. This means that the certification will capture any errors in the generated code, irrespective of faults in the generator.

The work of Denney and Fischer in [8] is similar to the Proof-Carrying Code (PCC) work of Necula [16]. In PCC, a compiler is extended to produce object code accompanied with proofs for safety policies that can be independently verified on a host system. In Certifiable Program Generation, the idea is extended to code generators, to provide assurances about the generated source code. Since they operate at the level of source code (as opposed to object code), the formulation of the safety properties is changed appropriately. In this paper, we extend this idea to model transformations, where we wish to provide assurances about the generated models. Consequently, the formulation of the safety policies and the verification methods will be different, but the basic architecture is comparable.

2.2 GReAT

GReAT [5] is a language for specifying model transformations graphically using elements of the meta-models of the constituent domains. The meta-models of the domains are specified using UML and OCL. GReAT belongs to the class of practical graph transformation systems such as AGG[9], PROGRES[17] and FUJABA[18].

One of the features of GReAT is the ability to link elements from the different meta-models, to create temporary cross-domain links. These links are called *cross-links*, and can be used to trace relations between model elements belonging to different domains during the course of the transformation.

2.3 Extended Hierarchical Automata

To demonstrate our idea of goal-directed certification, we will use Statecharts as the design language, and Extended Hybrid Automata (EHA) [14] as the analysis language. EHA has been chosen as the analysis language as it has a straightforward mapping into the PROMELA language used in SPIN[15]. EHA were used to give formal operational semantics for Statecharts, and they offer a simple hierarchical representation for Statecharts that was used in correctness proofs [19].

EHA models are composed of one or more *Sequential Automata*, which are non-hierarchical finite automata. The states of a Sequential Automaton (called *Basic States*) may be *refined* into further Sequential Automata, to express hierarchy in a flat notation. A Statechart model can be represented by a Sequential Automaton, with a finite automaton representing the top level states of the Statechart. Compound states in the Statechart must be represented as individual Sequential Automata, and marked as *refinements* of the corresponding Basic States in the EHA. The entire Statechart can be represented this way, using a set of Sequential Automata and a series of refinements.

Some transitions in the Statechart may cut across levels of hierarchy. Such transitions are said to be inter-level. Transitions in an EHA model, however, are always contained within one Sequential Automaton, and cannot cut across levels of hierarchy. Inter-level transitions my therefore be elevated based on the scope of the transition. An inter-level transition is placed in the Sequential Automaton corresponding to the Statechart state containing it, and is drawn between the Basic States corresponding to the top-most ancestors of the source and target states in the Statechart. The transition in the EHA is also annotated with special attributes called *source restriction* and *target determinator*, which keep track of the actual source and target states of the transition. Figure 1 shows the meta-model for EHA. The complete transformation from Statechart to EHA will be explained later.

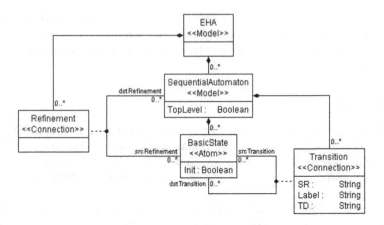

Fig. 1. EHA meta-model in UML

2.4 Bisimulation

Bisimulation is an equivalence relation between Labeled Transition Systems (LTS), which can conclude whether the two systems will behave identically. In other words, if two systems have a bisimulation relation, then one system simulates the other and vice versa. Given an LTS $(S, \Lambda, \rightarrow)$, a relation R over S is a *bisimulation* if:

$$(p, q) \in R \text{ and } p \xrightarrow{\alpha} p' \text{ implies that there exists a } q' \in S,$$
$$\text{such that } q \xrightarrow{\alpha} q' \text{ and } (p', q') \in R,$$

and conversely,

$$q \xrightarrow{\alpha} q' \text{ implies that there exists a } p' \in S,$$
$$\text{such that } p \xrightarrow{\alpha} p' \text{ and } (p', q') \in R.$$

If we considered the union two transition systems representing a Statechart model and an EHA model, and find a relation R relating each Statechart state to an EHA state, and proved that R is a bisimulation, we can conclude that the Statechart model and the EHA model will behave identically.

3   Verifying Model Transformations by Goal-Directed Certification

In goal-directed certification, we do not wish to provide a general correctness proof for the transformation. We try to solve the more tractable and useful question of trying to prove that a particular instance of a transformation preserved certain properties of interest for the instance models involved. Suppose we have a design modeling language that has convenient features for representing complex controller behaviors and designs, and we have a simpler analysis language that comes with sophisticated verification tools. In our case study, we will consider Stateflow [1] as our design language, and PROMELA (of the SPIN model checker [12]) as be the analysis language. We use the design language for expressing controller designs, and then translate the design models into the analysis language where the actual verification is done. We then try to answer the question, do the results of the verification on the PROMELA instance model hold on the Stateflow instance model? In other words, how can we be sure that the model transformation that maps design models into analysis models preserves the semantics of those models?

We wish to note that in some simple cases, we may be able to specify a transformation using a sequence of declaratively specified steps, and provide an argument for its correctness by construction. However, we do not yet have a model transformation tool that can take a purely declarative specification and produce an automated transformation. In a production scenario, it is usually not feasible to provide such assurances by construction, due to implementation complexity issues. We propose an automatable and reusable method to verify the correctness of the implementations of model transformations, which can be integrated into the transformation, but will perform the verification independent of the transformation itself. Thus, an incorrect implementation will not produce a valid certificate of correctness.

The above questions are difficult to answer in general, but we can possibly answer them if we restrict ourselves to single instances and specific properties. One such model property is reachability: what states are reachable/unreachable in the design model? We would like to answer this by translating the design model into an analysis model, executing the reachability analysis on the analysis model, and deducing that the reachability holds for the original design model given the model transformation is correct.

Reachability is checked by a model checker via state-space exploration. Thus, if we can somehow show that the state-space of the design model has an isomorphic mapping into the state-space of the analysis model, then the reachability properties checked on the analysis model have the same logical truth-value for some equivalent reachability properties in the design model. We can use our definition of bisimulation here, to find the relation R between the elements of the two instance models, and check if R is a bisimulation. If R is a bisimulation, we can conclude that the two models behave identically, when it comes to the property of reachability.

Figure 2 shows the basic architecture for this evaluation. The model transformation generates the target model from the source model, and the target model is verified by the model checker (SPIN). As described earlier, our model transformation language (GReAT) allows us to link source and target elements using *cross-links*. We will use these cross-links to trace the relation R which links states in the source (Stateflow) model to the corresponding items in the target (EHA) model. A straightforward *bisimilarity checker* is used to trace these relations and find whether R is a bisimulation. If the bisimilarity checker determines R to be a bisimulation, we can conclude that the results of the model checker for the analysis (EHA) model will be valid on the design (Stateflow) model.

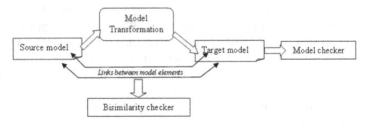

Fig. 2. Architecture for verifying reachability preservation in a transformation

Please note that there exist solutions that can perform reachability analysis on Stateflow/Simulink models, such as the OSC Embedded *Validator* [2] and TNI's Safety-Checker Blockset [4] that are available in the industry. Our aim is not to provide such a solution. We also do not wish to provide a method for defining the semantics of these languages. We simply wish to consider a simple model transformation as a case study to demonstrate our methodology.

The following subsections will describe in detail the transformation, construction of the cross-links and checking for bisimilarity.

3.1 Transforming Statechart Models to EHA

The model transformation was built using GReAT and GME [13]. We first defined meta-models in GME for the two languages, Statechart and EHA. The transformation uses the following steps (which are automatically executed by the GReAT transformation engine):

1. Every Statechart model is transformed into an EHA model, with one top level Sequential Automaton in the EHA model.
2. For every (primitive or compound) state in the Statechart (except for regions of concurrent states), a corresponding Basic State is created in the EHA.
3. For every composite state in the Statechart model, a Sequential Automaton is created in the EHA model, and a "refinement" link is added that connects the Basic State in the EHA corresponding to the state in the Statechart, to the Sequential Automaton in the EHA that it is refined to.
4. All the contained states in the composite state are further transformed by repeating steps (1) and (2). The top level states in the Statechart are added to the top level Sequential Automaton in the EHA.
5. For every non-interlevel transition in the Statechart model a transition is created in the EHA between the Basic States corresponding to the start and end states of the transition in the Statechart model.
6. For every inter-level transition in the Statechart model, we trace the scope of the transition to find the lowest parent state s_P that contains both the source and the target of the transition. A transition is created in the EHA, in the Sequential Automaton corresponding to s_P. The source of the transition in the EHA is the Basic State corresponding to the highest parent of the source in the Statechart that is within s_P, and the target in the EHA is the Basic

State corresponding to the highest parent of the target in the Statechart that is within sp. The transition in the EHA is further annotated, with the *source restriction* attribute set to the Basic State corresponding to the actual source in the Statechart, and the *target determinator* set to the basic state corresponding to the actual target in the Statechart.

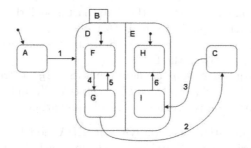

Fig. 3. A sample Statechart model

Figure 3 shows a sample Statechart model and Figure 4 shows the transformed EHA model. Transitions *2* and *3* are inter-level, and the *source restriction* and *target determinator* values for the EHA model are shown in the table on the top right.

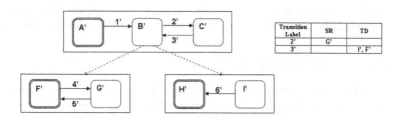

Transition Label	SR	TD
2'	G'	
3'		I', F'

Fig. 4. Sample EHA model

3.2   Verifying Behavior Equivalence

In order to define the verification problem we introduce the following concepts. A *state configuration* in a Statechart is a valid set of states that the system can be active in. If a state is part of an active configuration, then all its parents are also part of the active configuration. A transition in the Statechart can take the system from one state configuration to another state configuration, where the source and target states of the transition are subsets of the initial and final state configurations. Similarly, a state configuration in an EHA model is a set of Basic States. If a Basic State is part of an active configuration, and is part of a non-top-level Sequential Automaton, then the Basic State that is refined into this Sequential Automaton is also a part of the active configuration.

An EHA model truly represents the reachability behavior of a Statechart model, if every reachable state configuration in the Statechart has an equivalent reachable state configuration in the EHA and vice versa.

Definition. We can define a relation R between the Statechart and the EHA models, and check if the relation is a bisimulation as follows:

1. Given a state configuration S_A in the Statechart model, there exists an equivalent state configuration S_B in the EHA model
2. Given a transition t: $S_A \rightarrow S'_A$ in the Statechart, there exists an equivalent transition t': $S_B \rightarrow S'_B$ in the EHA
3. If for any two equivalent state configurations (S_A, S_B), there exist equivalent transitions $(t$: $S_A \rightarrow S'_A$, t': $S_B \rightarrow S'_B)$ such that S'_A and S'_B are equivalent (and vice-versa), then the relation R is a bisimulation.

If the R is a bisimulation, then verifying the EHA model for reachability will be equivalent to verifying the Statechart model for reachability. If not, it means that the models do not behave identically with respect to reachability, and that could be due to an error in the transformation.

When the model transformation algorithm outlined earlier is implemented, it is known which of the Basic States and Transitions in the EHA were created corresponding to which of the states and transitions in the Statechart. However, it is not certain whether all the states were represented, all compound states were refined correctly, all the transitions were connected correctly, and all the inter-level transitions were annotated correctly. To verify this, we need to keep track of the relation R between the two models, and check if there is a bisimulation.

3.3   Checking for Bisimilarity

We built a tool that checks the bisimilarity between the design and analysis models by validating the equivalence relation between the states and transitions of the two sides. The checking of bisimilarity is of linear complexity in the number of states and transitions considered. The checking was made possible by the model transformation approach we have used that uses graph rewriting with explicit links between source and target elements maintained throughout the transformation, as explained below.

During the model transformation, our model transformation tool allows us to create *cross-links* that link model elements in the source model to those in the target model. During the transformation process, when a transformation rule matches a state or a transition in the Statechart and creates the equivalent Basic State or transition in the EHA, a cross-link is created, which marks the relation R between the two elements. Figure 5 shows a sample GReAT rule which achieves this. The top part of the rule matches the Statechart element, and the bottom part creates the corresponding EHA element. The ✓ mark in *BasicState* indicates that it is newly created, along with the associated links (these appear in blue when seen in color). The link from *BasicState* to *PrimitiveState* is a *cross-link*. The *AttributeMapping* block allows us to add code to the rule, to perform some

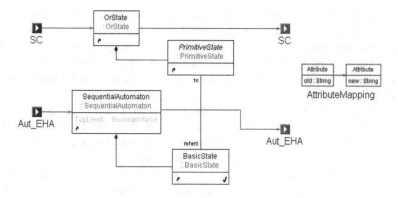

Fig. 5. Sample GReAT rule with cross-link

special actions such as set the attribute values for the newly created elements. When the transformation is complete, the equivalence relations can be accurately traced using these cross-links.

At the end of the transformation, we can check if the equivalence relation is a bisimulation. Rather than checking for all possible state configurations in the Statechart, it is more efficient to consider every transition in the Statechart and the minimal source state configuration. If we can confirm that every transition in the Statechart model has an equivalent transition in the EHA model for which the source and target state configurations are equivalent (and similarly from transitions in the EHA model to the Statechart model), then we can conclude that a state configuration in the Statechart is reachable if and only if its equivalent state configuration in the EHA model is reachable.

In our implementation of the bisimulation checker, we collect the set of all the transitions from the source graph. For each transition in this set, we find the equivalent transition in the EHA by following the cross-link. Now we can compute the minimal source state configuration S_A for the transition in the Statechart model, and the source state configuration S_B for the EHA model. We check the equivalence of S_A and S_B by taking every state s in S_A, finding its equivalent state s' from the EHA, and checking if s' is in S_B, and vice versa. The target states are checked similarly. If this check succeeds for all transitions in the Statechart, and there are no more transitions in the EHA, then the two systems can be said to be bisimilar with respect to reachability. In other words, if bisimilarity holds then we can determine reachability in the Statechart model by verifying it in the EHA model. If this check fails, then there may be errors in the transformation, and the generated EHA model does not truly represent the input Statechart model.

3.4 Conclusions from the First Case Study

The experimental setup used to demonstrate the approach was as follows. We created a set of models in the design language and translated them into the analysis language, marking the equivalence relations during the transformation using cross-links. After finishing the translation, the bisimulation checker was called, with the cross-links between the source and target models preserved. If this checker verified that there is a bisimulation relation between the models, then reachability properties verified on the analysis model will be guaranteed to hold for the source model.

Note that in this approach, the verification done on the analysis models *together* with the bisimilarity check provides the certification. Either one of them alone is not sufficient. Furthermore, the certificate is valid *only* for the particular model and *not* for the model transformation in general.

To illustrate this point, we deliberately introduced a small error in the transformation process that caused problems only if hierarchical states were used. This resulted in transformations that checked correctly for specific models (with no state hierarchy), but failed to check for others (i.e. hierarchical ones). Hence, models without hierarchical states where transformed correctly, while models with hierarchical states were not. The result of the verification could be accepted only if the bisimilarity check has succeeded. It is interesting to note that though the transformation had an error, in the instances where the check succeeded, the target models did truly represent the source models with respect to reachability. Thus, there would be no error in performing reachability analysis on the target models in these instances. In other words, our approach will capture instances where a transformation fails, rather than capture errors in the transformation itself.

The question that arises is whether a strict bisimulation relation is provable in a wider range of transformations, where there may not be a one-to-one mapping between the models that are representable in the source and the target languages. An important question is whether we even need to prove that a strict bisimulation exists. It would be useful to explore other less strong forms of equivalence, that can be applied to more generic cases.

To answer these questions, we will go to our next case study, where we will consider two Statechart variants that differ in certain features, and thus in the set of systems they can represent. We will study a transformation from one variant to the other, and try to prove that it preserved certain properties of interest. We will use *Semantic Anchoring* [6] and a slightly modified notion of bisimulation, called *weak bisimulation*.

4   More Background

4.1   Semantic Anchoring

The meta-model of a domain Specific Modeling Language (DSML) specifies its syntax and static semantics. Semantic Anchoring [7] [6] is a method for specifying the dynamic semantics of DSMLs. It relies on the observation that a broad category of behaviors can be represented by a small set of behavioral abstractions. The behavior of certain abstractions such as Finite State Machines or Timed Automata has been studied over several years in a wide range of applications.

Their behaviors are well understood and precisely defined. Such abstractions are called *Semantic Units*. Semantic Anchoring is the specification of the behavior of a DSML as a transformation from the DSML to a chosen semantic unit. The semantic unit is usually represented in some formalism, such as Microsoft's Abstract State Machine Language (AsmL) [3], for performing verification.

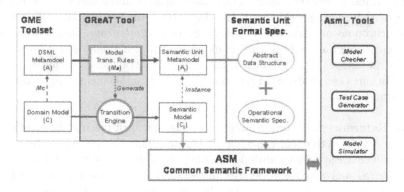

Fig. 6. Tool Architecture for Semantic Anchoring

Figure 6 shows the architecture used for semantic anchoring. In our case study, we will use FSMs as the semantic unit.

4.2 Statechart Variants

Statecharts [10] were first proposed by Harel to model the reactive behavior of systems. Since then, different variants of the formalism have been proposed to address specific problems. The result is that today we have several variants of the Statecharts formalism, such as iLogix Statecharts and MATLAB Stateflow. A number of such variants and the differences is studied in [20]. On some occasions, such as during tool integration, we may need to transform models from one variant of the formalism to another. It is very important in these cases that the behavior is preserved by the transformation.

Since the common commercial Statecharts variants vary in subtle issues, we will look at two hypothetical variants that will vary on a small but significant set of features. Let us call these hypothetical variants *SCA* and *SCB*. We will now look at the differences between *SCA* and *SCB*.

Compositional Semantics. Compositional semantics is the property of being able to define the semantics of a compound component completely from the semantics of its subcomponents, without looking at its internal syntactical structure. Having compositional semantics simplifies verification in many cases. Having transitions that cut across levels of hierarchy violates compositional semantics. Thus, if a Statechart variant allows inter-level transitions, then it will not have compositional semantics. For our case study, SCA will permit inter-level semantics, while SCB will not.

Note that SCA models which have inter-level transitions can also be represented in SCB, by using *self termination* and *self start* states [20]. These will be explained with examples later.

Instantaneous States. Some Statechart variants allow states to be entered and exited in a single time step (In the current case study we only consider the synchronous model). Such states are called *instantaneous*. Such a Statechart can step through a series of instantaneous states in a single time step, until a *non*-instantaneous state is reached. Such a series of transitions is called a *macro step*. For our case study, SCA will not permit instantaneous states, while SCB will permit them.

State References. In some Statechart variants, transitions may be guarded by referencing the activity of other parallel states. This is done using state references, which are special conditions denoting the activity of states. The condition *in(S)*, *en(S)* and *ex(S)* will be true in the time steps when the state S is active, entered and exited respectively. In our case study, SCA will permit state references, while SCB will not.

These are significant differences in the features offered by the variants. Representing a model in one variant in terms of the other variant will require some significant changes. This will be explained with an example later. It must be understood that all SCA models may not be representable in SCB (and vie versa), but our goal is to verify whether the transformation was correct in the specific cases that *were* representable.

4.3   Weak Bisimulation

Let us go back to our earlier definition of bisimulation. Given an LTS (S, Λ, $\rightarrow$), a relation R over S is a *bisimulation* if:

$$(p, q) \in R \text{ and } p \xrightarrow{\alpha} p' \text{ implies that there exists a } q' \in S,$$
$$\text{such that } q \xrightarrow{\alpha} q' \text{ and } (p', q') \in R,$$

and conversely,

$$q \xrightarrow{\alpha} q' \text{ implies that there exists a } p' \in S,$$
$$\text{such that } p \xrightarrow{\alpha} p' \text{ and } (p', q') \in R.$$

This defines a *strict* bisimulation, which enforces a strict one-to-one mapping of the state space. In some cases, two systems may have essentially the same behavior, but differ in their state spaces. One system may have intermediate states that are not observable externally, but truthfully reproduce the observable behavior of another system. If we modified our notions of what constitutes states, transitions and labels, we may find that the two systems are bisimilar. This leads us to the notion of *weak bisimilarity* [11]. For instance, in a system that allows instantaneous states, we can define weak bisimulation by considering only non-instantaneous states in the bisimulation definition, and by considering macro steps as a single transition. This gives a more practical and usable method to compare the behavior of two systems.

5 Verifying Transformations Using Semantic Anchoring

We now look at our modified architecture for goal-directed certification, using semantic anchoring and weak bisimulation.

We first define the behavior of the DSMLs of the transformation by semantic anchoring. This is used to generate the behavior model from the instance models. The behavior models will be in a common semantic unit (Finite State Machines). A tool is used to check if the generated behavior models are weakly bisimilar, based on a suitable definition of weak bisimulation which we will see later. Figure 7 shows an overview of this framework.

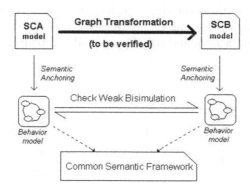

Fig. 7. Framework for verifying behavior preservation

5.1 Transformation from SCA to SCB

Figure 8 shows an SCA Statechart model, and Figure 9 shows the transformed SCB model. The transformation from SCA to SCB first represents all the states in the SCA model. The first issue to address is the presence of inter-level transitions. These are represented using self-termination and self-start states. The transition $T_2{:}b$ in the SCA model is an inter-level transition, triggered by an event b. This is represented in the transformed SCB model by adding a self-termination state D. The transition is broken into two parts, one from the start state to D, and another from the parent state Q to C. Neither of these transitions are inter-level, but their combined effect is similar to the inter-level transition in the SCA model.

For the semantics of the transition to be identical, the system must transition from state B to state C in a single time step. To achieve this, D is made an instantaneous state, and an instantaneous event i is generated. Thus, the D

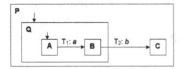

Fig. 8. A sample *SCA* model

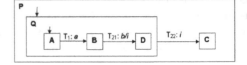

Fig. 9. A sample *SCB* model

can be exited and *i* will be available in the same time step. This will make the series of transitions T_{21} and T_{22} into a macro step that will be identical to the transition T_2 in the *SCA* model, to an external observer.

After copying the states, the transformation copies all normal transitions between the corresponding states. Inter-level transitions are then elevated to the common parent of both the start and the end states. Self-termination and self-start states are added on the source and target sides of the transition as necessary, using unique instantaneous states and actions. When state references are encountered in the *SCA* model, unique actions representing the state activity are added to all transitions entering or exiting the state. For instance, when a state reference *en(S)* appears, all its occurrences are denoted in the *SCB* model by a specially named action, and this action is added to all transitions entering state *S*.

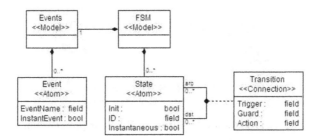

Fig. 10. Meta-model for FSM semantic unit

5.2   Behavior by Semantic Anchoring

We represent the behavior of both the Statechart variants using a common semantic unit, namely Finite State Machines. The meta-model for FSM is shown in the Figure 10.

The semantic anchoring is specified as a transformation from the Statechart variant to the FSM semantic unit. The FSM is enhanced with instantaneous states and actions, to represent the behavior of instantaneous states and actions of the *SCB* model. Figures 11 and 12 show the behavior models in terms of the FSM semantic unit, for the sample Statechart models described above. The FSM semantics are defined by an AsmL model generated from the FSM model. The AsmL model models the behavior of the states and transitions of the FSM, taking into account the instantaneous nature of some of the states. Here, we assume that the semantic anchoring has been correctly specified, and does not need to be verified. However, it may be possible to use the bisimulation techniques described earlier to verify that the semantic model correctly represents the source model.

Fig. 11. FSM semantic model for the SCA model

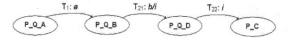

Fig. 12. FSM semantic model for the SCB model

5.3   Verifying Behavior Preservation

To provide a certificate for an instance of a transformation from SCA to SCB, we will compare the generated behavior models of the Statechart models, using the definition of weak bisimulation described below.

Weak Bisimulation. We establish the relation R between non-instantaneous states of the two transition systems. We then define a transition T as a transition from one non-instantaneous state to another, and its label as the aggregate of the events and actions of the constituent transitions, if instantaneous states are involved, ignoring the instantaneous actions (which will not be visible outside the macro step). Using these conditions, we redefine our bisimulation relation for weak bisimulation as follows. Given the relation R between non-instantaneous states p and q, R is a weak bisimulation if:

$$\forall\ (p,\ q) \in R \text{ and } \forall \alpha: p \overset{\alpha}{\Rightarrow} p', \exists\ q' \text{ such that } q \overset{\alpha}{\Rightarrow} q' \text{ and } (p',\ q') \in R,$$

and conversely,

$$\forall \alpha: q \overset{\alpha}{\Rightarrow} q', \exists\ p' \text{ such that } p \overset{\alpha}{\Rightarrow} p' \text{ and } (p',\ q') \in R.$$

The weak transition is represented by $\Rightarrow$, and its label α is represented as a comma-separated list of the triggers and actions involved. According to this definition, the FSMs shown in Figure 11 and Figure 12 are weakly bisimilar. Note that this notion of weak bisimilarity guarantees equivalence of behavior between the two models, for all practical purposes.

Checking for Weak Bisimulation. The relation R between corresponding (non-instantaneous) states of the two behavior models is traced by using specially coined labels to represent the states in the system. Having generated the behavior models, and given the relation R, we can modify our bisimulation checker to check for weak bisimulation. If the checker shows that the two behavior models are weakly bisimilar, we can conclude that the transformed SCB model truly represents the source SCA model.

6   Conclusions

We feel that goal-directed certification is more practical and achievable than providing a general correctness proof for a model transformation. Using the transformation itself to trace the equivalence relation R between the source and target elements makes it easier to check if the systems are bisimilar. We have also seen that weak bisimulation helps us to practically extend this approach to a wider range of systems. Semantic anchoring is a very powerful technique for specifying DSML behavior, and a combination of a well chosen semantic unit and a well defined weak bisimulation criterion can help us verify the semantic equivalence of models generated by a model transformation.

We may also choose to represent a small subset or a specific aspect of a system's behavior by semantic anchoring, and use suitably defined weak bisimulation criteria to verify the preservation of specific behaviors in model transformations between DSMLs that are otherwise very different. Further research in using this technique in a wide range of transformations will provide more insight into the nature of such behaviors. Other types of transformations that we wish to address in the future include abstractions and refinements, such as from a block diagram like representation (such as Simulink) to embedded code.

Acknowledgments. The research described in this paper has been supported by an NSF Grant, CNS-0509098, titled: Software Composition for Embedded Systems using Graph Transformations.

References

1. Matlab's Simulink/Stateflow, http://www.mathworks.com/products/stateflow/
2. OSC Embedded Validator, http://www.osc-es.de/index.php?idcat=17
3. The Abstract State Machine Language, http://www.research.microsoft.com/fse/asml
4. TNI Safety-Checker Blockset, http://www.tni.fr/en/produits/safety checkerblockset/index.php
5. Agrawal, A., Karsai, G., Ledeczi, A.: An end-to-end domain-driven software development framework. In: OOPSLA 2003: 18th annual ACM SIGPLAN conference on OOP, systems, languages, and applications, pp. 8–15. ACM Press, New York (2003)
6. Chen, K., Sztipanovits, J., Abdelwahed, S., Jackson, E.K.: Semantic Anchoring with Model Transformations. In: ECMDA-FA, pp. 115–129 (2005)
7. Chen, K., Sztipanovits, J., Neema, S.: Toward a semantic anchoring infrastructure for domain-specific modeling languages. In: EMSOFT 2005: Proceedings of the 5th ACM international conference on Embedded software, pp. 35–43. ACM Press, New York (2005)
8. Denney, E., Fischer, B.: Certifiable Program Generation. In: GPCE, pp. 17–28 (2005)
9. Göttler, H.: Attributed graph grammars for graphics. In: Proceedings of the 2nd International Workshop on Graph-Grammars and Their Application to Computer Science, London, UK, pp. 130–142. Springer, Heidelberg (1983)

10. Harel, D.: Statecharts: A visual formalism for complex systems. Science of Computer Programming 8(3), 231–274 (1987)
11. Harwood, W., Moller, F., Setzer, A.: Weak Bisimulation Approximants. In: Ésik, Z. (ed.) CSL 2006. LNCS, vol. 4207, pp. 365–379. Springer, Heidelberg (2006)
12. Holzmann, G.J.: The Model Checker SPIN. Software Engineering 23(5), 279–295 (1997)
13. Ledeczi, A., Bakay, A., Maroti, M., Volgyesi, P., Nordstrom, G., Sprinkle, J., Karsai, G.: Composing Domain-Specific Design Environments. Computer 34(11), 44–51 (2001)
14. Mikk, E., Lakhnech, Y., Siegel, M.: Hierarchical Automata as Model for Statecharts. In: ASIAN 1997, pp. 181–196. Springer, Heidelberg (1997)
15. Mikk, E., Lakhnech, Y., Siegel, M., Holzmann, G.J.: Implementing Statecharts in PROMELA/SPIN. In: WIFT 1998: Proceedings of the Second IEEE Workshop on Industrial Strength Formal Specification Techniques, Washington, DC, USA, p. 90. IEEE Computer Society Press, Los Alamitos (1998)
16. Necula, G.C.: Proof-carrying code. In: Proceedings of the 24th ACM SIGPLAN-SIGACT Symposium on Principles of Programming Langauges (POPL 1997), January 1997, pp. 106–119 (1997)
17. Schürr, A., Winter, A., Zündorf, A.: The PROGRES approach: Language and environment. In: Rozenberg [21], ch. 13, pp. 487–550, 15.
18. Nickel, U., Niere, J., Zündorf, A.: Tool demonstration: The FUJABA environment. In: The 22nd International Conferenceon Software Engineering (ICSE), Limerick, Ireland, ACMPress, Limerick (2000)
19. Varró, D.: A Formal Semantics of UML Statecharts by Model Transition Systems. In: Corradini, A., Ehrig, H., Kreowski, H.-J., Rozenberg, G. (eds.) ICGT 2002. LNCS, vol. 2505, pp. 378–392. Springer, Heidelberg (2002)
20. von der Beeck, M.: A Comparison of Statecharts Variants. In: ProCoS: Proceedings of the Third International Symposium Organized Jointly with the Working Group Provably Correct Systems on Formal Techniques in Real-Time and Fault-Tolerant Systems, London, UK, pp. 128–148. Springer, Heidelberg (1994)

An Instrumentation-Based Approach to Controller Model Validation

Rance Cleaveland[1], Scott A. Smolka[2], and Steven T. Sims[3]

[1] Department of Computer Science
University of Maryland
College Park, Maryland 20742, USA
rance@cs.umd.edu
[2] Department of Computer Science
Stony Brook University
Stony Brook, NY 11794-4400, USA
sas@cs.sunysb.edu
[3] Reactive Systems, Inc.
120-B East Broad Street
Falls Church, VA 22046, USA
sims@reactive-systems.com

Abstract. This paper discusses the concept of *Instrumentation-Based Validation* (IBV): the use of model instrumentation and coverage-based testing to validate models of embedded control software. IBV proceeds as follows. An engineer first formalizes requirements as *assertions*, or small models, which may be thought of as monitors that observe the behavior of the controller model as it executes. The engineer then instruments the model with these assertions and develops test suites with the aim of highlighting where assertion violations occur. To make our discussion of IBV more concrete, we also consider its implementation within the Reactis tool suite for the automated testing and validation of controller models given in Simulink® / Stateflow®.

1 Introduction

In the traditional V-process for software development depicted in Figure 1, artifacts at one stage, such as requirements, are used as a reference point for determining the adequacy of artifacts, such as subsystem specifications, at later stages. *Model-based development* (MBD) strengthens the V-process by allowing executable models to be used to convey system and subsystem design information. The behavior of these models may then be used to assess the eventual behavior of deployed systems. Tools such as the Simulink® / Stateflow® [1] modeling notations have proved very useful for MBD.

One may criticize existing industrial MBD approaches, however, for their relative silence on the question of *model validation*: the process of determining whether or not a given model satisfies its requirements. An executable model provides an excellent baseline for validating lower-level, more-detailed system descriptions, such as source code. In this case, one can check that the source code's executable behavior is consistent with

---

[1] MATLAB®, Simulink® and Stateflow® are registered trademarks of The MathWorks, Inc.

M. Broy, I.H. Krüger, and M. Meisinger (Eds.): ASWSD 2006, LNCS 4922, pp. 84–97, 2008.

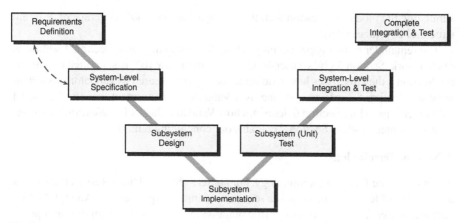

Fig. 1. The V-Process. The red line highlights the validation activity that is the subject of this paper.

that of the model. However, the eventually deployed system will only be satisfactory if the model itself can be shown to meet the requirements that have been defined for it. Requirements, by and large, are expressed in natural language, rather than in any sort of mathematical notation, and validating models against requirements has traditionally been a labor-intensive activity, with little tool support available.

In this paper, we show how *Instrumentation-Based Validation* (IBV) remedies this state affairs by automating the task of checking requirements against models. The basic usage scenario involves the following steps.

1. An engineer formalizes requirements as Simulink / Stateflow models that are intended to monitor a controller model for violations.
2. The engineer then instruments his or her controller model with these requirements and generates test suites that are then run on the model to determine whether violations can occur.
3. The test suites are designed to highlight any assertion violations that may occur.

The chief virtues of the instrumentation approach to requirements capture are the following.

1. Engineers can use the same notation for modeling and requirements formalization; there is no need to learn a new formalism.
2. Requirements models may themselves be simulated and debugged.
3. Requirements models may be linked deeply within a model in order to access internal values computed by the model; there is no need to expose internal model variables at the top level of the model purely so that requirements may "see" them.

To make our discussion of instrumentation-based validation more concrete, we consider the implementation of IBV within the Reactis tool suite for the automated testing and validation of controller models given in Simulink / Stateflow [1]. Specifically, Reactis Validator automates the process of instrumentation-based validation by thoroughly simulating the model in question with the aim of achieving 100% coverage of different structural coverage criteria.

The remainder of this paper develops along the following lines. Section 2 addresses related work. Section 3 gives a user-level viewpoint of how IBV is supported by Validator. Section 4 then discusses how requirements may be captured in Validator's *assertion* notation. Section 5 explains how one uses Validator to instrument a controller model with assertions, while Section 6 describes how Validator checks for assertion violations in instrumented models. Section 7 contains our concluding remarks.

A Note on Terminology

We shall use the following terminology. For an SUT (System Under Test), a *test suite* is a collection of tests, where a *test* is a sequence of input/output vectors. An input/output vector captures the SUT's response (the outputs) to a given set of stimuli (the inputs), and a test can now be understood as a simulation run of the SUT. When the SUT in question is a Simulink / Stateflow model, Reactis generates test suites exactly of this nature.

2   Related Work

Recent approaches to IBV for Simulink / Stateflow and related languages [2,3,4,5,6] attempt to *verify* whether or not a controller model satisfies a requirement specified as a safety property of the form "some undesirable system configuration never occurs." To perform the verification, some form of exhaustive state-space analysis is conducted. One such approach, and perhaps the closest in spirit to Reactis Validator, is that of [4]. There it is shown how safety properties can be captured as "model observers" in the SCADE graphical language for block diagrams and state machines. A SAT solver, along with arithmetic decision procedures and constraint solving, are used to determine if a SCADE model is compliant with an observer. A result of "indeterminate" is returned if the model or observer uses arithmetic expressions not supported by the underlying technology.

The techniques presented in [2,3,6] support the IBV of a restricted set of safety properties by allowing one to insert special "proof operator" blocks into Simulink models. In [7], the problem of searching the space of input sequences for test cases that violate a given safety property in a controller model is interpreted as an optimization problem. Evolutionary algorithms are then used to automate test-case generation.

Due to the problem of state explosion, approaches to IBV based on state-space exploration in general cannot handle complex controller models comprising large numbers of model components. In contrast, Reactis Validator does not perform an exhaustive state-space search; rather it aims to exhaustively cover all model coverage targets via testing. Consequently, Reactis Validator can be expected to handle models of much greater complexity, and our—and our customers'—experience with the tool lends credence to this claim.

In the context of Reactis Validator, the term *assertion* has its usual, English definition: a proposition that, at any given point in time, may be determined to be either true or false. Validator assumes that assertions should be invariantly true; if one becomes false, the tool treats this as evidence of deficiencies in the model. Validator assertions are thus different from the so-called "assertion blocks" found in the Model Verification block library in Simulink. Assertion blocks are similar to `assert` statements in C/C++; whenever the input signal to an assertion block becomes zero, simulation halts. Assertions in Validator, on the other hand, do not block simulation; it is possible to continue when an assertion becomes false.

3 Using Validator

Validator provides facilities for instrumenting Simulink / Stateflow controller models with assertions; checking whether or not instrumented models can violate assertions; and generating tests that demonstrate why assertions are violated. The tool does not modify the Simulink / Stateflow controller model itself; the instrumentation is maintained by Validator separately.

Figure 2 shows a screen shot of the top-level Reactis window, with an instrumented model loaded. The model is a simplified version of a cruise control and is included with the latest Reactis release. The utilities provided by Validator are accessed from this top-level window, as are those of the other main components of Reactis, Tester and

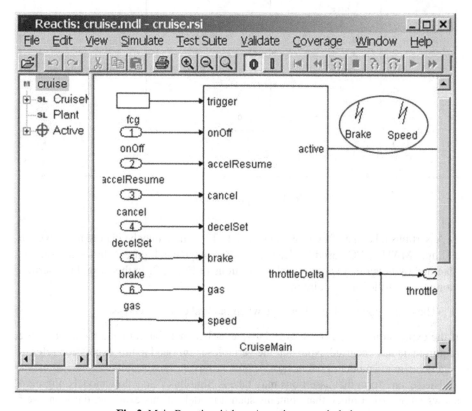

Fig. 2. Main Reactis window. Assertions are circled.

Simulator. In the screen shot, one may see two blocks containing zig-zag, "lightning-bolt" icons. These blocks are assertions that have been added into the model using Validator. The Reactis User Manual describes how this is done.

Although these blocks appear to be "unconnected" to the rest of the model, they in fact are able to "read" data items at the level of the model in which they are embedded.

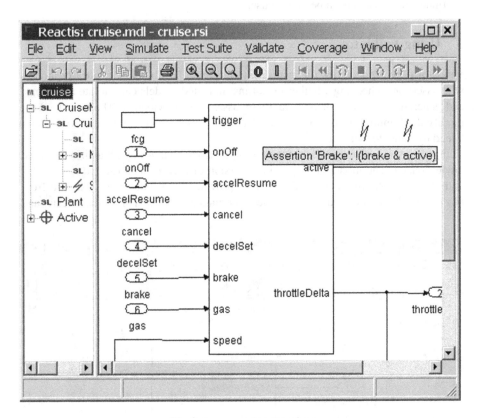

Fig. 3. An expression assertion

Assertions take one of two forms in Reactis. First, they may be expressions given in a simple MATLAB/C-based boolean expression language. Figure 3 shows an example obtained by hovering over one of the assertions in Figure 2. In this case the assertion monitors the following requirement:

The cruise control shall disengage when the brake pedal is pressed.

If the expression !(brake & active) ever becomes false, then a violation of the requirement has occurred. Note that the variables mentioned in this expression refer to data items in the model.

The second form that assertions may take is Simulink / Stateflow models. Figure 4 shows an assertion block that contains such a model. In this example, the icon itself

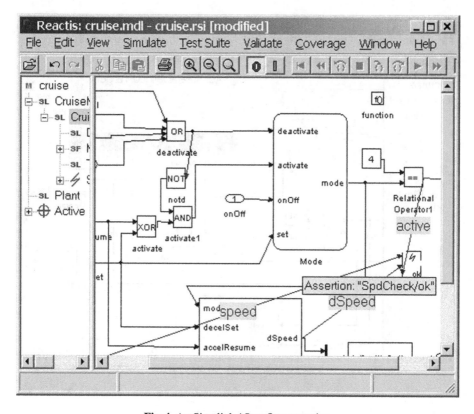

Fig. 4. An Simulink / Stateflow assertion

differs only slightly from the one for expressions (in this case, one may see the term
ok in the lower-right corner). Hovering over the icon, however, reveals the name of the
assertion (here SpdCheck/ok: SpdCheck is the name of the Simulink / Stateflow
model that implements the assertion, while ok is the name of the single outport in the
assertion). In addition, one may see *wiring information* showing which data items in
the model the inports of the assertion (here named active, speed and dSpeed) are
connected to.

Launching Validator is accomplished by clicking on the Validate pull-down menu
and selecting Check Assertions, as shown in Figure 5. This results in the launch
panel depicted in Figure 6 appearing. Clicking Check initiates the checking procedure.
When this finishes, one sees a panel like the one shown in Figure 7. In this case, the
tool has determined that 67% (two of three) assertions in the model were violated, and
that Validator constructed 8 tests containing a total of 349 steps to determine this. The
tests also covered the model to the displayed levels according to the various (Simulink-
specific, Stateflow-specific and generic, e.g., MC/DC) coverage criteria tracked by Reactis. The procedure Validator uses to check for the possibility of assertion violations
in instrumented models is explained more fully below in Section 6.

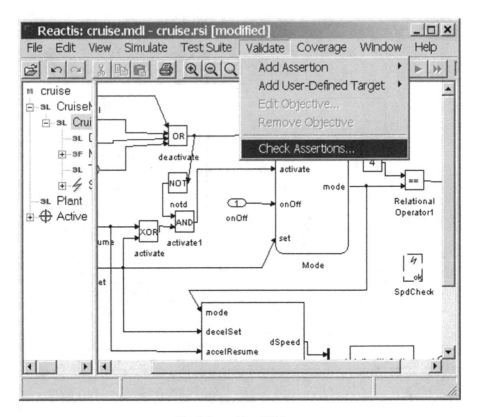

Fig. 5. Launching Validator

4 Encoding Requirements as Validator Assertions

This section concentrates on explaining how assertions, and more specifically Simulink / Stateflow assertions, may be used to encode requirements.

In the case of a cruise control, one might find the following requirement written in a requirements document.

> *"When active, the control mechanism shall not allow the set and actual speeds to differ by more than 1 km/h for more than three seconds."*

This requirement is in fact encoded within the SpdCheck assertion referred to earlier, the diagram for which is given in Figure 8. This view of the assertion was obtained from within Reactis by double-clicking on the icon for SpdCheck.

In general, one captures requirements as models by imagining how one might implement a *monitor* that observes the behavior of the controller model and reports when the requirement in question is violated. In the case of the sample requirement, a monitor might repeatedly sample the actual and set speeds. If the monitor notices a discrepancy of greater than 1 km/h, it might begin timing how long this discrepancy persists. If the difference dips below the allowed threshold of 1 km/h, then the monitor discontinues

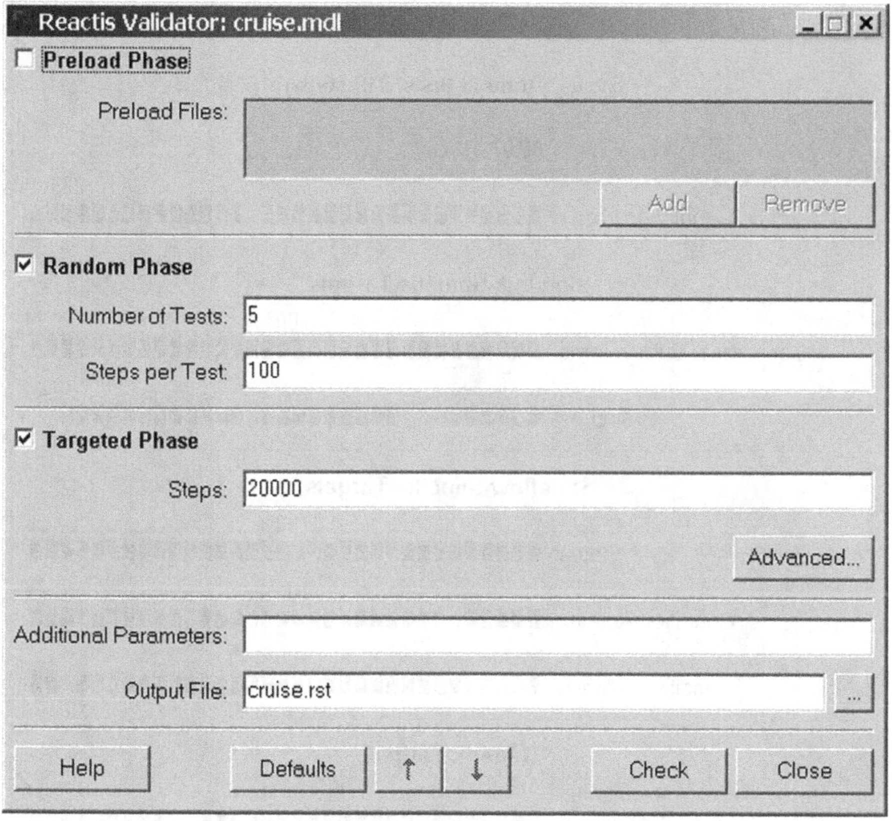

Fig. 6. The Validator launch panel

timing and reverts to its old mode of tracking values. If, however, three seconds elapse without the difference in the speeds being brought to within the acceptable range, then the monitor would report a violation of this requirement.

Note that the requirement imposes constraints on the speed differential only when the cruise control is active. If the cruise control is not engaged, then of course the controller has no obligation to control the speed of the vehicle. So the monitoring described above should only be in effect when the cruise control is "on".

The SpdCheck assertion is, in effect, an implementation of the above monitor in Stateflow. In the model, one may find a user-defined Stateflow graphical function, diff(), that is responsible for computing the difference between the values of speed and dSpeed (both of which are inputs to the model). Control resides initially in state Inactive; when active (another input to the model) becomes true, state Active is entered, together with its substate OkDiff. Intuitively, OkDiff remains the current state so long as the difference in the speeds remains within 1. Whenever the difference is larger than this value, substate BigDiff is entered, at which point counter cnt is initialized to 0. In every subsequent simulation step, if the difference in speeds remains too high, then the counter is incremented; when the counter value exceeds 3,

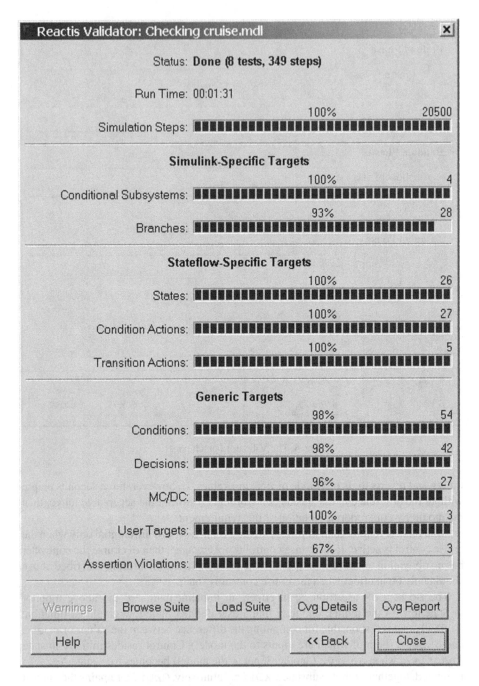

Fig. 7. The Validator results panel

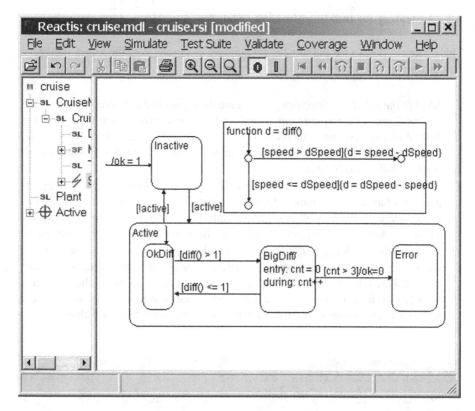

Fig. 8. The Stateflow model for the SpdCheck assertion, as seen from within Reactis

state Error is entered, and variable ok (the only output of the model) is set to 0. This act of "outputting 0" is how Simulink / Stateflow assertions "report" failure.

As a practical matter, Simulink / Stateflow assertions should be created using The MathWorks' Simulink / Stateflow tools and sorted in a model library. Validator may then be used to link specific assertion models in the library into the controller model. This strategy also facilitates the use of tools like DOORS to manage assertion models, so that they may be linked to the natural-language requirements from which they are derived.

4.1 How Simulink / Stateflow Assertions Are Constructed

To create the Simulink / Stateflow assertion models used by Validator, one uses The MathWorks' environment to create a library such as the one depicted in Figure 9. This library contains two models, one of which, DesiredSpeedCheck, corresponds to the assertion SpdCheck in the instrumented cruise-control model. Note the input/output interface to this model: there are three inports — speed, dSpeed and active — and one output — ok.

4.2   A Strategy for Building Simulink / Stateflow Assertions

This section outlines a simple strategy for building assertions from the natural-language statements that requirements are often given in.

1. *Identify the interface.* Specifically, what are the inputs to the assertion? In the case of SpdCheck, the requirement asserts a relationship between two speeds, so it is natural that the eventual "monitor" (i.e. assertion) will have, as two of its inputs, these speeds. Implicit in the requirement is another input that determines the on/off status of the cruise control.
2. *Identify the major "modes" for checking the requirement.* In the SpdCheck example, the behavior of the monitor depends foremost on whether or not the cruise control is active or not. This observation prompts the inclusion of the two main states, Inactive and Active, as well as the conditions for transitioning between them.
3. *Within major modes, identify key scenarios.* In the case of SpdCheck, one can identify three key situations: when the difference in speeds is tolerable, when it has exceeded the tolerance but for less than the allowed time, and when the difference has been too large for too long. Each of these scenarios is represented as a substate in Active, with transitions used to define when the substate should change.

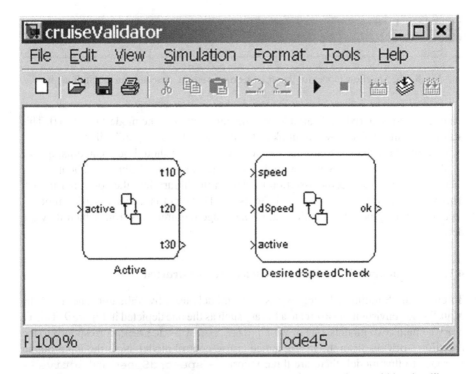

Fig. 9. The Stateflow model for the SpdCheck assertion, as given within the library cruiseValidator.mdl contained in the latest Reactis release

4.3 Expression-Based Assertions

Expression-based assertions may be seen as a simple short-hand for Simulink / State-flow assertions that contain (1) no Stateflow and (2) no state information that persists from one simulation step to the next. In particular, any expression-based assertion may also be rendered as a Simulink assertion. For this reason this report will not specifically address techniques for constructing them.

5 Instrumenting Models with Assertions

To annotate models with assertions, one uses the `Add Assertion` entry in the top-level `Validate` menu, as depicted in Figure 10. Selecting `Expression` or `Diagram` then invokes a dialog panel that allows one to enter an expression (in the former case), or import a model contained in a library (in the latter case), and "wire" it into the model. The Reactis User Manual contains more information about this.

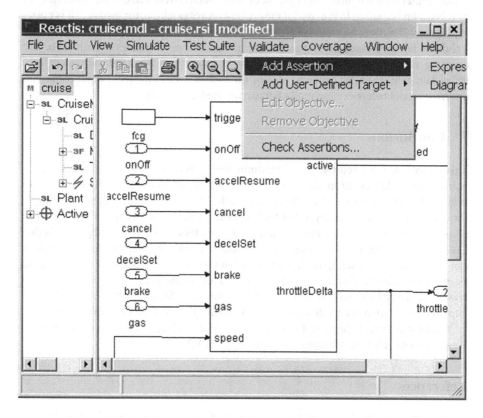

Fig. 10. Adding assertions into models

6   How Validator Works

This section describes how Validator checks for the possibility of assertion violations in instrumented models.

Validator uses the same underlying technology, *guided simulation*, that Reactis Tester uses to generate good test data. Specifically, Validator simulates the instrumented model thoroughly, with the goal of maximizing the same model-coverage criteria that Tester also attempts to maximize as it generates test cases. The guided-simulation strategy involves selecting input data at each simulation step that advance how much of the model has been exercised according to these criteria. While generating this input data, Validator also tracks whether any assertions are violated in the process.

Conceptually, then, Validator executes by (1) running Reactis Tester in order to get good test data, and (2) executing those tests on the model in order to determine if any assertions are violated. (In practice, these two steps are intertwined.) For this reason, Validator is not guaranteed to uncover all assertion violations; while test data may be thorough enough to give 100% coverage of the controller model, this does not ensure that all conceivable internal configurations of the model have been covered, and some subtleties can be missed on occasion. In the case of the cruise-control example, for instance, it is possible for SpdCheck to be violated. However, this violation is not uncovered in all runs of Validator. For this reason, it is advisable to run Validator several times on a model before deeming it violation-free. Like Tester, Validator contains a randomized component to its input-date generation, so different runs of the tool will yield different input data, with different model behavior potentially being exercised as a result.

7   Conclusions

This paper has discussed the use of Instrumentation-Based Validation to check for requirements violations in models, and the automation of IBV within the Reactis tool suite. IBV and Reactis Validator fill a niche in the model-based development paradigm for which there is little, if any, other tool support available: checking early-stage models against system requirements. Validator works by thoroughly simulating models that have been instrumented with assertions, in order to determine if any of these assertions can be violated. In general, one has an assertion for each requirement of interest; these assertions monitor the behavior of the model and report anomalies. The paper described how these assertions may be formulated as Simulink / Stateflow models and "wired into" models; it also briefly discussed how Validator then searches for violations.

Validator originally appeared in release V2003.2 of Reactis and is a component of all subsequent releases, the most recent of which is V2006.

References

1. Anonymous: Model-Based Testing and Validation of Control Software with Reactis. Reactive Systems, Inc. (2003), http://www.reactive-systems.com/papers/bcsf.pdf
2. Rau, A.: Model-Based Development of Embedded Automotive Control Systems. PhD thesis, Universitat Tubingen (2003)

3. Lepper, M.: An Algorithm for the Real-Time Evaluation of Temporal Trace Specifications. PhD thesis, Technische Universitat Belin (2004)
4. Bouali, A., Dion, B.: Formal verification for model-based development. In: Proceedings of SAE 2005 World Congress 05AE-235 (2005)
5. Anonymous: Embedded Validator Produktinformation. Embedded Systems AG (2006), http://www.osc-es.de/products/en/embeddedvalidator.php
6. Anonymous: Safety-Checker Blockset Documentation. TNI-Software (2006), http://www.vnvware.com/
7. Pohlheim, H., Conrad, M.: Evolutionary safety testing of embedded control software by automatically generating compact test data sequences. In: Proceedings of SAE 2005 World Congress 2005-01-0750 (2005)

TestML - A Test Exchange Language for Model-Based Testing of Embedded Software

Juergen Grossmann[1], Ines Fey[1], Alexander Krupp[3],
Mirko Conrad[4], Christian Wewetzer[2], and Wolfgang Mueller[3]

[1] DaimlerChrysler AG, Alt Moabit 96a, D-10559 Berlin
juergen.grossmann, ines.fey@daimlerchrysler.com
[2] dSPACE GmbH, Technologiepark 25, D-33100 Paderborn
christian.wewetzer@dspace.de
[3] Paderborn University/C-LAB, Fuerstenallee 11, D-33102 Paderborn
alexander.krupp, wolfgang.mueller@c-lab.de
[4] Member of the ACM
mirko.conrad@acm.org

Abstract. Test processes in the automotive industry are tool-intensive and affected by technologically heterogeneous test infrastructures. In the industrial practice a product has to pass tests at several levels of abstraction such as Model-in-the-Loop (MIL), Software-in-the-Loop (SIL) and Hardware-in-the-Loop (HIL) tests. Different test systems are applied for this purpose (e.g. dSPACE MTest, dSPACE Automation Desk, National Instruments Teststand) and almost each test system requests its own proprietary test description language. The exchange of tests between different test systems and the reuse of tests between different test levels is normally not possible. Efforts to integrate these heterogeneous test environments, to address test exchange in a general manner and to standardize and harmonize the existing language environment are still at the beginning and not tailored towards the requirements of the automotive domain. To keep the whole development and test process efficient and manageable, the definition of an integrated and seamless approach is required. TestML – the test exchange language we present in this article – is defined to overcome the technological obstacles (different test language syntax and semantics, different data formats and interface descriptions) that almost automatically accompany the application of heterogeneous test tools and test infrastructures. TestML supports the exchange of tests between different test notations in a heterogeneous tool environment. In this paper, we introduce the XML schema of TestML and demonstrate the efficiency of the interchange format by giving examples from the model-based development of electronic control units. Tool support is illustrated by an application with Simulink/Stateflow.

1 Introduction

Development processes in the automotive industry are highly distributed and fragmented. The Original Equipment Manufacturer (OEM) acts as the system

M. Broy, I.H. Krüger, and M. Meisinger (Eds.): ASWSD 2006, LNCS 4922, pp. 98–117, 2008.

integrator and solution provider. He is responsible for the development of high level specifications and the integration and quality assurance at system level. The software and hardware of the individual electronic control units (ECUs) are normally provided by different suppliers. Tools, methods and data formats used in the development processes of the suppliers and the OEMs are normally different.

Moreover, new development paradigms, such as model based development, have to be integrated into existing development processes and tool chains. Model-based specifications in development and the establishment of powerful code generators have led the development process to be noticeably more effective, and automated at a higher level of abstraction. Due to the availability of executable models, tests and analytical methods can be applied early and integrated into subsequent development steps. The positive effects — early error detection and early bug fixing — are obvious.

To keep the whole development and test process efficient and manageable, the definition of an integrated and seamless approach is required. Such an approach especially would address the subjects of test exchange, autonomy of infrastructure, methods, and platforms and the reuse of tests. The respective technological basis will be constituted by a domain specific test language, that is executable will unify the test infrastructure as well as the definition and documentation of tests. For this purpose, the BMBF project IMMOS (Integrated Methodology for Model-based ECU Development) was carried out by DaimlerChrysler AG, IT Power Consultants, dSPACE GmbH, Fraunhofer FIRST, FZI Karlsruhe and Paderborn University. We present the test exchange language TestML as a substantial project result.

In section 2 we give a short overview of the test processes in the automotive domain and address related work. Section 3 describes the overall purpose and ideas behind TestML whereas section 4 depicts the set-up and structure of the language itself. To illustrate the behavioral semantics of TestML we provide a mapping between TestML constructs and Matlab/Simulink constructs in Section 5. Section 6 provides a number of short test cases that exemplify the expressiveness of TestML. Section 7 summarizes the paper.

2   Related Work

In the industrial practice an automotive control system has to pass several kind of tests on different levels. Tests that go along with the integration of the complete vehicle system are mainly the responsibility of the OEM. These tests address the interaction between control units, the vehicle communication infrastructure and last but not least tests of the complete vehicle system. Tests on ECU level are mainly in the responsibility of the respective suppliers. They encompass the verification of the of the software driven functionality and the electronic characteristics of the ECU.

Actually a wide range of different test and simulation environments are used in the automotive domain. For tests on model level, so-called Model-in-the-Loop

(MIL) environments are used. To test the software itself, so-called Software-in-the-Loop (SIL) and Processor-in-the-Loop Environments are introduced[1]. In the end the integration between soft- and hardware (i.e. the complete ECU) is tested using Hardware-in-the-Loop- (HIL) Environments [1]. Besides software related tests (functionality, software integrity, software robustness), HIL environments allow to test the electronic characteristics and may simulate a complete network of interacting ECUs. Finally the OEM uses HIL Environments to test and simulate the complete electronic infrastructure of a vehicle.

Normally, different test systems are applied for the different simulation environments and almost each test system has individual requirements for methods, languages and concepts. The established test tools from National Instruments [2], dSPACE [3], Etas [4], Vector [5], MBtech [6] for example are highly specialized ones. They rely on proprietary languages and technologies and are mostly closed in respect to portability, extension and integration. In comparison, in the domain of Electronic Design standardization efforts have culminated in the definition of a set of verification and test languages: SystemVerilog [7], PSL [8], and e [9]. The languages and tool support facilitate the efficient creation of highly automated model-based testbenches [10]. This is achieved by a concise representation of interfaces including timing information, and by support for constraint based stimulus generation, and advanced (temporal) coverage and assertion facilities for evaluation. However, the current concepts focus on digital design, and they do not focus on testing of continuous domain models which are commonly applied in the automotive industry.

Efforts to address test exchange and test reuse in such heterogeneous environments are still in the beginning. The emerging IEEE standard ATML [11] is not finalized and not supported by the automotive tool chains. A new promising approach, that is based on TTCN-3 [12] and — among others — integrates the TestML concepts described in this paper, is already under definition but not yet available for industrial practice [13,14].

3   The TestML Principles

TestML is a tool-independent XML-denoted language, which was developed for the interchange of test descriptions. The language elements are represented by individual XML elements that are defined by an XML schema. The complete XML schema for TestML can be accessed in [15].

TestML was tailored specifically to meet the demands of model-based testing of embedded software in the automotive sector. The language covers the different test stages from the module to integration and system tests as well as test levels from MIL to HIL. Besides describing strictly functional tests, different comparative test approaches such as regression testing and back-to-back testing

---

[1] A SIL environment allows to test the compiled target software using environment models both running on standardized personal computers. A PIL platform additionally simulates the targets processor environment to allow tests that address special target platform issues.

are supported. Our aim is to realize an interchange format for the large spectrum of test description languages established in the automotive industry. This section describes the purpose of TestML and expands on the background and the demands of the language design.

3.1   A Unified Format for Test Exchange

Our basic assumption is that semantic similarities as well as overlaps exist between the different test description languages (see [16] for an overview). On the one hand, these similarities represent the indispensable precondition for the idea of interchanging test scenarios and test data across tool and language barriers. On the other hand, they offer the necessary foundation for the definition of a generic exchange format.

TestML was conceived as a language for exchanging test descriptions in the context of model-based testing of embedded automotive software. This includes software from different sub-domains like telematics, body control, power train and driving assistance. Whereas communication related issues are crucial for telematics, the majority of body control and driving assistance software belongs to feedback control systems that rely on sensors and actuators and have to deal with a large amount of continuous real world data. The general conditions of the different automotive sub-domains constitute a series of specific demands that have to be made on a technology-independent test description language spanning different tools in the automotive domain:

- specification of discrete and continuous (analogue) stimuli
- a concept of time to describe time-dependent events
- specification of reactive test cases to test feedback communication and control systems
- management of measurement data as inputs as well as reference data for comparative tests
- expressions for tests evaluation regarding the analysis of discrete and continuous signals.

The Basis of TestML is a self-contained language definition that makes it possible to cover test descriptions at different levels of abstraction (such as test scenarios and test data) independent from the respective tool environment.

The integrating effect of the language results from the potential to map the language constructs of existing test description languages to TestML and vice versa by using appropriate adapters. TestML itself acts as an intermediate notation that is interposed between the separate tool-dependent languages in the exchange of test data and test descriptions (see Fig. 1). The advantages are obvious. If multiple languages are to be supported, the complexity of integration increases only linearly for this solution. If integration is achieved through the realization of bilateral, point-to-point coupling without an intermediate format instead, the complexity increases quadratically.

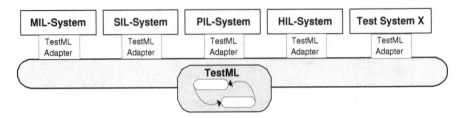

Fig. 1. Integration of different test descriptions using an intermediate language

3.2   Abstraction of Specific Test Systems

Complex test systems are used for the testing of control units. Test systems usually consist of multiple logical components (signal generators, capture/replay tools, test evaluation components, environment models etc.) that have to be coordinated and collectively controlled in the course of test execution. Setup and control of test systems differ contingent. In addition to the heterogeneous tool environment different test notations exist that can be used to describe the tests. For evaluation and categorization of existing test notations for model-based software testing of embedded software systems see [16].

In its function as an exchange language TestML enables operation of several different test systems. Because individual test systems differ greatly in their concrete technical specifications, it must be possible to abstract from the concrete realization of the respective source and target system for the exchange of test descriptions. Thus, we define one such abstraction termed TestML test system. A TestML test system consists of a combination of test components that we consider minimally necessary regarding the exchange of test descriptions. The individual components of the test system subsequently given below are, except for the test interface, represented implicitly by TestML means of description. The TestML test system itself is not an explicit part of the TestML language. Knowledge about setup and structure of the system help to better understand the subsequent annotation of individual means of description in TestML. Figure 2 shows a diagrammatic illustration of the TestML test system including TestML elements referring to the individual components.

The abstract test system for TestML consists of the following components:

- The system under test (SUT) represents the system that is to be tested. Mainly relevant for TestML is its test interface. From the perspective of TestML, the SUT itself is hidden behind the test interface.
- The stimulation unit is responsible for the generation of test stimuli; actual test execution takes place here.
- The capture unit records the system reactions and/or the system reactions as well as the test stimuli.
- The evaluation unit is responsible for the evaluation of test cases. It accesses all data recorded by the capture unit and can be operated temporally independent from the stimulation unit.

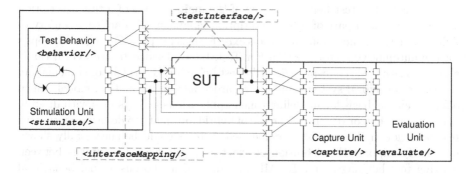

Fig. 2. Abstract test system for TestML

3.3 Test Behavior

The term test behavior subsumes processes that describe the stimulation of the test object at the moment of test execution. To serve its function as an exchange language, TestML has to cover and integrate the widest possible spectrum of different behavioral descriptions. Below we will specify a series of different criteria that can serve as the basis for the differentiation of varying classes of test behavior and fundamentally characterize the spectrum of TestML behavioral descriptions. The criteria are:

1. **Types of stimuli**
   The type of stimuli used for stimulation represents a basic criterion of differentiation in the stimulation of a test object. Four different types of stimulation signals are differentiated in literature ([17], [16]). Relevant at this point is the differentiation of *timed signals* and *timeless messages*.

2. **Determination**
   Test behavior can be specified as *reactive behavior* or as *determined behavior*. A test with reactive test behavior controls and changes the stimulation of the test object depending on how the test object reacts to the continuous stimulation. To do so, the output signals or output messages of the test object are interpreted, evaluated, and considered for the generation of new stimuli. In determined test behavior, the stimulation of the test object is established from the outset. The reaction of the test object is not considered for the generation of stimuli or is used only to abort the test at an appropriate time.

3. **Data synthesis**
   Another criterion for test behavior is the differentiation of *synthetically generated stimulation sequences* and recorded *measured data* that can later be replayed for test purposes. Synthetically generated stimulation sequences are usually described through programming techniques. Apart from the stimulation of a test object, recorded data is mainly used as a reference for test evaluation. Comparative approaches like regression testing or back-to-back testing explicitly require the existence of recorded reference data.

Specification of test behavior is one of the main aspects of a test description and is an essential part of a test description language. In practice, a variety of different methods, notations, and tools exist for this purpose. For a good synopsis for the automotive sector see [16]. For TestML we decided to use hybrid timed automata as a basic concept to describe test behavior. Hybrid automata emanate the theory of hybrid systems and are regarded as a mathematical model, which offers a reliable basis for modeling timed applications and systems with discrete and analog behavior (cf. [18]). The use of hybrid automata to describe continuous test behavior in the context of embedded systems could be successfully shown in [19]. To support the definition of exact and well-defined mappings between existing test languages and TestML we provided a rigorous formal behavioral semantics for TestML by means of Abstract State Machines (ASMs) [20].

4   Structure and Elements of TestML Test Descriptions

This section describes the elements and the setup of test descriptions with TestML. The most important basic elements of the language will be introduced individually and illustrated below. Each basic element represents an important concept and/or function from the field of testing and, as is common in XML, stands for a container that may contain further means of description and encapsulates them to the outside.

- The element *testml* forms the root element for each TestML description and represents a number of test cases. The element *testml* needs no further explanation from here on.
- The element *testInterface* serves to describe the interface to the SUT.
- The elements *testSequence* and *rtTestSequence* constitute test sequences that describe an operating scenario to be tested by means of test inputs.
- The elements *stimulate*, *capture* and *evaluate* describe stimulation, recording, and test analysis within one test sequence.
- The element *behavior* is used for the specification of test behavior.

A number of other means of description exist besides the mentioned basic elements that represent either data types, operators and/or mathematical expressions, structure the language and/or form the inner structure of the abovementioned elements. Figure 3 shows the section of the TestML schema in which the basic elements are defined.

4.1   The Test Interface

The test interface is described by the element *testInterface*. A large number of input and output channels represented by the element *port* in TestML are part of a test interface, ensuring type safe communication between the SUT and the test behavior defined modularly in TestML. Values can be written to the SUT and/or read by the SUT through each defined channel. The type of communication can be specified in more detail by stating the direction of communication and the data types supported by the individual channel.

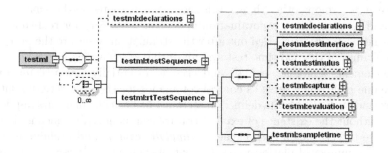

Fig. 3. The basic elements of a test description with TestML

Specification of a test interface

```
<testInterface ID="Testinterface_1">
  <port ID="P1_phi_Brake" type="double" direction="input"
  name="phi_Brake"/>
  <port ID="P2_phi_Gas" type="double" direction="input"
  name="phi_Gas"/>
  <port ID="P3_v_act" type="double" direction="input"
  name="v_act"/>
  <port ID="P4_BrakePedal" type="boolean"
  direction="output" name="BrakePedal"/>
</testInterface>
```

The listing above depicts the description of a test interface with 4 channels in TestML. The direction of communication, the type and the name of the port are annotated in the form of XML attributes to the element *port*.

4.2   Test Sequences

TestML represents test cases through the elements *testSequence* and *rtTestSequence*. To emphasize that test cases are usually complete application scenarios, they are identified as test sequences in TestML. While the element *rtTestSequence* can describe a real-time test case, the element *testSequence* represents a non real-time test case. Real-time test cases and non real-time test cases can be differentiated by the lack of temporal references within the element *testSequence*. The structural set-up of TestML test sequences otherwise remains the same.

A TestML test sequence usually consists of the elements *stimulate*, *capture* and *evaluate* as well as a modular behavioral description through elements of the type *behavior*. We will address this in more detail in section 3.3.

4.3   Stimulation, Recording and Evaluation

The specification of stimulation, recording, and evaluation in TestML is undertaken, with a strict conceptual separation, by the elements *stimulate*, *capture* and *evaluate*: Among other things, this separation is rooted in the separation of time- and resource-intensive evaluation operations necessary for real-time tests that usually have to be carried out after the stimulation to ensure the necessary reaction times of the real-time test system during stimulation.

The elements *stimulate, capture* and *evaluate* essentially have two functions. On the one hand, they serve as control commands for the abstract stimulation, capture and evaluation units defined in section 4.3. The control occurs implicitly, that is without the existence of explicit control commands. This means that for a concrete target system each element *stimulate, capture* and *evaluate* is interpreted as a number of platform-specific control commands. These are necessary to control the concrete test units provided by the concrete system.

On the other hand, the elements *stimulate, capture* and *evaluate* encapsulate the detailed expressions and statements of a TestML test description. The element *stimulate* contains the complete behavior specification to generate the required stimulus signals (see element *behavior* in section 3.3 for details). Moreover, the elements *stimulate* and *capture* contain mappings that map the input and output ports of a test interface (element *port*, see section 4.1) on the elements of a behavior signature (element *signature*, see section 3.3) or accordingly on capture variables. The mapping on a behavior signature is part of the stimulation description while mapping of capture variables is conducted in the element *capture*. Capture variables serve as references to access recording data and are later used within the element *evaluate* for test evaluation. Irrespective of it being used for stimulation or recording, mapping is specified through the element *interfaceMapping*. The following listing depicts mapping between channels of a test system and recording variables within an element *capture*.

Mapping of channels to capture variables

```
<interfaceMapping>
   <map>
     <portRef IDREF="P1_phi_Brake"/>
     <signalRef IDREF="Sig1_phi_Brake"/>
   </map>
   <map>
     <portRef IDREF="P2_phi_Gas"/>
     <signalRef IDREF="Sig2_phi_Gas"/>
   </map>
</interfaceMapping>
```

The element *evaluate* describes the test evaluation. Whereas the elements *stimulate* and *capture* are obligatorily started simultaneously at the beginning of test execution, the element *evaluate* can be started independent of the two other elements, even after test execution. In principle, test evaluation takes place based on the data recorded by the element *capture*. Test evaluation is carried out by specifically defined operators and commands. These operators and command allow the comparison of signal values and complete signal shapes and are explained in the following section.

4.4   Data Types, Operators and Expressions

In most programming languages the basic data types are bool, integer, double, and string. Naturally, they are supported by TestML. They may be represented according to their corresponding type as defined in the W3C XML schema, i.e. xs:integer for an integer. Also, test specific special data types are offered, such as time and signal. Times are given as a double value and a time unit. The possible units are day, hour, second, millisecond, and microsecond represented by their common abbreviations "d", "h", "s", "ms", and "us". The following listing shows the declaration of a double variable and, following the declaration, a write operation to set the variable to the value of 100. All declared variables are referenced within TestML by their ID.

Instantiation of data types

```
<double ID="var1" name="Examples variable"/>
<write>
  <doubleRef IDREF="var1"/>
  <value><double>
    <value>100</value>
  </double></value>
</write>
```

The data type signal is special in that it may not only describe a singular value, but a time-dependent wave-form. Most of the times, the value data type of a signal is double. The waveform is represented by means of simple signal expressions or TestML automata, which are introduced in section 3.3. The next listing shows a simple signal expression specifying a ramp which rises from 0 to 100 within 10 seconds.

Instantiation of a signal

```
<signal>
  <time>
    <unit>s</unit> <double><value>10</value></double>
  </time> <ramp>
    <start><double><value>0</value></double><start>
    <end><double><value>100</value></double></end>
  </ramp>
</signal>
```

For expression evaluation a set of simple operators is provided. Table 1 shows a selection of operators. The four basic arithmetic operations are provided, as well as equality, comparison, and logical operators. The operators may be combined to form expressions as usual. They may be applied in an extended form to signals, which represent a time series of values.

Table 1. List of Operators

Operator	Meaning	Operator	Meaning
$<add/>$	addition	$<and/>$	logical and
$<sub/>$	subtraction	$<or/>$	logical or
$<mult/>$	multiplication	$<not/>$	logical not
$<div/>$	division	$<xor/>$	logical xor
$<abs/>$	absolute value	$<equ/>$	equality
$<max/>$	maximum value	$<grt/>$	greater
$<min/>$	minimum value	$<geq/>$	greater or equal

An example of a comparison expression is shown in the next listing, which compares two signals with the identifiers $Data1\_v\_act$ and $Data2\_v\_act$.

comparison expression

```
<cond>
  <grt>
    <signalRef IDREF="Data1_v_act"/>
    <signalRef IDREF="Data2_c_act"/>
  </grt>
</cond>
```

4.5   Behavioral Constructs

The structure and elements of the element *behavior* are depicted in Fig. 4. They all together form a so-called TestML automaton. The most important elements of a TestML automaton are the elements *signature*, *step* and *switch*. The element *signature* provides an interface to the internally specified and encapsulated behavior. The element itself consists of a number of signal declarations (much like the ports in the test interface) that can individually be accessed in reading or writing depending on the specification.

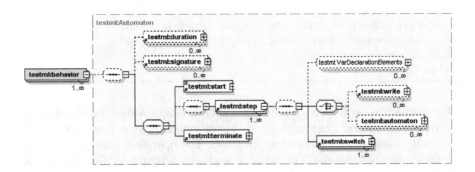

Fig. 4. The element behavior

The element *step* describes a defined state within a TestML automaton. Each *step* in turn is either defined by a TestML automaton or contains one or more commands that define test behavior directly — either through arithmetic equations, time-based signal primitives or alternatively for timeless messages. The element *switch* defines a transition that marks the passage between two *steps*. By use of the element *cond* every transition can be annotated by conditions for a time- or value-dependent control of automata. If the transition condition evaluates to true, the transition fires and the *step* referenced by the element *succ* will be processed next. For each step one transition without condition is allowed. A transition without condition fires after all time-dependent instructions that are defined within the respective step have been terminated.

5   Mapping TestML Automata to Matlab Simulink

This section provides an executable TestML implementation using Simulink/Stateflow [21]. We mainly emphasize on behavioral aspects and introduce a detailed mapping that maps the TestML constructs defined in section 4.5 to the well-defined behavioral constructs of Simulink/Stateflow. For a concise TestML semantics refer to [20].

In TestML we generally distinguish between timed automata and non-timed automata. Timed automata reside inside TestML real-time test cases and non-timed automata reside inside non real-time test cases. Each top level TestML automaton, independent of its type, can be mapped to a Stateflow chart, that resides inside a Simulink Stateflow block. The signature of a TestML automaton is represented by the input and output ports of the Stateflow block. Hence the mapping between the automaton signature and an arbitrary test interface can be simply realized by drawing lines between Simulink ports. Figure 5 shows a Stateflow block called "TestML_Automaton", which provides four data output ports *phi_Brake*, *phi_Gas*, *v_des*, *leverPos* and one data input port *v_act*.

Each Stateflow chart that represents a TestML Automaton consists of a top level state with the same name as the TestML automaton. This top level state contains further states and transitions, which each represent either a TestML *step* or a TestML *switch*. For time control the top level state provides a local time property called *time*. We define local time with

$$time = t - startTime$$

in which *time* represents the local time, *t* holds the global time, and *startTime* represents the point in time that the automaton has started. In general global time progress is realized by Simulink simulation time using a discrete simulation solver. Moreover, each TestML step — except a final or start step — is realized by a Stateflow state, which provides a local time property called *stepTime*. Local step time is defined in the same way as local automaton time. The property *startTime* here represents the point in time when the step has started. As we will see later on, TestML steps have to control the running status of all embedded entities (write statements and embedded automata). Hence we

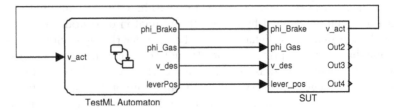

Fig. 5. A TestML automaton represented by Stateflow

introduce a step property called *runningEntities*. This property is initialized when a step is entered and holds the number of all embedded entities (e.g. *en* : *runningEntities* = 2). It is decremented whenever an embedded entity stops and sends the *EntityStopped* event.

$$on\ EntityStopped : runningEntities - -$$

TestML *start* steps are simply realized as Stateflow default transitions. TestML *final* steps are denoted as empty states with the name "final".

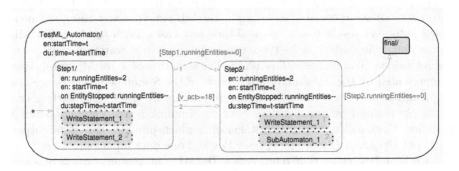

Fig. 6. Base structure of a TestML automaton in Stateflow

We have to provide an equivalent Stateflow transition for each TestML *switch*. A switch is composed of the elements *cond* and *next*. The element *next* can simply be interpreted as transition end, which refers to the next Stateflow state to be executed when the respective transition condition evaluates to *true*. The element *cond* expresses a switch condition that can in most cases be mapped directly to a Stateflow transition condition. The sole exception is the absence of a switch condition. In TestML the absence of a switch condition defines a so-called "default switch" which fires when all embedded entities of the current step have been finished. In contrast a Stateflow transition without any annotations fires immediately after its source state is activated.

We can not use the empty Stateflow transition to implement the TestML default switch. Instead we have to check the status of all embedded entities.

When all entities are finished the property *runningEntities* of a TestML step is zero. We can use this as a switch condition of a Stateflow transition.

$$[< Stepname > .runningEntities == 0]$$

Figure 6 shows the base structure of a TestML automaton implemented with Stateflow. The Automaton consists of two steps with two switches in between: a TestML default switch and a switch listening on the input port *v_act*. The main functional behavior of a TestML step is defined by its embedded entities. These are either embedded TestML automata or write statements which assign signals or simple values to ports. Embedded TestML automata are implemented almost in the same way as top-level automata. Sole difference: Embedded automata have to provide the *EntityStopped* event that will be fired when the execution of the automaton has finished. The event is triggered by the final state and can be realized by *en : EntityStopped* using the Stateflow Action Language. The concrete implementation of TestML write statements depends on the type of the enclosing automaton. Inside timed automata we assign timed signals to ports. Timed signals have a distinct duration. When executing write operations, one has to consider and control the duration of the signal that is written. In contrast, non-timed automata only provide simple value assignments that have no duration. Temporal control is not necessary here.

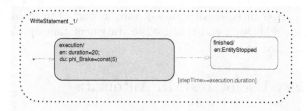

Fig. 7. Timed write statement which applies a constant signal to *phi_Brake*

We start with the implementation of write statements that reflect duration. For each write statement we provide a top level state that contains a controller structure that manages temporal and functional behavior. Multiple write statements that belong to the same TestML step are realized as multiple parallel executed top level states (see section 6). The enclosed controller structure consists of two states. The "execution state" is responsible for signal execution and its application to a port. When activated, an execution state calculates signal values as part of its during action and applies the calculated value to a specified port (e.g. *du : phi_Brake := const(4)*). We may use graphical functions for value calculation that each represent a signal of a certain kind which is parameterized by a set of signal-specific parameters (e.g. *ramp(offset, slope, limit)*, *const(constval)*, *sinewave(offset, frequency, amplitude)*). The "finished" step is triggered when the actual step time exceeds the signals duration. We implement this using the following transition condition:

$$[executer.duration > stepTime]$$

During its entry a finished step fires an *EntityStopped* event *en* : *EntityStopped* so that the enclosing step is informed about the signals end. Figure 7 shows the implementation of a write statement that applies a constant signal with the length of 20 seconds to a port called *phi_Brake*.

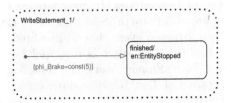

Fig. 8. Non-timed write statement which applies a constant signal to *phi_Brake*

Non-timed automata contain write statements that do not reflect duration. For this kind of write statements we adopt the structure of timed write statements and simply omit the execution state. The value calculation and its application to a port are realized as an action defined as part of the Stateflow default transition. Figure 8 shows a non-timed write statement that applies a constant value to a port called *phi_brake*.

6   Exemplary Use of TestML Automata

In the following, the description potential of TestML is shown and illustrated by means of short examples taken from practice. The samples selected each represent a specific type of test behavior mentioned in section 3.3. In the following examples, the TestML automata are not depicted in their XML representation but as annotated states in an UML alike notation[2].

6.1   Specification of Timed, Deterministic Test Stimuli

We now examine a typical test sequence taken from a cruise control test. The focus of the test is on accelerator pedal interpretation, i.e. the unit which is responsible for interpreting the driver interaction via brake and gas pedal. For this

---

[2] We deliberately avoid to depict the XML representation here, since this quickly becomes too large even for short examples. The use of graphical representations makes a more compact visualization possible. In the following the TestML element *step* is depicted as a state and the element *switch* is presented as a transition. Statements which are used within the element *step*, either for the definition of signals or simple values or to assign these definitions to a port, are annotated in the form of pseudo code inside the states. For further information on XML representations, refer to the enclosed schema.

example, the test interface was deliberately kept small. The port v_act describes the current vehicle speed in m/s, phi_Acc represents accelerator pedal travel and is given in percent and phi_Brake represents brake pedal travel and also given in percent. In order to test the acceleration pedal interpretation the following timed test scenario is used:

1. Within the first second, the current vehicle speed is kept constantly at -10 m/s and afterwards the value for v_act is set to -5 m/s for a second.
2. In the course of the test, the accelerator pedal travel is raised from 0% to 100% and then lowered linearly from 100% to 0%.
3. In the course of the test, the brake pedal travel is linearly lowered from 100% to 0% and then raised from 0% to 100%.

Figure 9 shows both the individual signal forms and the description used for the generation of signal forms with TestML. Every state of the TestML

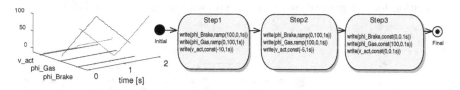

Fig. 9. Specification of synthetic stimulation sequences with TestML automata

automaton depicted above defines a time interval with its length being determined by the duration of instructions within the respective state. The example mentioned above contains for the state "Step1" the following three instructions:

– Write a ramp signal with the value course from 100 to 0 and the length of one second on the channel called phi_Brake $[write(phi\_Brake, ramp(100, 0, 1s))]$.
– Write a ramp signal with the value course from 0 to 100 and the length of one second on the channel called $[phi\_Gas\ (write(phi\_Gas, ramp(0, 100, 1s))]$.
– Write a constant signal with the value -10 and the length of one second on the channel called v_act $[write(v\_act, const(-10, 1s))]$.

After the statements have been executed a change into the next state, called "Step2", takes place via the output transition. For the state "Step2" we have the following three instructions. The complete execution stops as soon as the final state is reached.

– Write a ramp signal with the value course from 100 to 0 and the length of one second on the channel called phi_Brake $[write(phi\_Brake, ramp(0, 100, 1s))]$.
– Write a ramp signal with the value course from 0 to 100 and the length of one second on the channel called phi_Gas $[write(phi\_Gas, ramp(100, 0, 1s))]$.
– Write a constant signal with the value -10 and the length of one second on the channel called v_act $[write(v\_act, const(-5, 1s))]$.

6.2   Specification of Timed, Reactive Test Stimuli

In order to be able to show the use of TestML automata for the specification of reactive test behavior, the example mentioned above needs to be modified. Here, it is not the pedal interpretation which is tested rather than the cruise control. The test interface is expanded by an input and an output channel. The port v_target is an input port and describes the desired vehicle speed; v_act is an output port and represents the current vehicle speed. The reactive test behavior may be described as follows:

1. Set target speed v_target at 18 m/s
2. Use gas pedal until vehicle speed is greater than or equals 18 m/s.
3. Switch on cruise control.
4. Use brake pedal until vehicle speed equals 0 m/s.

Figure 10 shows the individual signal forms (left-hand side) as well as the description for the generation of the signal forms with (right-hand side).

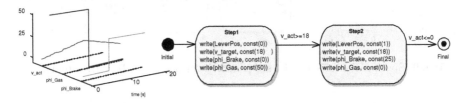

Fig. 10. Specification of reactive stimulation sequences with TestML automata

In contrast to the example from the previous section, the transition between the states "Step1" and the state "Step2" is equipped with a condition. The condition defines the switching characteristics between "Step1" and "Step2". The instructions are executed until the transition condition for "Step1" is fulfilled. Then the instructions from "Step2" are executed.

- Write a constant signal of 50 on phi_Gas [$write(phi\_Gas, const(50))$] and a constant signal of 0 on phi_Brake [$write(phi\_Brake, const(0)$]. The cruise control is switched off [$write(LeverPos, const(0))$] and the velocity of the target vehicle is set to $18m/s$ [$write(v\_target, const(18))$].
- If the channel v_act has taken on a value greater or equal 18 m/s, write a constant signal of 0 on the channel phi_Gas [$write(phi\_Gas, const(0))$], a constant signal of 70 on the phi_Brake channel [$write(phi\_Brake, const(70))$] and switch on the cruise control [$write(LeverPos, const(1))$]. The velocity of the target vehicle remains at $18m/s$ [$write(v\_target, const(18))$].

With a basic set of signal primitives and their suitable combinations, the use of TestML automata supports the definition of complex signal forms.

6.3   TestML Automata for Timeless Test Stimuli

Apart from systems working with timed test stimuli, there are frequently systems found in practice which are controlled solely by timeless stimuli, so-called messages. A test description for such a system consists of a set of actually timeless messages, which – by all means in a given order – are sent to different channels of the test system. The message sequence depicted below stands as an example for the discontinuous test case description as it can be used in this case for the AutomationDesk tool from dSPACE [3]. Again, we define the test of a cruise control function. Besides the already known phi_Brake input the brake pedal flag BrakePedal is also read.

A possible hysteresis of the brake pedal recognition is tested. First, a rising edge from 0 to 100 for the *phi_Brake* input is created and then the *ped_min* value is set. The *ped_min* value is the highest value in which the *BrakePedal* output again takes on the value 0, provided that there is no hysteresis. The test description to be represented in the TestML looks as follows:

1. Writing 0.0 to *phi_Brake*
2. Waiting for *time_step* seconds
3. Writing 100.0 to *phi_Brake*, this way a rising edge from 0.0 to 100.0 is created
4. Waiting for *time_step* seconds
5. Calculation of *ped_value* according to $ped\_value = ped\_min - tol$
6. Writing of *ped_value* to *phi_Brake*
7. Reading *BrakePedal* and saving of the value in the *brake_flag* variable

The following automaton shows the implementation of the simulation by a TestML automaton. Reading the model output (last point of list mentioned above) is carried out by the capture element, which will not be depicted at this point.

Fig. 11. Specification of message based test sequences with TestML automata

Individual states of the automaton describe the activation of individual messages. Because of the use of timers, which can be defined locally on the automata, the transitions between the states are time-controlled and define temporal distances between messages.

7   Summary and Outlook

TestML is a XML-noted test exchange language that is tailored towards the requirements of model-based testing of embedded vehicle software throughout the course of development. The reason for this development can be found in the need for test definitions, which can be reused during the whole development process, both in different test phases and different test environments as well as in the exchange between suppliers and the OEM. Thus, the aim of the language design was to be able to map a spectrum as broad as possible of the test description languages established in the automotive industry. With this, an exchange of tests between different tool platforms for the MIL, SIL and HIL test is made possible. TestML supports, besides classical functional tests, also comparative test approaches, such as regression testing and back-to-back tests, which are based on the existence of recorded reference data.

Test scenarios capable of real-time use are an important functionality of HIL test beds. As a major extension over most existing means for test description, TestML provides language constructs for tests under real-time conditions. This enables support of the entire development process by the test exchange language.

Special care was taken to provide a flexible test behavior description language covering different levels of abstraction. The concept of hybrid automata used to capture test behavior permits the mapping of common classes of automotive test descriptions, including deterministic and reactive test stimuli with or without temporal references as well as the use of recorded data streams as they accrue out of test drives. The decision to map all test aspects on automata made it possible to avoid an overloading of the exchange language with manifold constructs, which ultimately would have led to semantically redundant definitions. We would like to thank our participants in the IMMOS project for their contribution to TestML, especially S. Sadeghipour and H.-W. Wiesbrock from ITPower Consultants, Prof. H. Schlingloff and M. Friske from Fraunhofer FIRST.

References

1. Schäuffele, Zurawka (ed.): Automotive Software Engineering. Vieweg & Sohn Verlag, Wiesbaden (2006)
2. National Instruments: Web pages of the National Instruments corporation (2007)
3. dSpace AG: Web pages of the dSpace corporation (2005)
4. Etas Group: Web pages of the Etas Group (2007)
5. Vector Informatik GmbH: Web pages of the Vector Informatik GmbH (2007)
6. MBtech Group: Web pages of the MBtech Group (2007)
7. IEEE: IEEE Std.1800-2005 - Standard for SystemVerilog Unified Hardware Design, Specification and Verification Language (2005)
8. IEEE: IEEE Std.1850-2005 - IEEE Standard for Property Specification Language (PSL) (2005)
9. IEEE: IEEE Std.1647-2006 - Standard for the Functional Verification Language 'e' (2006)
10. Bergeron, J., Cerny, E., Nightingale, A., Hunter, A.: Verification methodology manual for SystemVerilog. Springer, Heidelberg (2006)
11. SCC20 ATML Group: IEEE ATML specification drafts and IEEE ATML status reports (2006)
12. ETSI: ES 201 873-1 V3.2.1: Methods for Testing and Specification (MTS). The Testing and Test Control Notation Version 3, Part 1: TTCN-3 Core Language (2007)

13. Schieferdecker, I., Großmann, J.: Testing of Embedded Control Systems with Continous Signals. In: Dagstuhl-Workshop MBEES: Modellbasierte Entwicklung eingebetteter Systeme II, TU Braunschweig, pp. 113–122 (2006)
14. Schieferdecker, I., Bringmann, E., Grossmann, J.: Continuous TTCN-3: testing of embedded control systems. In: SEAS 2006: Proceedings of the 2006 international workshop on Software engineering for automotive systems, pp. 29–36. ACM Press, New York (2006)
15. IMMOS Project: TestML schema definition version 1.0.3 (2006)
16. Conrad, M.: Modell-basierter Test eingebetteter Software im Automobil. PhD thesis, TU-Berlin (2004)
17. Conrad, M., Sax, E.: Mixed signals. In: Testing Embedded Software, pp. 229–249 (2003)
18. Alur, R., Courcoubetis, C., Henzinger, T.A., Ho, P.-H.: Hybrid automata: An algorithmic approach to the specification and verification of hybrid systems. In: hybrid systems, pp. 209–229 (1992)
19. Lehmann, E.: Time Partition Testing Systematischer Test des kontinuierlichen Verhaltens von eingebetteten Systemen. PhD thesis, TU-Berlin, Berlin (2004)
20. Grossmann, J., Mueller, W.: A Formal Behavioral Semantics for TestML. In: Proc. of IEEE ISoLA 2006, Paphos Cyprus, pp. 453–460 (2006)
21. The MathWorks: Web pages of Simulink - Simulation and Model-Based Design (2006)

Towards Integrated Model-Driven Verification and Empirical Validation of Reusable Software Frameworks for Automotive Systems *

Venkita Subramonian and Christopher Gill

Department of Computer Science and Engineering
Washington University, St. Louis, MO, USA
{venkita,cdgill}@cse.wustl.edu

Abstract. Software for automotive systems is rapidly increasing in complexity and scale, and leveraging reusable software frameworks in the development of these systems offers significant potential to reduce engineering costs and cycle times. However, the development of practical models and verification and validation techniques for automotive software built with reusable frameworks remains an open research challenge. This paper makes three main contributions to the state of the art in software engineering for automotive systems. First, it summarizes ways in which reusable software frameworks are relevant to automotive software engineering. Second, it describes an approach to verification and validation of reusable software frameworks which we have developed for other application domains. Third, it presents an evaluation of our approach in the context of an illustrative verification and validation scenario.

1 Introduction

The increasing complexity and scale of software for automotive systems argues for increasing re-use of software in the development of those systems. Because interacting software functions are increasingly distributed across many embedded micro-controllers in automotive systems, leveraging reusable middleware in the development of these systems offers significant potential to reduce engineering costs and cycle times.

However, these benefits only can be realized if the reusable middleware can be specialized through configuration and customization to address constraints, optimizations, and trade-offs in timing and other quality of service (QoS) dimensions that are specific to the automotive software applications being developed. Furthermore, system developers must be able to verify designs involving middleware prior to investing in their implementation, and to validate those implementations prior to investing in their commercial deployment.

Model checking can play a valuable role in verifying automotive applications' increasingly heterogeneous constraints, e.g., for safety-critical functions like computer assisted steering and braking and for comfort functions such as in-vehicle navigation

---

* Research supported in part by NSF CAREER award CCF-0448562.

M. Broy, I.H. Krüger, and M. Meisinger (Eds.): ASWSD 2006, LNCS 4922, pp. 118–132, 2008.

and entertainment systems. As we discuss in Section 5, model checking also can generate verification traces to guide validation experiments, and the comparison of verification and validation traces can be valuable to assess and improve the fidelity of the models with respect to the actual behavior of the implemented software.

Our previous research has focused on specializing reusable middleware frameworks to address footprint and timing trade-offs in networked embedded systems [1], enforcing run-time timing [2] and liveness [3] constraints at run-time, and developing high-fidelity timed automata [4] models of canonical reusable software building blocks that are widely used in practice [5]. In this paper we describe our most recent research on the integrated verification and validation of systems built with reusable software frameworks. The results of that investigation (which we summarize in Section 5) demonstrate the need for careful co-design in both the models and the reusable software itself to ensure that (1) scientifically valid comparisons are made between the software and the models, (2) irrelevant differences between the software and the models are abstracted away to reduce the effort required for verification and validation, and (3) relevant differences between the software and the models are preserved and analyzed to reveal important mis-matches between the software, the models, and the application requirements, which at least must be documented and where possible corrected .

The rest of this paper is structured as follows. Section 2 summarizes other research related to our approach, and to its application in the automotive software application domain. Section 3 summarizes software platforms, frameworks, and design patterns that are relevant to automotive applications. Section 4 describes our solution approach, in which timed automata models of reusable middleware building blocks are used to verify properties of software built using them, and to generate traces used for integrated verification and validation. Section 5 presents an illustrative example drawn from our previous research in the avionics software domain, and shows how our approach can be used to verify and validate that example: our results show that (1) checking models of reusable middleware building blocks can verify timing properties of software that uses those building blocks, (2) verification and validation can be integrated through collection and comparison of detailed time and event traces, and (3) observed differences between the verification and validation traces can be used to refine models to reflect more accurately the actual software implementations they represent. Section 6 concludes the paper with a summary of observations and recommendations arising from this research, and describes remaining open research challenges and future work for verification and validation of automotive software built upon reusable software frameworks.

2   Related Work

DREAM [6,7,8] provides an open-source tool and methodology that allows distributed real-time embedded (DRE) system designers to do model-based schedulability analysis of time and event-driven DRE systems. DREAM offers a computational model called the DRE semantic domain [7]. The key elements in this computational model are tasks, timers, event channels and schedulers. Tasks are triggered either by a timer or by external aperiodic events, and tasks communicate among themselves by means of an event channel. Within this computational model, DREAM considers the problem of deciding the schedulability of a given set of tasks with time and event-driven interactions. By using timed automata models for each of the elements in the computational model, the schedulability problem is converted [8] into a reachability problem in the composed model through a model checking tool like UPPAAL. DREAM also provides a model transformation facility by which a model of the DRE system is expressed using a domain specific modeling language (*e.g.*ESML [9]), and is transformed using model transformation [6] tools to create timed automata models in the DRE semantic domain.

Even though our approach is similar to DREAM in that we use timed automata models to verify system properties, the problems that these two bodies of research address are different. Whereas DREAM addresses the problem of deciding schedulability of a set of tasks under the DRE semantic domain, our research addresses the problem of correct composition of reusable software elements that are at a finer level of granularity than the elements in the computational model offered by DREAM. Both these kinds of analysis are important - while the higher level computational model provided by DREAM helps the DRE systems designer to address the schedulability problem in time and event-driven systems, our approach helps the system designer choose configurations that are appropriate for the specific application. Moreover, the computational model in DREAM makes an assumption that all communication between tasks uses an event channel, and the communication between tasks and event channels themselves are abstracted away using synchronized transitions in UPPAAL. During actual implementation, these synchronized transitions are realized using reusable software which could have different configurations that impact the timing and liveness properties of a DRE system in different ways. Hence a more detailed model of the fundamental reusable software elements is necessary, which has been the focal point of our research.

Automotive Software Verification [10,11] uses a design pattern based approach to build reusable software that provides high-level communication services to higher layer automotive software tasks. A middleware architecture for communication is realized in the context of the OSEK/VDX operating system. The communication activities carried out by the middleware are mapped on to tasks in OSEK/VDX. [12] discusses code generation from a high level RT-UML [13] model for OSEK/VDX. That work identifies key issues in mapping of UML models where some annotations in RT-UML cannot be mapped directly to the constructs and primitives offered as part of OSEK/VDX.

AUTOSAR (AUTomotive Open System ARchitecture) [14] is an open standard for automotive software architecture that specifies standardized interfaces for communication among automotive electronic components. It aims to alleviate the complexity involved in developing and upgrading software based control systems in the automotive domain. The use of abstract concepts that are fundamental building blocks in a particular domain combined with adequate modeling techniques and models based on these fundamental building blocks can have a valuable and sustainable impact on automotive software engineering.

3   Automotive Software Engineering

Fine-grained reusable middleware frameworks like ACE [15] address the challenge of providing common domain-specific building blocks that can be used to build higher level software abstractions. For example, the ACE framework provides building blocks like Reactor, Acceptor, Connector and Active Objects, which have been used to build a wide range of reusable middleware frameworks and services for distributed real-time embedded systems - *e.g.*, for real-time scheduling (Kokyu [16]), distributed communication (TAO [17], nORB [18,19,20]), and component middleware (CIAO [21]). The presence of such foundational fine-grain abstractions is not limited to reusable software built on ACE. For example, in the sensor networks application domain, TinyOS [22] provides building blocks like Timer, ADC, RFM, Active Messages, *etc.* for building different kinds of sensor network middleware - *e.g.*, for reconfiguration, scheduling, group communication, and self-stabilization. We now discuss a similar low-level framework in the context of automotive software engineering.

Operating System Features. OSEK VDX [23] is a set of interface specifications for operating systems, communication, and network management in the automotive domain. The OSEK operating system is targeted to run on micro-controllers and is therefore designed to require a minimum of hardware resources (e.g., CPU and memory). These specifications enable automotive OEM and third-party ECU (electronic control unit) suppliers to use a standardized set of APIs to facilitate system integration, thus making automotive applications more portable, reusable and interoperable. A customized version of the OSEK OS can be generated by using the OSEK Implementation Language (OIL), through which one can specify a portable description of all OSEK-specific objects (*e.g.*, events, tasks, resources).

An OSEK compliant operating system implementation provides automotive application developers with a set of reusable primitive building blocks that include (1) tasks, (2) event objects, and (3) messages. Tasks are the equivalent of threads in general purpose operating systems. They are the basic schedulable entities in the OSEK/VDX and forms the basis for enforcing the various real-time requirements of automotive applications. Event objects are used to inform tasks of various events occurring in the system - *e.g.*, arrival of messages on a communication link, or expiration of a timer. Messages are used to communicate between software components residing within an ECU.

POSA2 Abstractions. A task in OSEK/VDX can wait on multiple events at a time using the *WaitEvent* function, which is a key feature of the Reactor pattern [24]. Reactor is an event handling design pattern used in network programming (*e.g.*, in ACE [15]) to demultiplex events from multiple sources, possibly using just a single thread. This design pattern is used in low level reusable middleware to demultiplex and dispatch incoming requests and replies from peers. Event handlers like request and reply handlers are registered with a reactor. The reactor uses a synchronous event demultiplexer, *e.g.*, the UNIX *select* system call, to wait for data to arrive from one or more peers. When data arrives, the synchronous event demultiplexer notifies the reactor, which then dispatches the appropriate event handler based on the event source.

The Active Object pattern, which separates method invocation from method execution, is also relevant. Since the thread of execution is separate from the thread of invocation, this pattern can be used to serialize access to resources used by multiple threads. This pattern can be used, as is discussed in [10,11], to separate the communication subsystem from the automotive application by using different tasks for each of these layers of the system.

4   Solution Approach

In previous research [25,5], we have developed timed automata [4] models of reusable software building blocks that have been used to implement a wide range of software frameworks and applications. These lower-level timed automata models of the reusable building blocks can be combined with higher-level formal models of the applications and frameworks that use them to provide a faithful model of a system *including the reusable software platform on which the system is deployed*, such that the composite models can be verified for correctness with high fidelity to the implemented system.

Our focus has been on creating timed automata models of reusable software objects provided by ACE [15]. ACE is a portable C++ framework used for developing high-performance concurrent and real-time software using threads, sockets, and other mechanisms provided by a wide range of OS platforms. By developing high fidelity formal models at a level of abstraction that is just above the operating system, our approach adds rigor to other model-based approaches currently being pursued by the systems research community, which target reusable software architectures at higher levels of abstraction. Our approach also provides sound and composable models of foundational reusable software building blocks to the formal methods community, offering new opportunities for innovation in formal methods that can directly impact the design, implementation, verification, and validation of real-world software systems.

In Section 4.1 we first present a simple example drawn from our previous research in the avionics software domain, which serves to illustrate and motivate our approach. In Section 4.2, we then give an overview of the ACE building blocks we have modeled, and discuss the suitability of several model checking tools for verification of timing and liveness properties in software built using those building blocks.

4.1   Illustrative Example

In this section, we illustrate how timed automata models can be used to analyze timing and liveness properties in software built upon reusable software building blocks. We first present a motivating example [26] - a simple distributed real-time embedded subsystem from the domain of avionics mission computing [27] - and describe how our modeling approach presented in Section 4.2 can be used to describe the reusable ACE software building blocks incorporated within that example. In Section 5 we then show how our approach can be used to analyze timing properties of this example subsystem *taking into account the semantics of the reusable software building blocks with which this system is implemented.*

Figure 1 shows the elements of our example avionics system: (1) a *Rate Generator*, which wraps a hardware timer and sends periodic events to event consumers that register for those events; (2) a *GPS Subsystem*, which wraps one or more hardware devices for navigation and caches a periodically refreshed location value to provide low-latency response; (3) a *Graphical Display*, which wraps the hardware for a heads-up display device in the cockpit to provide visual information to the pilot and a location value that is updated by querying an interface on the GPS component when the controlling software receives a triggering event.

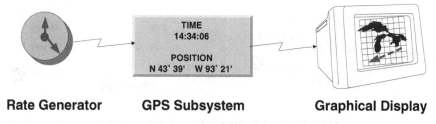

Rate Generator   **GPS Subsystem**   **Graphical Display**

Fig. 1. Example Avionics System

This example is representative of a broader class of distributed real-time embedded systems where clusters of closely-interacting components are connected via specialized networking devices, such as VME-bus backplanes. Although the functional characteristics of these systems may differ, they often share the rate-activated computation and display/output timing constraints illustrated here.

Both control flow (rate generator to GPS and GPS to display) and data flow (display to GPS) interactions occur in this subsystem. An event push style of communication is used by the rate generator (to send a timer-driven triggering event to the GPS), and by the GPS (to communicate the availability of data to the display). A data pull style of communication is then used by the display subsystem (to obtain location data from the GPS). In the middleware-based software framework from which this example was drawn, the push style of communication is typically implemented using a publish-subscribe event channel, and the pull style of communication is typically implemented using a remote function call.

Even though middleware-based software architectures currently are not prevalent in the automotive software engineering domain, the low-level software building blocks that are the focus of our work are directly relevant there, as we have discussed in greater detail in Section 3. Furthermore, as reducing development costs and cycle times becomes increasingly important, specialized reusable middleware solutions designed for stringent timing and footprint constraints [18,19,20] may be adapted further for the automotive software engineering domain. Therefore, the observations and lessons learned from our verification and validation studies of this example, which we present in Section 6, are relevant to automotive software engineering.

Figure 2 illustrates how reusable low-level building blocks like the reactors, event handlers, and thread pools provided by ACE, are incorporated into the example shown in Figure 1. Each communication channel in the example subsystem illustrated in Figure 1 has a corresponding event handler. For example, the Timer_EC_EH event handler handles requests sent from the rate generator to the Event Channel (EC), the GPS_EC_EH event handler handles requests sent from the GPS unit to the EC, etc.

To illustrate how timed automata models of reusable software can be used to analyze timing and liveness properties in practice, we now consider a simple but representative example scenario using the low-level models of reusable ACE building blocks described in Section 4.2 in order to (1) capture the semantics of the reactor and event handler models, (2) illustrate how interference with specified constraints on timing can arise in software built with those reusable software building blocks, and (3) show how the particular form of interference that may arise can be analyzed through model checking.

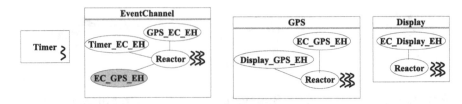

Fig. 2. Reusable Software in the Avionics Example

In many distributed real-time embedded systems, correct operation can depend on satisfying stringent but relatively simple timing constraints, such as receiving the result from a remote method invocation before a relative deadline. In this example, system timing is affected by interference between nominally independent call sequences, when they must contend for shared resources such as the CPU. We consider a scenario where a single thread is used by a reactor to demultiplex events to its registered event handlers. The extent to which the event handlers contend for shared resources impacts whether or not a deadline miss can occur. Using our models we then can determine (1) whether any deadline misses *can* occur due to interference between call sequences, and (2) if a deadline miss is possible, which sequences of actions can cause it to occur. For example if the rate generator and GPS push events at roughly the same time, then whichever event handler (Timer_EC_EH or GPS_EC_EH) is dispatched first could delay the other event handler, potentially resulting in a missed deadline.

4.2   Modeling in ACE

To be able to verify the correctness of customized reusable software in the context of each specific application, we have developed detailed and formal models of common reusable software building blocks found in the widely used ACE [15] framework, such as reactors, thread pools, event handlers, and interaction channels, which can be composed and checked rigorously to evaluate timing and liveness properties in each particular application and its supporting reusable software configuration. A crucial challenge is to determine the appropriate level of abstraction at which to model system software. To answer this question, one must look at the kinds of abstractions used in state-of-the art system implementations. For example, distribution middleware services such as CORBA [28] object request brokers (ORBs) provide a level of abstraction that promotes portability and reusability and hence makes an appealing candidate for formal modeling. Since many state-of-the-art distribution middleware implementations expose sets of configuration options used to tailor the reusable software for particular applications, modeling the combinations of configuration options [29] is a useful and necessary step toward model-driven construction and verification of distributed real-time embedded systems. We contend, however, that to evaluate issues such as timing and liveness, which are crucial to many distributed real-time embedded systems, finer-grained models of lower-level reusable software building blocks are needed to capture (and supplement analysis of) crucial details related to concurrency and interaction.

Results of our previous experience with system software construction indicate the efficacy of such a fine-grained approach. In that work we built a special-purpose ORB called *nORB* [18,19,20], with support for real time operation dispatching in the context of memory constrained networked embedded systems. We took a fine-grained bottom-up approach to the development of nORB, starting with lower level elements of the ACE [15] framework: Reactor, Acceptor, Connector, CDR Stream, *etc.* Along with taking a fine-grained approach to building nORB, we used the application itself as a guide for making fundamental design and implementation trade-offs. That work has given us insights into application-driven construction and customization of reusable software for this and other domains, allowing us to define composable models with a high degree of fidelity to how reusable software is built in practice.

Our modeling approach is designed specifically for analysis of timing and liveness in concurrent software with real-time constraints. We rely first on model checking to ensure soundness. Due to the potential size of the state spaces that need to be checked, we then apply several optimizations: (1) building highly modular models, by sub-dividing them into fine-grain composable automata; (2) encoding our models in formats used by model checkers that allow automata to be added to a model, or removed from it, dynamically; and (3) adopting a hybrid approach in which parts of the analysis are provided by other analysis techniques [30,3] thus reducing the state space that must be explored through model checking. Model checkers such as UPPAAL [31], IF [32], Bogor [33], and SPIN [34] each have their particular features and restrictions. For example, among these four tools, timed automata models are supported only by UPPAAL and IF, whereas only Bogor supports object-oriented and concurrent constructs explicitly. UPPAAL uses a rendezvous model of communication whereas in IF communication is asynchronous. Because our models must capture time, concurrency, and asynchronous interactions between system elements that can be added and removed dynamically, we selected IF as the most suitable model checking environment for our needs in that work.

Figure 3 shows our model architecture, which is implemented using the IF tool set [32,35,36]. We specify our fine-grained models as IF *processes* that run in parallel and interact through shared variables and asynchronous signals. The behavior of these processes is represented formally in IF as *timed automata with urgency* [37] and the semantics of a system modeled in IF is the Labeled Transition System (LTS) obtained by interleaving the executions of its processes.

Our models are divided into three layers: (1) models of network and OS level abstractions such as channels for interprocess communication; (2) models of semantically rich reusable software building blocks like reactors; and (3) models of the application functionality implemented in the form of event handlers. Although Figure 3 shows a static view of our models, the models themselves are executable in the IF environment and can be checked against system property specifications. The unshaded rectangular boxes shown in Figure 3 are modeled using timed finite state automata specified using the IF language. The shaded rectangular boxes shown in Figure 3 are data structures that are shared by the different automata in the models. Automata with timed transitions (transitions that are guarded with conditions based on clock variables) are indicated in Figure 3 by timer icons. [38] and [39] provide detailed explanation of these models.

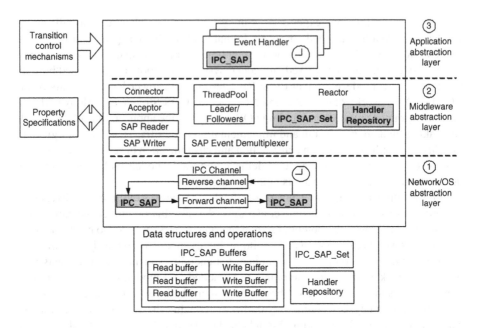

Fig. 3. Model Architecture

5   Integrated Verification and Validation

We now summarize the results of a verification and validation study we conducted to evaluate the fidelity of the reusable middleware models developed in our previous research [5] by instrumenting both the models and the software they represent, and comparing the execution traces produced by that instrumentation in both cases. To do this, we recorded events via instrumentation points in the kernel, middleware, and application layers using data streams [40]. We also added output to timed automata transitions corresponding to the middleware instrumentation points. We then collected traces from the execution of the models and of the software, and post-processed those traces to generate time-lines for comparison. We compared the two timelines in terms of (1) the sequence of events that occurred in each case, and (2) the time at which each event occurred. The models were realized and executed using IF 2.0 (with bug-fixes) on a 2.8GHz Pentium 4 with 2GB RAM running Enterprise Linux with a 2.6.9-22 kernel. All validation experiments were run on a 1.4GHz Pentium 3 with 1GB RAM and running Fedora 2 with a LibeRTOS [41] 2.6.12 kernel.

Figure 4 shows a short extract from the sequence of events generated by post-processing traces from model and actual executions of the example scenario described in Section 4.1. In that scenario, two clients each send a request to the same server and the server hosts two event handlers each processing the requests from one client. We logged the following events along with their time stamps - (1) a client sending a request, (2) the request arriving at the socket buffer on the server, (3) the upcall to the event handler, and (4) the receipt of reply from the event handler by the client. The sequence of events

```
0: BEFORE_CLIENT_SEND_REQUEST(2)        0 : BEFORE_CLIENT_SEND_REQUEST(2)
0: EVENT_SOCK_DEF_READABLE(4)           0 : EVENT_SOCK_DEF_READABLE(4)
0: BEFORE_CLIENT_SEND_REQUEST(1)        0 : BEFORE_CLIENT_SEND_REQUEST(1)
0: EVENT_SOCK_DEF_READABLE(2)           0 : EVENT_SOCK_DEF_READABLE(2)
0: HANDLE_INPUT_BEGIN(2)                0 : HANDLE_INPUT_BEGIN(2)
25: EVENT_SOCK_DEF_READABLE(1)          25 : EVENT_SOCK_DEF_READABLE(1)
25: AFTER_CLIENT_RECV_REPLY(1)          25 : AFTER_CLIENT_RECV_REPLY(1)
25: HANDLE_INPUT_BEGIN(4)               25 : HANDLE_INPUT_BEGIN(4)
50: EVENT_SOCK_DEF_READABLE(3)          51 : EVENT_SOCK_DEF_READABLE(3)
50: AFTER_CLIENT_RECV_REPLY(2)          51 : AFTER_CLIENT_RECV_REPLY(2)
50: BEFORE_CLIENT_SEND_REQUEST(2)       51 : BEFORE_CLIENT_SEND_REQUEST(2)
50: EVENT_SOCK_DEF_READABLE(4)          51 : EVENT_SOCK_DEF_READABLE(4)
50: BEFORE_CLIENT_SEND_REQUEST(1)       51 : BEFORE_CLIENT_SEND_REQUEST(1)
50: EVENT_SOCK_DEF_READABLE(2)          51 : EVENT_SOCK_DEF_READABLE(2)
50: HANDLE_INPUT_BEGIN(2)               51 : HANDLE_INPUT_BEGIN(2)
75: EVENT_SOCK_DEF_READABLE(1)          76 : EVENT_SOCK_DEF_READABLE(1)
75: AFTER_CLIENT_RECV_REPLY(1)          76 : AFTER_CLIENT_RECV_REPLY(1)
75: HANDLE_INPUT_BEGIN(4)               77 : HANDLE_INPUT_BEGIN(4)
100: EVENT_SOCK_DEF_READABLE(3)         102 : EVENT_SOCK_DEF_READABLE(3)
100: AFTER_CLIENT_RECV_REPLY(2)         102 : AFTER_CLIENT_RECV_REPLY(2)
```

Fig. 4. Comparison of timelines between model (left) and actual (right) executions

shows that that the model and actual executions are reasonably close both in terms of the order of events and the time at which they occur. However, one key difference between the model and actual execution traces is the execution time of event handler processing. During model execution, the progress of time is controlled by the model checker and unless it is specified explicitly (as we show later), there is no execution jitter. However, during actual software execution we recorded the execution jitter shown in Figure 5.

As part of our experiments, we ran 25 iterations of the above flow - *i.e.*, with the client sending a request and the event handler responding with a reply - in both model and actual execution. Based on the generated timeline traces, we then plotted the events generated against their timestamps for both model and actual executions to obtain the

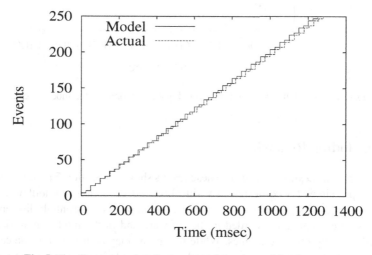

Fig. 5. Timeline comparison between model and actual implementation

graph shown in Figure 5. This figure shows visually how close the model is to the actual execution in terms of the times at which various events occur.

We also observed that the cumulative effect of jitter during actual execution becomes more pronounced as time progresses, which suggests that modeling the execution jitter as random noise would be a reasonable first approximation. To make the composed verification model reflect the actual system more closely, we added a jitter interval of 1ms to the event handler execution time in our model, which caused a significant increase in state space explored by the model checker. For exhaustive simulation, the model without jitter produced 2325 states, 2380 transitions, and took 1 second, whereas with jitter the model produced 217885 states, 225130 transitions, and took 181 seconds to explore exhaustively. The exhaustive simulation with jitter produced 288 traces of possible executions of the example scenario described in Section 4.1. To illustrate the range of variability added to the model by the jitter interval, we generated timelines for each of the 288 verification traces from the model with jitter, and then superimposed them in a new graph with the event numbers on the y-axis and timestamps on the x-axis. The result, shown in Figure 6, confirms that the model checker explores various combinations of execution jitter as it moves from state to state during exhaustive simulation.

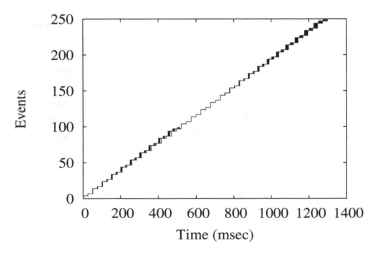

Fig. 6. Timeline with execution jitter for all paths explored by the model checker

6   Concluding Remarks

Observations and Lessons Learned. These results shown in Section 5 highlight several important principles for co-design of verification and validation in middleware models and software. First, the choice of instrumentation points is essential: discrepancies between where events are recorded in the software and in the models may skew the relationships between the timelines. While fixing this may be trivial in some cases, in other cases it may be necessary to expand a single model state into a more nuanced automaton to capture software semantics in more detail.

Second, observational equivalence must be evaluated subject to the constraints being checked. Relevant non-determinism in the software must be reflected in the model to ensure that the model is not over-constrained (and thus fails to check important cases) but irrelevant non-determinism should be eliminated from the model to reduce model checking complexity and to increase correspondence between the timeline representations for the model and software traces. Because the same model elements may be re-used for a variety of software configurations, doing this in practice can be aided greatly by (1) the ability to turn model and software instrumentation points on and off together, through a set of common configuration descriptors, (2) post-processing predicates for both time-lines that filter out irrelevant variations while detecting relevant ones, and (3) classifiers that annotate the timelines to indicate regions where event timing and ordering correspond between them, and regions where event timing or ordering differ.

Third, the ability to conduct scientifically valid evaluations of the correspondence between verification and validation results, especially in the face of concurrency [42], requires that (1) the sources of non-determinism in the model be the same as those in the software, (2) the equivalence classification of traces from the model be the same as the equivalence classification of traces from the software, (3) for every specific trace generated from the model, a trace in the same equivalence class must be generated by the software experiments, and vice versa, and (4) the likelihood of generating a particular trace from the model or the software should be appropriate even if the generation of every trace is impractical or intractable. The last two points highlight a very important relationship between (1) exerting more control (e.g., through scheduling [2]) over when events occur and in what order to (re)produce specific scenarios, and (2) allowing a wider variety of scenarios to be explored to avoid repeated verification or validation of essentially equivalent scenarios.

Open Problems and Future Work. Several open problems will shape our future work on model-based verification and validation of reusable software frameworks. First, the need for automated instrumentation of both models and software *with respect to particular constraints to be checked* motivates the development of automated analysis and aspect weaving techniques. Second, the need for round-trip co-design and engineering of models and software is demonstrated by our results in Section 5, which emphasizes the need to develop integrated tools for software design, implementation, verification, and validation, into which different sets of reusable software building blocks and fine grained formal models for those building blocks can both be incorporated. Third, the ability to configure schedulers and other means of controlling software execution at run-time must also be integrated within these software tools, in terms of both models and software implementations.

References

1. Subramonian, V., Xing, G., Gill, C., Lu, C., Cytron, R.: Middleware specialization for memory-constrained networked embedded systems. In: Proceedings of 10th IEEE Real-time and Embedded Technology and Applications Symposium (RTAS) (2004)
2. Aswathanarayana, T., Subramonian, V., Niehaus, D., Gill, C.: Design and performance of configurable endsystem scheduling mechanisms. In: Proceedings of 11th IEEE Real-time and Embedded Technology and Applications Symposium (RTAS) (2005)

3. Sanchez, C., Sipma, H.B., Manna, Z., Subramonian, V., Gill, C.: On Efficient Distributed Deadlock Avoidance for Real-time and Embedded Systems. In: 20th IEEE International Parallel and Distributed Processing Symposium (IPDPS 2006) (2006)
4. Alur, R., Dill, D.L.: A theory of timed automata. Theoretical Computer Science 126(2), 183–235 (1994)
5. Subramonian, V., Gill, C., Sanchez, C., Sipma, H.B.: Composable Models for Timing and Liveness Analysis in Distributed Real-time Embedded Systems Middleware. Technical Report WUCSE-2005-54, Computer Science and Engineering Department, Washington University in St.Louis (2005)
6. Madl, G., Abdelwahed, S., Schmidt, D.C.: Verifying distributed real-time properties of embedded systems via graph transformations and model checking. International Journal of Time-Critical Computing Systems (2005)
7. Madl, G., Abdelwahed, S.: Model-based analysis of distributed real-time embedded system composition. In: EMSOFT 2005: Proceedings of the 5th ACM international conference on Embedded software, pp. 371–374. ACM Press, New York (2005)
8. Madl, G., Abdelwahed, S., Karsai, G.: Automatic Verification of Component-Based Real-time CORBA Applications. In: The 25th IEEE Real-time Systems Symposium (RTSS 2004), Lisbon, Portugal (2004)
9. Karsai, G., Neema, S., Bakay, A., Ledeczi, A., Shi, F., Gokhale, A.: A Model-based Front-end to ACE/TAO: The Embedded System Modeling Language. In: Proceedings of the Second Annual TAO Workshop, Arlington, VA (2002)
10. Marques, R.S., Simonot-Lion, F.: Guidelines for the development of a communication middleware for automotive applications. In: Proceedings of the 3rd Workshop on Object-oriented Modeling of Embedded Real-Time Systems (OMER3 2005) (2005)
11. Marques, R.S., Simonot-Lion, F.: Design-Patterns based development of an automotive middleware. In: Proceedings of the 6th IFAC International Conference on Fieldbus Systems and their Applications (FeT 2005) (2005)
12. Gu, Z., Wang, S., Shin, K.G.: Issues in Mapping from UML Real-Time Profile to OSEK API. In: Proc. Workshop on Specification and Validation of UML models for Real-Time and Embedded Systems (SVERTS 2003) (2003)
13. Object Management Group: UML Profile for Schedulability. Final Draft OMG Document ptc/03-03-02 edn. (2003)
14. AUTomotive Open System ARchitecture: AUTOSAR (2005), www.autosar.org
15. Institute for Software Integrated Systems: The ADAPTIVE Communication Environment (ACE) (Vanderbilt University), www.dre.vanderbilt.edu/ACE/
16. Gill, C.D., Levine, D.L., Schmidt, D.C.: The Design and Performance of a Real-time CORBA Scheduling Service. Real-time Systems, The International Journal of Time-Critical Computing Systems, special issue on Real-time Middleware 20(2) (2001)
17. Institute for Software Integrated Systems: The ACE ORB (TAO) (Vanderbilt University), www.dre.vanderbilt.edu/TAO/
18. Group, D.: nORB - Special Purpose Middleware for Networked Embedded Systems (2005), deuce.doc.wustl.edu/nORB/
19. Subramonian, V., Xing, G., Gill, C., Lu, C., Cytron, R.: Middleware Specialization for Memory-Constrained Networked Embedded Systems. In: Proceedings of the 10th IEEE Real-time and Embedded Technology and Applications Symposium (RTAS), Toronto, Canada, IEEE, Los Alamitos (2004)
20. Subramonian, V., Gill, C.: Middleware Design and Implementation for Networked Embedded Systems. In: Zurawski, R. (ed.) Embedded Systems Handbook, CRC Press, Boca Raton (2006)
21. Institute for Software Integrated Systems: Component-Integrated ACE ORB (CIAO) (Vanderbilt University), www.dre.vanderbilt.edu/CIAO/

22. Hill, J., Szewczyk, R., Woo, A., Hollar, S., Culler, D., Pister, K.: System architecture directions for networked sensors. In: Proceedings of the ninth international conference on Architectural support for programming languages and operating systems, pp. 93–104. ACM Press, New York (2000)

23. OSEK Consortium: OSEK/VDX communication specification (2004), http://www.osek-vdx.org

24. Schmidt, D.C., Stal, M., Rohnert, H., Buschmann, F.: Pattern-Oriented Software Architecture: Patterns for Concurrent and Networked Objects, New York, vol. 2. Wiley & Sons, Chichester (2000)

25. Subramonian, V., Gill, C., Sanchez, C., Sipma, H.B.: Composable timed automata models for real-time embedded systems middleware. Technical Report WUCSE-2005-29, Computer Science and Engineering Department, Washington University in St.Louis (2005)

26. Wang, N., Gill, C., Schmidt, D.C., Subramonian, V.: Configuring Real-time Aspects in Component Middleware. In: OTM 2004. LNCS, vol. 3291, pp. 1520–1537. Springer-Verlag, Heidelberg (2004)

27. Sharp, D.C., Roll, W.C.: Model-Based Integration of Reusable Component-Based Avionics System. In: Proc. of the Workshop on Model-Driven Embedded Systems in RTAS (2003)

28. Object Management Group: The Common Object Request Broker: Architecture and Specification. 3.0.2 edn. (2002)

29. Balasubramanian, K., Balasubramanian, J., Parsons, J., Gokhale, A., Schmidt, D.C.: A Platform-Independent Component Modeling Language for Distributed Real-time and Embedded Systems. In: Proceedings of the 11th Real-time Technology and Application Symposium (RTAS 2005), San Francisco, CA, pp. 190–199. IEEE, Los Alamitos (2005)

30. Sanchez, C., Sipma, H.B., Subramonian, V., Gill, C., Manna, Z.: Thread Allocation Protocols for Distributed Real-Time and Embedded Systems. In: Wang, F. (ed.) FORTE 2005. LNCS, vol. 3731, pp. 159–173. Springer, Heidelberg (2005)

31. Behrmann, G., David, A., Larsen, K.G.: A Tutorial on Uppaal. In: Bernardo, M., Corradini, F. (eds.) SFM-RT 2004. LNCS, vol. 3185, pp. 200–236. Springer, Heidelberg (2004)

32. Bozga, M., Graf, S., Ober, I., Ober, I., Sifakis, J.: The IF Toolset. In: Bernardo, M., Corradini, F. (eds.) SFM-RT 2004. LNCS, vol. 3185, pp. 237–267. Springer, Heidelberg (2004)

33. Robby, Dwyer, M., Hatcliff, J.: Bogor: An Extensible and Highly-Modular Model Checking Framework. In: In the Proceedings of the Fourth Joint Meeting of the European Software Engineering Conference and ACM SIGSOFT Symposium on the Foundations of Software Engineering (ESEC/FSE 2003), Helsinki, Finland, ACM, New York (2003)

34. Holtzman, G.J.: The Model Checker SPIN. IEEE Transactions on Software Engineering 23(5), 279–295 (1997)

35. Bozga, M., Graf, S., Ober, I., Mounier, L.: IF-2.0: A Validation Environment for Component-Based Real-Time Systems. In: Brinksma, E., Larsen, K.G. (eds.) CAV 2002. LNCS, vol. 2404, Springer, Heidelberg (2002)

36. Bozga, M., Fernandez, J.C., Ghirvu, L., Graf, S., Krimm, J.P., Mounier, L.: IF: A Validation Environment for Timed Asynchronous Systems. In: Proceedings of CAV 2000 (2000)

37. Bornot, S., Sifakis, J., Tripakis, S.: Modeling Urgency in Timed Systems. In: de Roever, W.-P., Langmaack, H., Pnueli, A. (eds.) COMPOS 1997. LNCS, vol. 1536, pp. 103–129. Springer, Heidelberg (1998)

38. Subramonian, V.: Timed Automata Models for Principled Composition of Middleware. PhD thesis, Washington University in St. Louis, Computer Science and Engineering Department Technical Report WUCSE-2006-23 (2006)

39. Subramonian, V., Gill, C., Sánchez, C., Sipma, H.B.: Reusable models for timing and liveness analysis of middleware for distributed real-time and embedded systems. In: Sixth ACM/IEEE International Conference on Embedded Software (EMSOFT 2006), pp. 252–261 (2006)

40. Buchanan, B., Niehaus, D., Dhandapani, D., Menon, R., Sheth, S., Wijata, Y., House, S.: The data stream kernel interface. Technical Report ITTC-FY98-TR11510-04, Information and Telecommunication Technology Center, University of Kansas (1998)
41. Linutronix: LibeRTOS (2004), http://www.linutronix.de/linutronix/e/libertos.html
42. Niehaus, D., James, J., Gill, C.: Closing the Programmer's Universe: A Pattern Language for Reproducibility in Concurrent Programming Environments. In: Pattern Languages of Programs Conference, Allerton Park, IL (2003)

Modeling with the Timing Definition Language (TDL)

Wolfgang Pree and Josef Templ

C. Doppler Laboratory Embedded Software Systems
University of Salzburg, 5020 Salzburg, Austria
{pree,templ}@SoftwareResearch.net
preeTEC GmbH,
Nico-Dostal-Str. 6, 5020 Salzburg, Austria
www.preeTEC.com

Abstract. This paper describes the model-based development process of hard real-time software with the Timing Definition Language (TDL): modeling and simulation of TDL components in Matlab®/Simulink®, their mapping to a specific platform and finally the code generation.

1 TDL Components

Model-based development requires appropriate domain abstractions. They allow developers to ignore nasty details in the process of modeling automotive software systems. On the one hand, the challenge is to find abstractions that are high-level so that as many details as possible can be ignored. On the other hand, these abstractions must not be too disconnected from the underlying system so that efficient code can be generated out of the models.

In case of general purpose programming, imperative languages turned out to represent an appropriate level of abstraction from the von-Neumann computer architecture. In case of hard real-time systems, such abstractions have to consider the timing behavior as well as concurrency and have only been proposed recently. Synchronous languages such as Esterel [1] assume that infinitely fast computers exist that can immediately react to sensor input. Though composition of Esterel software is straightforward in theory, it encounters barriers in practice, in particular for distributed systems [2]. Giotto [3, 4, 5] and the Timing Definition Language (TDL) [6] share the same basic programming model which relies on the Logical Execution Time (LET) [5] abstraction. LET means that the observable temporal behavior of a task is independent from its physical execution. It is only assumed that physical task execution is fast enough to fit somewhere within the logical start and end points. The following figure shows the relationship between logical and physical task execution.

The inputs of a task are read at the release event and the newly calculated outputs are available at the terminate event. Between these, the outputs have the value of the previous execution. LET provides the cornerstone to deterministic behavior, platform abstraction as basis of portability and well-defined interaction semantics between parallel activities. It is always defined which value is in use at which time instant and there are no race conditions or priority inversions involved.

M. Broy, I.H. Krüger, and M. Meisinger (Eds.): ASWSD 2006, LNCS 4922, pp. 133–144, 2008.
© Springer-Verlag Berlin Heidelberg 2008

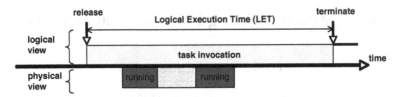

Fig. 1. Logical Execution Time (LET) abstraction

In addition to expressing LET semantics in a more convenient syntax than Giotto, and slightly simplifying the mode switching semantics, TDL has introduced the module (= component) as a top level language construct. This represents a significant step towards a component model for hard real-time systems. A TDL component provides a namespace for the definition of constants, types, sensors, actuators, tasks and modes. For the formal specification of the TDL constructs and their semantics we refer to the language report [6]. The TDL component construct serves multiple purposes:

1) it supports information hiding,
2) it acts as a static specification of components and dependencies,
3) it serves as the unit of distribution of functionality over a network of electronic control units.
4) it represents a partitioning of the set of actuators and control logic available in a system, and
5) it may serve as the unit of dynamic loading of system extensions

The TDL component construct is the precondition for another enhancement of LET-based languages. LET introduces a delay for observable outputs which poses a problem for controllers whose behavior would be better if outputs are provided as fast as possible without LET delays. With the TDL component construct it became possible to introduce globally asynchronous, locally synchronous (GALS) behavior. In this context 'globally' means between TDL components and 'locally' means within a TDL component. In order to avoid delays within a TDL component for the benefit of digital controller applications, a task's functionality code may be split in two parts: (a) a fast step and (b) a slow step, where the fast step is executed in logical zero time right at the release time of the task and the slow step is executed regularly. Output ports updated in the fast step are available immediately for a component's actuator updates or as inputs to other tasks within a TDL component.

Transparent Distribution. The TDL component in combination with the LET abstraction also forms the basis of what we call *transparent distribution*: Due to the LET semantics (1) the observable functional and temporal behavior of a system is the same no matter on which node of a distributed platform a TDL component is executed and (2) the developer does not have to care about the differences of local versus distributed execution of a TDL component. We refer to (1) and (2) as transparent distribution [7]. Transparent distribution facilitates, for example, what the automotive industry calls Electronic Control Unit (ECU) consolidation. The implementation of transparent distribution has required solutions of non-trivial communication scheduling problems as described in [10].

TDL is a textual language. We show the TDL code of a sample TDL component after Figure 8. In addition to the textual version we have developed a visual and inter-active TDL editor tool, called the TDL:VisualCreator, that offers exactly the same constructs as the textual version of TDL. The user of the TDL:VisualCreator tool can view the corresponding textual version of the TDL component at any time. The TDL:VisualCreator and other TDL tools are available as products from preeTEC.com and have been built on the basis of research results in the realm of the Giotto project [3] at the University of California, Berkeley and the MoDECS project [8] at the Uni-versity of Salzburg, Austria. The following section exemplifies TDL development with the TDL:VisualCreator tool. In section 3 we illustrate how TDL components are automatically mapped to a sample FlexRay platform, illustrating the benefits of trans-parent distribution. TDL with its component model and the transparent distribution of TDL components cut the overall development time of FlexRay software by a factor of 20 compared to tools that require a manual or slightly automated specification of communication schedules and that do not abstract from the platform.

2 Modeling Sample TDL Components

A case study for controlling an Active Rear Steering (ARS) system illustrates the advantages of the straight-forward modeling process with TDL. The ARS system is courtesy of MagnaSteyr Fahrzeugtechnik [9].

A TDL module (= component) corresponds to a control application that periodi-cally reads sensor values, calculates output values and writes these to actuators. Thus, a TDL module consists of a set of sensors, a set of actuators and a set of modes. Each mode consists of a set of periodic task invocations and other periodic activities such as actuator updates or mode switch checks. A module can be in one mode at a time.

In the ARS case study we use the TDL:VisualCreator tool that also allows TDL modeling within Matlab®/Simulink®. This has the advantage, that TDL components can be simulated. Note that the developer specifies the TDL modules and their timing behavior, that is the LET of the tasks, independent of a specific execution platform.

To edit a TDL module we drag the TDL module block from the Simulink® Library Browser (see Figure 2) and drop it on to a model.

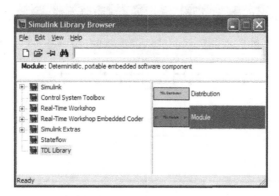

Fig. 2. TDL module as block in Matlab®/Simulink®

A double-click on the module block opens the TDL:VisualCreator where you can edit the various elements of a module (see Figure 3). The tree on the left hand lists the possible TDL constructs: the imported modules (see below) in folder Imports, the constants, types, sensors, actuators, the task declarations in folder Tasks, and the modes of the TDL module. Figure 3 shows that we have defined three sensors (delta_r_act, angular_rate, current) and one actuator (voltage) of the TDL module RearActuatorController. The developer edits the properties of a TDL construct by clicking on it. Figure 3 shows the properties of the selected sensor *current*. The corresponding properties and the corresponding values are displayed below the tree.

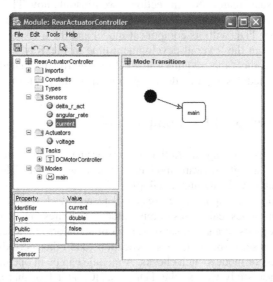

Fig. 3. Editing a TDL module in the TDL:VisualCreator

The TDL module RearActuatorController has only one task DCMotorController (see also Figure 3). In this simplified case study the mode main is the only mode of operation in this TDL module.

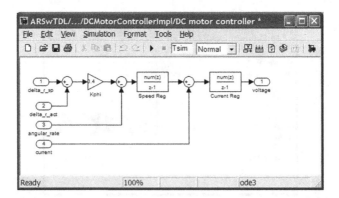

Fig. 4. Modeling a task's functionality with Matlab® /Simulink®

Let us now illustrate how we define the functionality of task DCMotorController and its timing behavior, that is, its LET. A double-click on the task opens a Simulink editor. The developer can use any of Matlab®/Simulink®'s discrete blocks to model the controller behavior. Figure 4 exemplifies this for the DCMotorController.

In the next step we define the timing behavior of the task DCMotorController in mode main and how it gets its inputs and to where it provides its output. For that purpose we click on mode main in the tree. Now we can define the period of mode main as one of its properties. In this example we set it to 1ms (see Figure 5). In the data flow editor, shown on the right-hand side of the window, we define the input and the output connections of task DCMotorController.

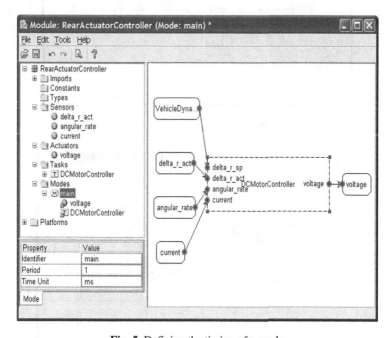

Fig. 5. Defining the timing of a mode

Finally, we define the LET of task DCMotorController within mode main. This is done by specifying the invocation frequency in relation to the mode period (see Figure 6). As the Frequency property is set to 1 it means that the LET of task DCMotor-Controller is 1ms (mode period) divided by 1 (frequency), thus 1 ms.

Figure 7 shows the overall Matlab®/Simulink® model of the ARS system, consisting of the two TDL modules RearActuatorController and VehicleDynamics and a subsystem Vehicle that represents the 'plant', that is, the relevant aspects of the vehicle that needs to be controlled. What we did not show was the definition of the import relationship between the two modules. Module RearActuatorController imports VehicleDynamics and uses the output port delat_r_sp of VehicleDynamics' public task dynamicsController. TDL module imports are discussed below.

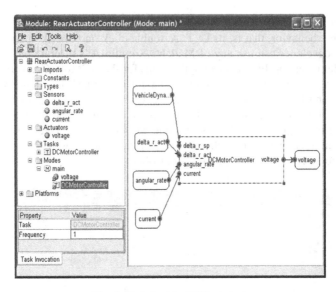

Fig. 6. Defining the LET of a task

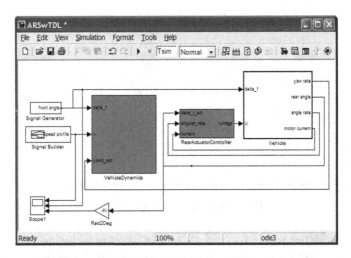

Fig. 7. ARS system model

The output of the Scope block (see Figure 8: speed, front angle, rear angle) illustrates the controller behavior: at low speeds steering operations cause the wheels on the rear axis to point in the opposite direction of the front wheels, whereas at higher speeds the wheels on the front axis and the rear axis point in the same direction.

The following listing shows the textual version of the TDL module RearActuator-Controller. As stated above this module imports the other TDL module VehicleDynamics. The sensor, actuator, task and mode declarations correspond exactly to the

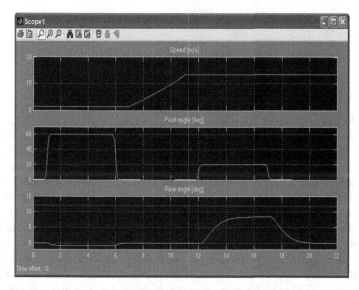

Fig. 8. ARS scenario

definition in the TDL:VisualCreator described above. The *uses* keyword marks an external function that implements platform-specific behavior. For example, the sensor delta_r_act is read by means of the external function getDelta_r_act. The implementation of sensor reading and actuator writing depends on the hardware and is thus separated from the platform-independent TDL code.

```
module RearActuatorController {

    import VehicleDynamics;

    public sensor double delta_r_act uses getDelta_r_act;
    sensor double angular_rate uses getAngular_rate;
    sensor double current uses getCurrent;

    actuator double voltage uses setVoltage;

    public task DCMotorController {  // task declaration
        input
            double delta_r_sp;
            double delta_r_act;
            double angular_rate;
            double current;
        output
            double voltage;
        uses DCMotorControllerImpl(delta_r_sp,delta_r_act,
                                    angular_rate,current,voltage);
    }

    start mode main [period=1 ms] {
        task
        [freq=1] DCMotorController { // task invocation with LET = 1 ms
            delta_r_sp := VehicleDynamics.dynamicsController.delta_r_sp;
            delta_r_act := delta_r_act;
```

```
        angular_rate := angular_rate;current := current;
        }
    actuator
      [freq=1] voltage := DCMotorController.voltage;
  }

}
```

Module Import. In order to allow the decomposition of large applications into smaller parts and to allow expressing dependencies between modules statically, the module concept provides an import mechanism, which allows a client module to specify that it depends on a service module and to access public elements of the imported module. In the ARS case study module RearActuatorController imports VehicleDynamics. Thus module RearActuatorController can use any of the exported items, that is, those that have the property Public set to true.

While it is obvious that using imported constants, types and sensors does not pose any semantic difficulties, it is not a priori clear how to treat constructs such as tasks and actuators. Multiple applications may read the same sensors, for example, but what happens if multiple applications write to the same actuators? Note that any of the parallel running TDL modules may be in one of several modes and it is not statically defined which actuators are under control of which application at which time. Therefore it must be prevented that multiple modules write to the same actuator. The module construct comes in handy to solve this problem. We simply restrict actuator updates to the module the actuator is declared in. Thus, the module construct also acts as a partitioning of the set of actuators. In a large application, sensors could be declared in a common service module, from where they can be used in any client module. A client module declares a subset of the actuators of the complete system and provides the functionality and timing to set their values.

Tasks form the units of computation. They are invoked periodically with a specified frequency. They deliver results through task output ports to actuators or to other tasks, and they read input values from sensor ports or from output ports of other tasks. A task whose visibility property Public is set to true exports all of its output ports. Thus, client modules can access the results delivered through a task's output ports, but it is not possible to invoke tasks from client modules.

Separation of Concerns. A TDL module expresses only the timing behavior with LET semantics: when tasks read inputs and when they provide outputs, when mode switch conditions are checked and when actuators are updated. The functionality is separated and specified as functions external to TDL: that is, how sensors are read, how actuators are updated, how tasks process their inputs. These external functions can be implemented in any programming language. In case of using TDL within Matlab®/Simulink® as illustrated in the realm of the TDL modeling by means of the TDL:VisualCreator above, the task functionality can be specified with Simulink® blocks (see Figure 5). For these Simulink® subsystems the developer generates C code with one of the available code generation tools so that the system can be mapped to a specific execution platform. Currently, TDL supports language bindings for ANSI C and Java.

We view this separation of timing and functionality as a precondition of an appropriate component model, in particular in the automotive industry. It allows the protection of intellectual property rights of the supplier companies. The supplier companies still can implement the specific control laws and provide that functionality as object code. On the other hand, the Original Equipment Manufacturers (OEMs) can integrate the components from various different suppliers based on the TDL component model—they do not have to know about the implementation of the functionality. We will exemplify one aspect of the integration process, the TDL module-to-node mapping, in more detail in the next section.

3 Sample TDL Component Deployment on a FlexRay Cluster

The TDL component model offers another separation of concerns that we have called transparent distribution: the behavior of a component is independent of the execution platform. With TDL the platform can also be considered *after* a component has been developed. This is in stark contrast to the current development practice which produces software that is strongly intertwined with the platform it was developed for. The good news for the developer is that the mapping to a specific platform, no matter whether it is distributed or not, becomes a straight-forward assignment of TDL modules to nodes (ECUs). preeTEC's automatic schedule and code generators and the TDL run-time system guarantee that the executable code exhibits exactly the same timing behavior as in the simulation, provided that the target platform offers sufficient computing resources. If not, no code is generated and the developer gets hints why this was not possible.

In order to map a set of TDL modules to a specific platform, the user puts a Distribution block from the Simulink® Library Browser to the particular model by dragging it from the library and dropping it onto the model (see Figure 9). In our

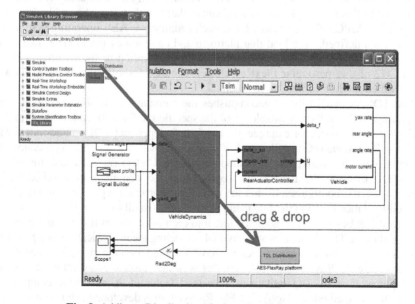

Fig. 9. Adding a Distribution block to the ARS system model

example, we name the block *AES-FlexRay platform* as we want to map the two TDL modules to a FlexRay cluster [11] with the socalled AES operating system [12]. Note that any number of platform mappings could be defined for a model, simply by putting further Distribution blocks to a model with TDL modules.

A double-click on the TDL Distribution block opens the TDL:VisualDistributor tool (see Figure 10). It already contains the TDL modules RearActuatorController and VehicleDynamics defined in the ARS model where the Distribution block was inserted.

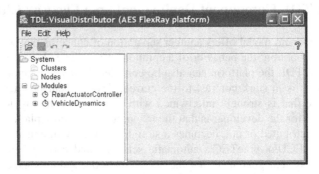

Fig. 10. TDL:VisualDistributor tool with the TDL modules defined in the Simulink® model

In order to assign the TDL modules to the nodes of a platform we now have to define the platform. The TDL:VisualDistributor offers the editing features to define the topology and properties of potentially distributed platforms that are common in the automotive domain. For a demo video that illustrates how to define a FlexRay platform we refer to the Web [13]. The TDL:VisualDistributor can also save and load platforms. In this case study we assume that a platform that describes a FlexRay cluster with two MPC5554 nodes as ECUs, each running the AES operating system, has already been defined. We load that platform and can then assign the two TDL modules by means of a straight-forward drag & drop operation to the two nodes ECU1 and ECU2 of that particular FlexRay cluster. Figure 11 shows the resulting view of the specified module-to-node assignment.

The TDL:VisualDistributor accomplishes the automatic generation of all files that are required to build the executable(s) for the specific platform. In case of the FlexRay-AES platform we need, for example, the platform-independent TDL source code for the modules RearActuatorController and VehicleDynamics, the C code (generated, for example, with the Real-Time-Workshop Embedded Coder) for each task function of each TDL module, the FIBEX file representing the communication schedule, the FlexRay-specific configurations and the makefiles. For that purpose we simply choose the Build All menu item in the File menu of the TDL:VisualDistributor tool.

After compiling the code and uploading it to each of the nodes the system behaves as simulated in the TDL:VisualCreator. As TDL modeling means basically setting the LET periods of tasks, and as the user does not have to define a communication schedule and the numerous FlexRay details, TDL together with the automatic generators reduces the development time by a quantitatively measured factor of 20 and more compared to state-of-the-art methods and tools, if a FlexRay-system is developed from scratch.

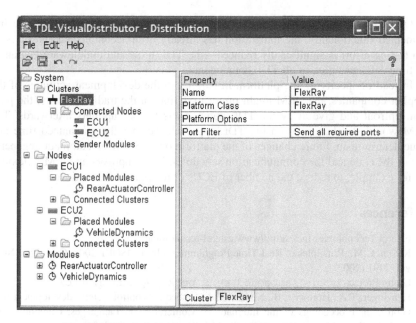

Fig. 11. TDL module-to-node assignment for a FlexRay cluster

4 Opportunities for the Automotive Industry Resulting from a TDL-Based Development Process

Besides significant development and maintenance cost savings, for example, for FlexRay software, a TDL-based development process could provide the desired flexibility for automakers to change the execution platform when required and at the same time redefine the OEM-supplier relationship.

Remember that the TDL components can be modeled and simulated without knowing on which platform they will be executed. One key benefit of the TDL-based development process is that an Original Equipment Manufacturer (OEM) would not have to worry from the beginning on which node of a distributed platform a TDL component will be executed.

Let us assume a sample scenario of how the automotive industry could harness the TDL technology: An OEM and a supplier agree about the coarse-grained system structure by means of TDL components. Each TDL component corresponds to a system function, such as automatically maintaining the distance to other vehicles. The OEM and its suppliers only have to refine each system so far as required by TDL, that is, the definition of the timing. The suppliers then implement the functionality of the TDL components, that is, typically the control laws, and error handling as well as accomplish the component validation and testing.

Parallel to this activity the OEM selects the computing and communication platform. For example, the OEM wants to reduce the number of ECUs (Electronic Control Units) and use more powerful computing nodes instead. The OEM can finetune the platform configuration with a tool such as the TDL:VisualDistributor.

Once the supplier companies return the TDL components together with the implemented functionality, the integration has already been accomplished and the system testing effort is significantly reduced—the TDL tools and middleware guarantee the time-safe execution of all TDL components.

Instead of specifying the platform in parallel to the development activities of the supplier companies, the OEM might prefer to define, in the traditional way, the platform upfront and give away the TDL components to the suppliers afterwards. The OEM would still benefit from the TDL approach: besides the guaranteed time and value determinism, future changes of the platform only require an automatic regeneration of the code and the communication schedules. This improves an OEM's flexibility, for example, to reduce the number of ECUs or to upgrade the hardware.

References

1. Esterel Technologies Inc., http://www.esterel-technologies.com
2. Kirsch, C.M.: Principles of Real-Time Programming. In: EMSOFT 2002. Grenoble LNCS, vol. 2491 (2002)
3. Giotto Project, http://embedded.eecs.berkeley.edu/giotto/
4. Henzinger, T.A., Horowitz, B., Kirsch, C.M.: Embedded control systems development with Giotto. In: Proceedings of the International Conference on Languages, Compilers, and Tools for Embedded Systems (LCTES), ACM Press, New York (2001)
5. Henzinger, T.A., Kirsch, C.M., Sanvido, M.A.A., Pree, W.: From control models to real-time code using Giotto. IEEE Control Systems Magazine 23(1), 50–64 (2003)
6. Templ, J.: Timing Dfinition Language (TDL) 1.2 Specification. Technical Report, on the Web -> Technology -> Further Documents (2007), at http://www.preeTEC.com/
7. Farcas, E., Farcas, C., Pree, W., Templ, J.: Transparent Distribution of Real-Time Components Based on Logical Execution Time. In: Proc. of ACM SIGPLAN/SIGBED Conference on Languages, Compilers, and Tools for Embedded Systems (LCTES), pp. 31–39. ACM Press, New York (2005)
8. MoDECS (Model-Based Development of distributed, Embedded Control Systems) Project, http://www.MoDECS.cc/
9. MagnaSteyr Fahrzeugtechnik, a global brand-independent engineering and manufacturing partner of automakers, http://www.MagnaSteyr.com/
10. Farcas, E., Pree, W., Templ, J.: Bus Scheduling for TDL Components, Dagstuhl conference on Architecting Systems with Trustworthy Components. LNCS, Springer, Heidelberg (2006)
11. FlexRay Web site, http://www.FlexRay.com/
12. DeComSys/Elektrobit Web site, http://www.decomsys.com/
13. preeTEC Web site, http://www.preeTEC.com/

Towards Model-Driven Development of Hard Real-Time Systems

Integrating ASCET and aiT/StackAnalyzer

Christian Ferdinand[1], Reinhold Heckmann[1], Hans-Jörg Wolff[2],
Christian Renz[2], Oleg Parshin[3], and Reinhard Wilhelm[3]

[1] AbsInt Angewandte Informatik GmbH
Science Park 1, D-66123 Saarbrücken, Germany
info@absint.com
http://www.absint.com

[2] ETAS GmbH, Borsigstraße 14, D-70469 Stuttgart, Germany
Christian.Renz@etas.de
http://www.etasgroup.com

[3] Universität des Saarlandes, Postfach 15 11 50, D-66041 Saarbrücken, Germany
wilhelm@cs.uni-sb.de
http://rw4.cs.uni-sb.de

Abstract. Software developers in the automotive sector must achieve high quality objectives. Many design and implementation errors are avoided by synthesizing code from model-based software specifications using automatic code generators such as ETAS' **ASCET**. To verify non-functional properties of the implementation, model-based design processes should be complemented with static program analysis tools like **AbsInt's StackAnalyzer** and timing analyzer **aiT**. AS-CET, **StackAnalyzer** and **aiT** can be integrated in a way that the **aiT/StackAnalyzer** analysis results for code generated by **ASCET** are conveniently accessible from within the **ASCET** development environment. This gives **ASCET** users a direct feedback on the effects of their design decisions on resource usage, allowing them to select more efficient designs and implementation methods. In the paper, we present the tools, the experimental integration, preliminary results and plans for further tool integration.

1 Introduction

Software developers in the automotive sector face some specific challenges: Many software systems are safety-critical and, thus, must achieve high quality objectives. On the other hand, competitive markets require software and hardware that can be mass-produced using a minimum of resources. Additionally, today's cars feature complete networks of Electronic Control Units (ECUs), which require highly collaborative software development. Therefore, even from the start, safety and budget considerations influence the design and specification of automotive software systems.

M. Broy, I.H. Krüger, and M. Meisinger (Eds.): ASWSD 2006, LNCS 4922, pp. 145–160, 2008.

Often these challenges induce conflicting goals concerning reduction of component costs, of development costs, and of development complexity. One example would be reduction of component costs by using cheaper ECUs without floating point units, where all calculations need to be performed using integers. However, due to the additional scaling and converting needed due to the representation of floating point numbers by integers, this can become an additional source of defects during the actual implementation of the system, leading to an increase in development costs and complexity.

There are different approaches to deal with the development problems in the automotive context. Standards like MISRA-C [1] attempt to minimize the amount of errors introduced by manual coding. Following such guidelines, however, may increase the time needed for coding and incur a cost in higher resource usage.

Model-based design tries to satisfy the high safety requirements in combination with good development productivity by starting with a software specification. The implementation process is not necessarily automatic. It is therefore still possible to introduce software defects through misinterpretation of design and specification documents or through human error during the manual coding process. Automatic code generators such as the one provided by **ASCET** are increasingly used to generate the implementation from the specification. By creating C code directly from the model-based specification, these code generators avoid the typical translation problems that occur in the implementation stage.

Many design and implementation errors are avoided by synthesizing code from specifications. However, non-functional properties such as absence of memory overflow and timer overruns are still an issue. To verify such properties of the implementation, unit tests and runtime measurements are currently used in the industry. Assuming sufficient test coverage of the system, some information about the typical runtimes of the software processes can be obtained. However, to acquire a higher level of confidence and to aid the development process, it is necessary to gather reliable and precise information about the code. Recent advances in the area of static program analysis based on abstract interpretation led to the development of tools to automatically detect upper bounds on resource usage like worst-case execution times (WCET) and worst-case stack usage, and of tools to prove the absence of runtime errors like null pointer dereferencing and out-of-bounds array accesses.

When using automatic code generation, tools checking for runtime errors are of minor importance – the code generator is expected to produce correct code given its knowledge about the model. Tools to determine safe and precise bounds on resource usage, however, can be very helpful for the users of modeling and automatic code generation tools. Tools of this kind include **AbsInt's Stack-Analyzer** and timing analyzer **aiT**. Other timing tools, including academic prototypes, are described and discussed in [2].

In the context of safety-critical hard real-time applications, the standard use of tools like **aiT** and **StackAnalyzer** is to demonstrate and prove that pieces of code are guaranteed to always execute within limited time intervals and resource bounds.

In our work, we propose to complement model-based design processes with static program analysis tools. This guarantees the satisfaction of safety requirements, and it helps to speed up the project by aiding in the establishment of general guidelines, the configuration of the build environment used as well as the coordination of distributed development and the development itself. We argue that to develop hard real-time systems, model-driven development coupled with detailed analysis of the implemented software is much better suited than traditional development methods that rely on programming C code.

The users of **ASCET** usually work on a much more abstract level than the producers of manual code. **ASCET**, **StackAnalyzer** and **aiT** can be integrated in a way that the **aiT/StackAnalyzer** analysis results for code generated by **ASCET** are conveniently accessible from within the **ASCET** development environment. This gives **ASCET** users a direct feedback on the effects of their design decisions on the resource usage, allowing them to select more efficient designs and implementation methods.

In the following, we present the tools, the experimental integration, preliminary results and plans for further tool integration.

2   Model-Based Design and Automatic Code Generation

In the automotive industry, model-based design has rapidly become a standard technology for system development. Complex automotive functions are usually based on abstract function models that make use of domain-specific knowledge. In this context, model-based CASE tools can offer significant development benefits as they allow for an easier transfer of domain-specific knowledge into a software engineering context. A comprehensive study of different model-based CASE tools can be found in [3].

2.1   Model-Based Development for Real-Time Applications

Software development using C offers many degrees of freedom that make it more difficult to verify the fulfillment of safety and real-time requirements. It is therefore necessary to provide a more abstract and more clearly defined specification of the system to be developed.

To solve this problem, ETAS' **ASCET** offers graphical specification editors to model control and data flow and state machines for state-based algorithms, as well as textual specification using **ESDL**, a programming language with a syntax based on Java that operates on the model level. Working with these specifications allows the developers to abstract away from the concrete variables on the target and deal with (physical) model variables instead, each with a well-defined representation in terms of concrete variables. These specifications can then be used to generate C code both for rapid-prototyping as well as ECU targets. The code generator will take care of the translation of model variables to program variables (according to the chosen representation of model variables) and of implementing operations on the model variables in a way that is consistent with their concrete representation, thereby eliminating a lot of possible oversights on the side of the developer. The code generators intended for producing C code used in series production were the first world-wide to be certified according to IEC 61508, the international standard for "functional safety of electrical/electronic/programmable electronic safety-related systems".

The improvements offered by this approach are demonstrated in [4]. To verify the correctness of their active steering model, BMW developed a formal verification tool that operates on components developed using **ASCET**.

To reduce the effort needed for verification, **ASCET** strongly supports modular development through so-called classes, encapsulated modules closely related to object-oriented programming concepts (while avoiding dynamic memory allocation and inheritance). Components can be reused by using multiple data sets and implementations depending on the project context. **ASCET** offers strong separation of algorithm, data and implementation details (memory classes, types, etc.), thus facilitating the software engineering process and the verification and testing process.

These improvements are especially useful in the context of fixed-point integer calculations on low-cost platforms, where manual coding typically introduces many bugs that can be avoided using code generation. To verify the model during different stages of development, **ASCET** offers several code generators to aid the developer in a step-by-step transition from model to production code. This allows verification of the code against the model on the PC using PC simulation of the generated code, and on real time-capable rapid-prototyping hardware similar to the target platform, but with additional resources. Finally the code can also be run on the target platform, either as a complete model or (using bypassing) as newly developed functions integrated into already released versions of the software.

2.2 Model-Based Development in the Context of Large Applications

To be usable for large-scale automotive applications, model-based tools need to integrate themselves tightly into existing toolchains. Amongst different tools, ANSI C code has established itself as a quasi standard for embedded development. Since **ASCET** allows for the integration both of models developed using Matlab/Simulink as well as legacy C code, we focused our analysis on compiled binaries as well as annotated C code.

3 Code Performance in Real-Time Systems

3.1 Stack Usage

Stack overflow is a possible cause of catastrophic failure that usually leads to run-time errors that are difficult to diagnose. The problems stem from the fact that the user needs to specify the amount of memory that should be reserved for the stack. Underestimating the maximum stack usage leads to stack overflow and thus system failure, overestimating means wasting valuable memory resources.

One approach to solve this problem is to measure the maximum stack usage using a debugger. However, even when running the program several times using a test suite, it is not guaranteed that the maximum stack usage is ever observed.

AbsInt's **StackAnalyzer** is able to provide a general worst-case estimate. By performing a value analysis on the stack pointer, the tool can figure out how the stack increases and decreases along all possible control-flow paths. This information can be used to derive the maximum stack usage of a task.

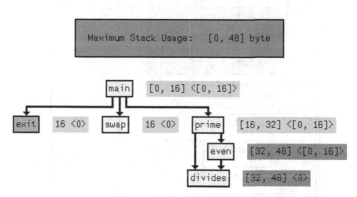

Fig. 1. Call graph with stack analysis results

The results of **StackAnalyzer** are presented as annotations in a combined call graph and control-flow graph. Figure 1 shows the call graph of a small application, with stack analysis results at routines and for the entire application (at the top). On this level, the results of stack analysis are displayed in boxes located to the right of the boxes representing the routines of the application. Each result box carries two results: a *global result*, coming first, and a *local result*, following in angular brackets. Each result is an interval of possible stack levels.

The local result at a routine R indicates the stack usage in R considered on its own: It is an interval showing the possible range of stack levels within the routine, assuming value 0 at routine entry. The local result for a routine is derived from the results at individual instructions, which are shown in Figure 2 for one of the routines of this example.

The global result for routine R indicates the stack usage of R in the context of the entire application. It is an interval providing bounds for the stack level while the processor is executing instructions of R, for all call paths from the entry point to R. Thus, the global result at routine R does not include the stack usage of the routines called by R.

The predicted worst-case stack usages of individual tasks in a system can be used in an automated overall stack usage analysis for all tasks running on an Electronic Control Unit, as described in [5] for systems managed by an OSEK/VDX real-time operating system.

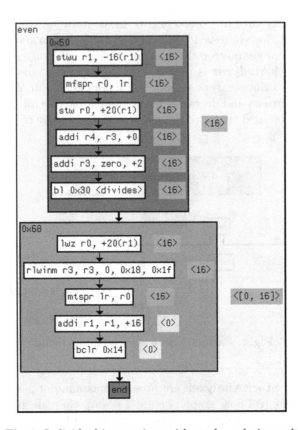

Fig. 2. Individual instructions with stack analysis results

3.2 Worst-Case Execution Time

Many tasks in safety-critical embedded systems have hard real-time character-istics. Failure to meet deadlines may be as harmful as producing wrong output or failure to work at all. Yet the determination of the worst-case execution time (WCET) of a task is a difficult problem because of the characteristics of modern software and hardware [6]. Underestimating the execution time leads to systems that are prone to errors because of timing failures, whereas overestimating might lead to the wrong conclusion that the system designed will not be able to run on the selected hardware or that so much capacity is already used that no new functionality can be added.

Embedded control software (e.g., in the automotive industries) tends to be large and complex. The software in a single electronic control unit typically has to provide different kinds of functionality. It is usually developed by several people, several groups or even several different providers. It is typically combined with third-party software such as real-time operating systems and/or communication libraries.

Caches and branch target buffers are used in virtually all performance-oriented processors to reduce the number of accesses to slow memory. Pipelines enable acceleration by overlapping the executions of different instructions. Consequently the timing of the instructions depends on the execution history.

The widely used classical methods of predicting execution times are not generally applicable. Software monitoring and dual-loop benchmark modify the code, which in turn changes the cache behavior. Hardware simulation, emulation, or direct measurement with logic analyzers can only determine the execution time for some fixed inputs. They cannot be used to infer the execution times for all possible inputs in general.

In contrast to that, abstract interpretation can be used to efficiently compute a safe approximation for all possible cache and pipeline states that can occur at a program point in any program run with any input. These results can be combined with ILP (Integer Linear Programming) techniques to predict a safe upper bound of the worst-case execution time (WCET bound) and a corresponding worst-case execution path.

AbsInt's WCET tool **aiT** determines the WCET of a program task in several phases [7] (see Figure 3).

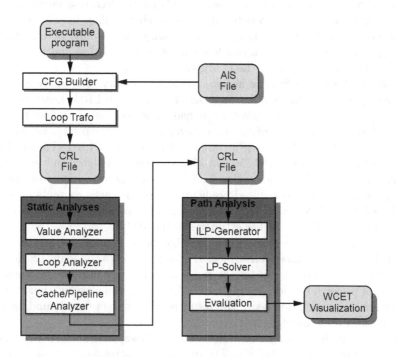

Fig. 3. Phases of WCET computation

The starting point of **AbsInt**'s analysis framework is a binary program and additional information about numbers of loop iterations, upper bounds for recursion, etc. This information may appear in a separate parameter file called

AIS file, or as special comments in the C source that can be generated by **ASCET**.

In the first step a *decoder* reads the executable and reconstructs the control flow [8]. This requires some knowledge about the underlying hardware, e.g., which instructions represent branches or calls. The reconstructed control flow is annotated with the information needed by subsequent analyses and then translated into CRL (Control-Flow Representation Language) – a human-readable intermediate format designed to simplify analysis and optimization at the executable/assembly level. This annotated control-flow graph serves as the input for micro-architecture analysis.

Then, *value analysis* tries to determine the values in the processor registers for every program point and execution context. Its results are used in loop bound analysis and in cache analysis (possible addresses of indirect memory accesses). Value analysis can also determine that certain conditions always evaluate to true or always evaluate to false. As consequence, certain paths controlled by such conditions are never executed. Therefore, their execution time does not contribute to the overall WCET of the program, and need not be determined in the first place.

WCET analysis requires that upper bounds for the iteration numbers of all loops be known. **aiT** tries to determine the number of loop iterations by *loop bound analysis*, but succeeds in doing so for simple loops only. Bounds for the iteration numbers of the remaining loops must be provided as specifications in the AIS file or annotations in the C source.

Cache analysis classifies the accesses to main memory. The analysis in **aiT** is based upon [9], which handles analysis of caches with LRU (Least Recently Used) replacement strategy. However, it had to be modified to reflect the non-LRU replacement strategies of common microprocessors: the pseudo-round-robin replacement policy of the ColdFire MCF 5307, and the PLRU (Pseudo-LRU) strategy of the PowerPC MPC 750 and 755. The modified algorithms distinguish between sure cache hits and unclassified accesses. The deviation from perfect LRU is the reason for the reduced predictability of the cache contents in case of ColdFire 5307 and PowerPC 750/755 compared to processors with perfect LRU caches [10,11], leading to higher estimates of the WCET.

Pipeline analysis models the pipeline behavior to determine execution time bounds for sequential flows (basic blocks) of instructions as done in [12]. It takes into account the current pipeline state(s), in particular resource occupancies, contents of prefetch queues, grouping of instructions, and classification of memory references by cache analysis. The result is an execution time bound for each basic block in each distinguished execution context.

Using the results of the micro-architecture analyses, *path analysis* determines a safe upper bound of the WCET. The program's control flow is modeled by an integer linear program [13,14] so that the solution to the objective function is the predicted worst-case execution time bound for the input program. A special mapping of variable names to basic blocks in the integer linear program enables execution and traversal counts for every basic block and edge to be computed.

aiT's results are written into a report file from which they may be extracted by the **ASCET** system. In addition, **aiT** produces a graphical description that can be visualized by the **aiSee** tool [15] to view detailed information delivered by the analysis.

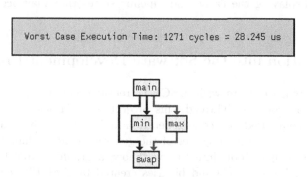

Fig. 4. Call graph with WCET bounds

Figure 4 shows the graphical representation of the call graph for a small example. The calls (edges) that contribute to the worst-case runtime are marked by the color red. The computed WCET bound is given in CPU cycles and in microseconds provided that the cycle time of the processor has been specified.

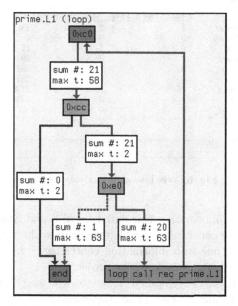

Fig. 5. Basic block graph in a loop, with timing information

Figure 5 shows the basic block graph of a loop. The number sum # describes the number of traversals of an edge in the worst case, while max t describes the execution time bound determined by **aiT** for the basic block from which the edge originates (taking into account that the basic block is left via the edge). The worst-case path, the traversal numbers and timings are determined automatically by **aiT**. Upon special command, **aiT** provides information on the origin of these timings by displaying the cache and pipeline states that may occur within a basic block.

4 Integration into the Software Development Process

When developing software with **ASCET**, reusable components are typically combined into a project. Through this project, the various operating system tasks can be configured and code generation and build can be started. Therefore, the project is the main center of the generate/compile/link-workflow. To integrate the analysis tools into this workflow, a graphical tool has been developed that takes the code and binaries created by **ASCET**, calls **aiT** and **StackAnalyzer** and displays the results in a window of its own (see Figure 6). This tool can be called directly from the project window. It fetches the information needed about the project via **ASCET**'s extensible tool API.

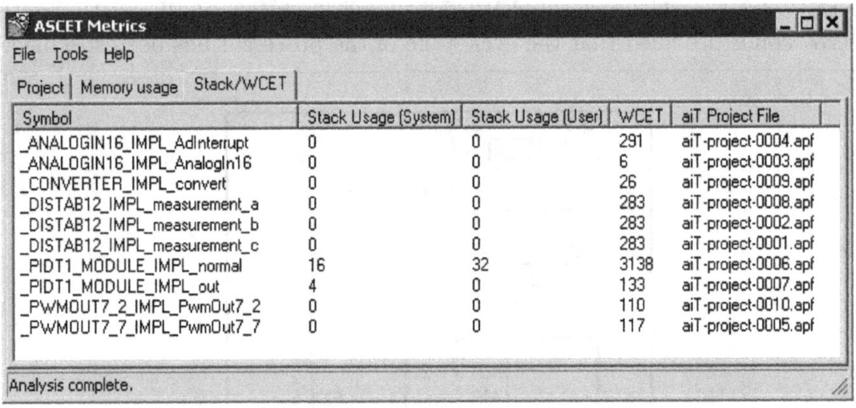
ASCET Metrics
File Tools Help
Project | Memory usage | Stack/WCET
Symbol | Stack Usage (System) | Stack Usage (User) | WCET | aiT Project File
_ANALOGIN16_IMPL_AdInterrupt 0 0 291 aiT-project-0004.apf
_ANALOGIN16_IMPL_AnalogIn16 0 0 6 aiT-project-0003.apf
_CONVERTER_IMPL_convert 0 0 26 aiT-project-0009.apf
_DISTAB12_IMPL_measurement_a 0 0 283 aiT-project-0008.apf
_DISTAB12_IMPL_measurement_b 0 0 283 aiT-project-0002.apf
_DISTAB12_IMPL_measurement_c 0 0 283 aiT-project-0001.apf
_PIDT1_MODULE_IMPL_normal 16 32 3138 aiT-project-0006.apf
_PIDT1_MODULE_IMPL_out 4 0 133 aiT-project-0007.apf
_PWMOUT7_2_IMPL_PwmOut7_2 0 0 110 aiT-project-0010.apf
_PWMOUT7_7_IMPL_PwmOut7_7 0 0 117 aiT-project-0005.apf
Analysis complete.

Fig. 6. Window with analysis results

In addition to the information calculated by **aiT** and **StackAnalyzer**, our tool also analyzes the generated map file to calculate the total memory usage. This tool serves as a one-stop information center that can be used to quickly review the effects of changes made to the project.

The **ASCET** software development framework is specifically suited for the development of real-time systems. The configuration of the operating system necessary for embedded development is directly built into **ASCET** projects. Processes and messages allow interfacing with real-time operating systems based on the OSEK standard. We therefore decided to base our integration on the pre-existing structure of operating system tasks and processes (called by the tasks). This way, the user can quickly check whether the actual worst-case task runtimes clash with the task scheduling periods chosen. It is planned to improve the integration by communicating the calculated WCET information back into **ASCET** to correct or improve the operating system configuration.

4.1 Improving Function Development

For the developer, the immediate and detailed feedback provided helps to find the critical areas of the project where most of the resources are spent. It also can help to decide between different alternatives to solve a given problem. Using model-based design, different modeling techniques can lead to strongly varying code. Here, the information provided by **aiT** and **StackAnalyzer** can help to prototype and develop software more rapidly.

An application of this is given in [16]. For his thesis, Abhik Dey has used our integration of **aiT** into **ASCET** to identify the components of a lambda probe model that need to be optimized for code size and performance. He was able to measure the impact of different modelling techniques as well as compiler settings precisely and managed to reduce the WCET of his complex lambda probe task down by 87% and the code size by 54%.

4.2 Improving the Complete Process

Through our tool, the project manager receives the information necessary to make choices for the project regarding modelling guidelines, code generation settings, compiler tools and compiler settings. By analyzing a set of representative projects, the complete tool chain can be optimized. As **aiT** also takes into account the exact hardware configuration and memory layout, various alternative platforms and configurations can easily be tested to achieve optimal resource usage.

Static analysis tools are also a valuable addition for managers coordinating the development of several pieces of software that will need to work together or even will be distributed on the same ECUs. By establishing memory and runtime quotas for individual parts of the software and checking and enforcing them using **ASCET**, **aiT** and **StackAnalyzer**, it is possible to prevent divergence of the efforts of several teams working on the same project.

4.3 Additional Improvements over Manual Coding

For the calculated WCET and stack usage to be useful, they need to be as close to the realistic model values as possible. Therefore, it is important to improve the precision of the calculation.

Instead of just relying on the C source code, we can make use of the additional information provided by the model, which is usually much more rigidly defined than the resulting C code. One example would be the implementation of physical values as integer values in the program: A temperature ranging from -20.0 to +50.0 in the model might be implemented as a 16 bit integer value in the C code, with appropriate conversions. Such implementations are used even when developing using C. In this case, the developer has to take care that conversions take place in all cases where the value is used. When using model-based development coupled with a code generator, all conversions are taken care of by the code generator automatically. After specifying the range and number of digits, the developer can work with a physical view of the variable.

In this example, the implementation of the physical value does not make use of the full range of the 16 bit integer. Depending on the way that the conversions are performed, this might or might not be obvious to the static analysis tool (and to a less careful human reader of the source code). Model-based development tools are able to supply exact information on the value range used, therefore allowing for higher precision of the analysis results. Further information to be supplied could be the maximum iteration number of loops, possible values of pointers, etc. Normally, **aiT** tries to find such information by static analysis, but relies on user annotations in cases where static analysis does not succeed.

Conversely, the results of **aiT** and **StackAnalyzer** are meant to be used to improve the C code used in the project. A developer working on C code discovering a certain coding pattern to be inefficient has to change every instance of this pattern as well as monitor future changes for instances of the pattern. Using model-based development, this information can be used to improve the implementation of the code generator. To update the C code, it is enough to regenerate it using the new version of the code generator. In addition to this manual improvement process, there are a few instances where it could be possible to use the information gained by static analysis to automatically configure the code generator. One example would be in- and outlining of state machines. Here, there are few rules to choose the implementation with the best performance that apply for all state machines. Instead, the developer could generate different variants of the state machine and choose the parameter setting that results in the code performing best.

We were able to use additional information supplied by the code generator in the context of interpolation routines for characteristic tables. Here, a special loop construct is used in the C code where the loop iteration count depends on the size of the data structures involved. This special loop construct could not be resolved by static analysis, rendering the calculation of loop bounds impossible. By providing annotations on the nature of the loop bounds, we were able to calculate the WCET for the table accesses.

4.4 Experiments

The software used in the experiments was an engine throttle control module specified in **ASCET** and compiled with Tasking compiler v7.5. The compiled code was run on an STM ST10F269 microcontroller board. Run-times were extracted from bus traces made with the ISYSTEMS ILA 128 logic analyzer.

In general, finding a worst-case input for each procedure can be very challenging. In our experiments, we used worst-case path information provided by **aiT** to manually construct a corresponding input.

In order to allow a fully automatic analysis, some adaptations were necessary that are described in the following.

Volatile Variables. Some data structures in the generated code were statically initialized with the `volatile` qualifier. **aiT** uses the values from the initialized data segment of the executable for value analysis, in particular to find infeasible paths and to determine loop bounds. Since **aiT** works on the binary level on which no information about volatile variables is preserved, it requires that all volatile variables be declared as volatile by means of annotations. Without these annotations, the initializations for variables produced by **ASCET** do not lead to the worst-case path.

For example, in the following (simplified) code the variables `active` and `noOfTransfers` were both initialized to zero. Without annotations, **aiT** would consider the `true` branch of the `if` statement as infeasible and derive a loop iteration count of zero.

```
if (active) {
    ...
    dst_ptr = ...;
    adr_ptr = ...;
    end_dst_ptr = dst_ptr + noOfTransfers;
    while (dst_ptr < end_dst_ptr) {
        *dst_ptr++ = *adr_ptr++;
    }
}
```

Currently, volatile annotations must be written manually. For the future, **AS-CET** is expected to pass information about volatiles to **aiT** automatically.

Synchronization. In the following example the boolean variable `_condition` is set externally by another process.

```
while (_condition) {
    ...
}
```

In such a case, an upper bound for the number of loop iterations cannot be determined statically.

This code is used to synchronize processes. Here we use an annotation specifying that this condition is never true. The cost for the synchronization should be taken into account by a system-wide schedulability analysis.

Interpolation Functions. The generated code contains lots of interpolation routines using iterative search algorithms like binary search or linear search. The loop bounds for these algorithms usually depend on some parameters, e.g., the size of the problem in case of binary search. Therefore, **aiT** has been extended by parametric loop bounds featuring an expression instead of a fixed number, for instance

```
loop here max  ceil (log2 (R4/2));
```

In this case, value analysis tries to determine the contents of register R4 at the place of the annotation, and if successful evaluates the expression to obtain a concrete loop bound. Parametric loop bounds can thus be used to specify automatic loop bounds for **ASCET** interpolation routines without effort for **ASCET** users.

4.5   Discussion of the Results

Table 1 shows the results of practical experiments for **aiT**. The measured and analyzed times are given in processor cycles. Overall, the predicted WCET bounds are very precise.

Table 1. Comparison of maximal measured run-times and WCETs predicted by **aiT** (in cycles)

Procedure name	Measured	aiT	Overestimation
_ANALOGIN16_IMPL_AdInterrupt	291	291	0.0%
_ANALOGIN16_IMPL_AnalogIn16	6	6	0.0%
_CONVERTER_IMPL_convert	26	26	0.0%
_DISTAB12_IMPL_measurement_a	263	283	7.6%
_DISTAB12_IMPL_measurement_b	263	283	7.6%
_DISTAB12_IMPL_measurement_c	263	283	7.6%
_PIDT1_MODULE_IMPL_normal	2980	3138	5.3%
_PIDT1_MODULE_IMPL_out	133	133	0.0%
_PWMOUT7_2_IMPL_PwmOut7_2	109	110	0.9%
_PWMOUT7_7_IMPL_PwmOut7_7	116	117	0.9%

Table 2. Comparison of maximal simulated system/user stack usage and usage as predicted by **StackAnalyzer** (in bytes)

Procedure name	Simulated	StackAnalyzer	Overestimation
_ANALOGIN16_IMPL_AdInterrupt	0/0	0/0	0.0%
_ANALOGIN16_IMPL_AnalogIn16	0/0	0/0	0.0%
_CONVERTER_IMPL_convert	0/0	0/0	0.0%
_DISTAB12_IMPL_measurement_a	0/0	0/0	0.0%
_DISTAB12_IMPL_measurement_b	0/0	0/0	0.0%
_DISTAB12_IMPL_measurement_c	0/0	0/0	0.0%
_PIDT1_MODULE_IMPL_normal	16/32	16/32	0.0%
_PIDT1_MODULE_IMPL_out	4/0	4/0	0.0%
_PWMOUT7_2_IMPL_PwmOut7_2	0/0	0/0	0.0%
_PWMOUT7_7_IMPL_PwmOut7_7	0/0	0/0	0.0%

Table 2 compares the results of stack usage analysis with results obtained from simulator runs, showing that the analysis results are precise. All stack sizes are given in bytes. The user stack usage is 0 in most routines since the generated code rarely contains local variables that would be stored on the stack. The system stack usage is 0 in those routines that do not call other routines and therefore never push a return address on the stack.

5 Conclusion

Tools based on abstract interpretation can perform static program analysis of embedded applications. Their results hold for all program runs with arbitrary inputs. Employing static analyzers is thus orthogonal to classical testing, which yields very precise results, but only for selected program runs with specific inputs. The usage of static analyzers enables one to develop complex systems on state-of-the-art hardware, increases safety, and saves development time. Precise stack usage and timing predictions enable the most cost-efficient hardware to be chosen. As recent trends in the automotive industry (e.g., X-by-wire, time-triggered protocols) require knowledge of the WCETs of tasks, a tool like **aiT** is of high importance.

Combined with model-based design and automatic code generation, the potential of static analysis tools is increased greatly: More strict specification and development guidelines enforced by tools like **ASCET** allow for a high precision of the analyzers' estimates as demonstrated by our experiments. The resulting combination allows for the development of more secure and better-performing systems while decreasing time-to-market through enhancing development productivity.

Since memory class information is only finalized in the linking stage, **aiT** and **StackAnalyzer** currently operate on completely linked binaries. This is not always convenient for the user. Many companies rely on a complicated toolchain to create binaries for the embedded platforms. It would be a huge overhead to use this toolchain just to analyze the performance of a single component. We currently research different ways of analyzing single compiled object files, either through direct analysis of the object file or through linking just the object file, ignoring or providing undefined symbols. In both cases, the calculated WCET bounds will be higher (and therefore less exact) due to the information missing from the linking stage. But even those less exact results might help users to improve the performance of their component.

We plan to further improve on the solution that we have developed so far by integrating static analysis tools like **aiT** and **StackAnalyzer** even more tightly into **ASCET**'s development environment. By allowing developers to analyze smaller parts of a model without integrating them into a project, we would be able to decrease turn-around-times for function development even more. We also hope to use the results obtained by **aiT** for semi-automatic OS configuration of the whole project.

Acknowledgments

The collaboration between AbsInt GmbH and Universität des Saarlandes was supported by the Network of Excellence on Embedded Systems Design **ARTIST2**. Collaboration between AbsInt GmbH and ETAS GmbH has been partially supported by the FP6 STREP project **INTEREST** (INTEgrating euRopean Embedded Systems Tools).

References

1. The Motor Industry Software Reliability Association: Guidelines for the Use of the C Language in Critical Systems (2004), ISBN 0-9524156-2-3
2. Wilhelm, R., Engblom, J., Ermedahl, A., Holsti, N., Thesing, S., Whalley, D., Bernat, G., Ferdinand, C., Heckmann, R., Mitra, T., Mueller, F., Puaut, I., Puschner, P., Staschulat, J., Stenström, P.: The worst-case execution time problem - overview of methods and survey of tools. ACM Transactions on Embedded Computing Systems 5, 1–47 (2007)
3. Schätz, B., Hain, T., Prenninger, W., Rappl, M., Romberg, J., Slotosch, O., Strecker, M., Wisspeintner, A., et al.: CASE tools for embedded systems. Technical Report TUMI-0309, Fakultät für Informatik, TU München (2003)
4. Damm, W., Schulte, C., Wittke, H., Segelken, M., Higgen, U., Eckrich, M.: Formale Verifikation von ASCET Modellen im Rahmen der Entwicklung der Aktivlenkung. In: INFORMATIK 2003 – Innovative Informatikanwendungen. Lecture Notes in Informatics, vol. 34, pp. 340–344 (2003)
5. Janz, W.: Das OSEK Echtzeitbetriebssystem, Stackverwaltung und statische Stackbedarfsanalyse. In: Embedded World, Nuremberg, Germany (2003)
6. Wilhelm, R.: Determining bounds on execution times. In: Zurawski, R. (ed.) Handbook on Embedded Systems, pp. 14–23. CRC Press, Boca Raton (2005)
7. Ferdinand, C., Heckmann, R., Langenbach, M., Martin, F., Schmidt, M., Theiling, H., Thesing, S., Wilhelm, R.: Reliable and Precise WCET Determination for a Real-Life Processor. In: Henzinger, T.A., Kirsch, C.M. (eds.) EMSOFT 2001. LNCS, vol. 2211, pp. 469–485. Springer, Heidelberg (2001)
8. Theiling, H.: Extracting Safe and Precise Control Flow from Binaries. In: Proceedings of the 7th Conference on Real-Time Computing Systems and Applications, Cheju Island, South Korea (2000)
9. Ferdinand, C.: Cache Behavior Prediction for Real-Time Systems. PhD thesis, Saarland University (1997)
10. Heckmann, R., Langenbach, M., Thesing, S., Wilhelm, R.: The influence of processor architecture on the design and the results of WCET tools. In: Proceedings of the IEEE, vol. 91(7), pp. 1038–1054 (2003) (Special Issue on Real-Time Systems)
11. Reineke, J., Grund, D., Berg, C., Wilhelm, R.: Predictability of cache replacement policies. Reports of SFB/TR 14 AVACS 9, SFB/TR 14 AVACS, ISSN: 1860-9821 (2006), http://www.avacs.org
12. Schneider, J., Ferdinand, C.: Pipeline Behavior Prediction for Superscalar Processors by Abstract Interpretation. In: Proceedings of the ACM SIGPLAN Workshop on Languages, Compilers and Tools for Embedded Systems, vol. 34, pp. 35–44 (1999)
13. Theiling, H., Ferdinand, C.: Combining abstract interpretation and ILP for microarchitecture modelling and program path analysis. In: Proceedings of the 19th IEEE Real-Time Systems Symposium, Madrid, Spain, pp. 144–153 (1998)
14. Theiling, H.: ILP-based interprocedural path analysis. In: Sangiovanni-Vincentelli, A.L., Sifakis, J. (eds.) EMSOFT 2002. LNCS, vol. 2491, pp. 349–363. Springer, Heidelberg (2002)
15. AbsInt Angewandte Informatik GmbH: aiSee Home Page (2006), http://www.aisee.com
16. Dey, A.: Implementation of control algorithms in production code projects, using case tools with automated code generation. Master's thesis, FHT Esslingen (2006)

Reusable Services and Semi-automatic Service Composition for Automotive Software*

Holger Giese

Hasso Plattner Institute for Software Systems Engineering
at the University of Potsdam,
Prof.-Dr.-Helmert-Str. 2-3,
D-14482 Potsdam,
Germany
holger.giese@hpi.uni-potsdam.de

Abstract. Automotive software has become an important factor in the development of modern and innovative high-end vehicles. More and more functions can only be realized by the cooperation of different control devices. In addition, not only a single product but a number of basic configurations and a large number of optional functions for each new type series have to be addressed by the software. While product lines are a promising approach to address known variability within a car series, the reuse of functions across type series is not feasible with the current proposals. In this paper, a service-oriented approach is sketched which exploits that functions in automotive systems only have to be recombined in a restricted manner in order to enable reuse across car series. Components are used as basic units which provide localized basis functionality, patterns represent reusable assets which capture the interaction and protocols in between several roles, and services capture complex reusable functionality which requires the interaction of multiple units. It is sketched how all phases of the development process can benefit from a service-oriented approach and that advanced synthesis techniques can be employed to reuse the components, patterns and services and compose them with only minimal manual efforts.

1 Introduction

Automotive software has become an important factor in the development of modern high-end vehicles. The size of the software is growing at an exponential rate. Today, about 70% of the innovations in these cars are software driven and an increase of the percentage of costs due to the development of software is expected from 20-25% up to 40% in the next few years (cf. [1,2]).

While, in the past, single control devices had to fulfill a single task only and had been connected to other devices only in rare cases, today more and more

---

* This work was developed in the course of the Special Research Initiative 614 – Self-optimizing Concepts and Structures in Mechanical Engineering – University of Paderborn, and was published on its behalf and funded by the Deutsche Forschungsgemeinschaft.

M. Broy, I.H. Krüger, and M. Meisinger (Eds.): ASWSD 2006, LNCS 4922, pp. 161–181, 2008.

functions can only be realized by the cooperation of different control devices which results in dramatically increasing complexity (cf. [1]).

The software of automotive systems is in fact even more complex, as a car vendor typically offers not only a single product but a number of basic configurations and a large number of optional functions for each new type series. In order to be able to customize the cars such that they are better suited to the specific needs of each customer, not only single software versions but a number of software configurations have to be mastered.

In addition, due to short innovation cycles and high time and costs pressure, productivity is of major importance for automotive software. Increasing reuse at all levels is therefore a valuable objective. The fact that the development of new functions is an exception rather than the regular case in automotive software [3] indicates a high potential for reuse. However, today an open and flexible software architecture which facilitates reuse is often missing and thus many functions are nearly built from scratch for each vehicle model (cf. [1]).

Initiatives such as AUTOSAR[1] are the first step towards and open and flexible software architecture. The definition of standard interfaces for the software components ensures that components from different suppliers and vendors can technically interoperate. However, at the application level the need for an application-specific design of the coordination between these components still hinders reuse.

Also software product families for automotive software (cf. [4]) are a promising direction for different variants of software for a type series. However, the resulting reuse is restricted to a single product family as the software components can only be reused if the architectural context is quite similar. Thus the product-line approach in general can only solve the problem of reuse for a single vendor or when the same standard product-line architecture is employed by all vendors.

However, as innovative solutions in software are a main competitive factor, we cannot assume that for these solutions integration into standard product-line architectures is already at hand when required. This is particularly problematic, as the different software components of a car or car series are developed by a multitude of suppliers within a complex vendor supplier network. Thus in contrast to standard software interfaces, the interfaces must not only serve as means to protect and decouple the components of the developed system from each other in order to handle the development complexity, but to also guarantee that the division of labor can really take place. Thus a solution is required where reuse can also happen at each stage of a complex supplier chain.

The observed limitation for reuse and the needed support for multiple system configurations result in great challenges for the software engineering of automotive software. At first, an approach for the development of the software is required which enables reuse across multiple type series and different software architectures in order to support the requirements of vendors and suppliers. Therefore, the approach must support adjusting of the software such that the required configurations can be derived with minimal effort. In addition, the software design

---

[1] www.autosar.org

and implementation has to be supported in such a manner that each component can be configured to be adjusted to the needs of specific architectures and configurations which might either mean that different levels of service have to be supported or that depending on the configuration a coordination with different other components might be required. Finally, when it comes to the verification of the system, an approach is required such that the verification efforts can be restricted to a limited number of feasible steps for the development artifacts and integrated system which guarantee that each type series and all delivered configurations operate as expected.

This paper outlines how a service-oriented approach can enable the reuse of automotive software within and across type series.[2] It is further discussed which existing solutions can be employed to achieve the outlined goals and how requirements engineering, architectural design, detailed design, implementation, and verification are affected by the proposed service-oriented proceeding.

It is important that the outlined approach does not really introduce a new style of modeling but employs the architectural views as they are already intuitively employed by the engineers when describing the different functions of automotive systems. Instead, the existing views are made explicit by means of the service concept.

The paper is organized as follows: At first in Section 2 an advanced function for a modern vehicle in the form of an intelligent energy-management system is introduced. It is employed in the following Section 3 to introduce and define step-wise the basic concepts for a component-based architecture, its extension with patterns, and finally the employed notion of services and the resulting architecture. Then, in Section 4 the implications of a service-oriented approach are discussed for the life-cycle phases requirements (Section 4.1), architectural design (Section 4.2), fine-grained design and implementation (Section 4.3), and verification & validation (Section 4.4). Finally, the paper discusses related work in Section 5 and some conclusions and an outline of planned future research is presented. Some formal prerequisites are provided in the Appendix.

2   Application Example

The ongoing electrification of more and more vehicle functions such as electric steering, driver-assistance systems, ABS, ESP, etc. creates a plus in functionality but also results in a steadily increasing need for electrical energy. Therefore, today in advanced cars all energy storage devices and energy producers are equipped with monitoring capabilities to ensure proper supervision of the

---

[2] The presented results extend the MECHATRONIC UML approach which supports the description and compositional verification of the real-time coordination by means of components and patterns [5] and the integrated description and modular verification of discrete behavior and continuous control with components [6,7]. As introducing all the required MECHATRONIC UML notations would not be possible with the given space constraints, we will however use standard UML notations and timed automata instead.

power supply for safety-related functions. Examples are systems such as Dynamic Electrical Energy Management[3] from Siemens VDO or eBalance [8] from Hella KGaA Hueck & Co., which guarantee that the storage devices are always properly charged and that, in case of problems, the energy consumption of comfort functions is restricted.

The specific functions such advanced energy-management systems provide are: (1) In specific operation scenarios, it is possible that the energy provided by the generator is not sufficient and the battery has to be used to handle the overload. If a critical load status of the battery and such an overload is detected, the loads due to comfort functions are shut down gradually so that sufficient energy can be provided to primary and safety-relevant systems like the braking system or steering. This reduces the energy load in the vehicle and guarantees that the battery can be properly charged in order to guarantee the long-term operation of the car. (2) Another scenario occurs if the engine is in its idle state. If such a situation and an overload are detected, the energy management system can request to increase the revolutions per minute (rpm) in idle state in order to ensure that the battery is not discharged beyond the safety margins. (3) To allow a safe operation of the electrical safety-critical functions, it is mandatory that these functions are 100% available even if all conventional energy systems fail. Therefore, such systems require a second independent energy storage device that is activated when the standard storage is not available.

In the following we will focus only on the first function and how the realization of the energy management system (EMS) in software is accomplished.

3   Software Architecture

The introduced example of intelligent energy management is now employed to introduce the concepts required for the service-oriented architecture of automotive systems step-wise. Besides introducing the concepts informally, we also provide some basic formalization in order to clarify the introduced concepts.

3.1   Component-Based Architecture

A component-based architecture ensures that the components only interact with their environment via well-defined interfaces (cf. [9]) and thus provide a reasonable decoupling of the different components. Following this principle, an architecture for an intelligent energy-management system inspired by the eBalance system [8] can be derived as depicted in Figure 1 using the UML standard notation for components, ports, and connectors.

A core component serves as the central management unit which controls all consumers and observes all producers. The core may in addition interact with the higher-level vehicle control by providing relevant status information and

---

[3] http://www.siemensvdo.com/products_solutions/chassis-
carbody/body_chassis_electronics/battery-energy-management/Battery-and-
energy-management-BEM.htm

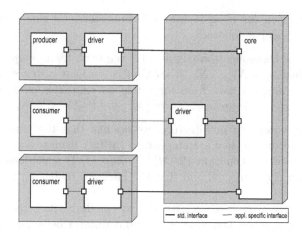

Fig. 1. Component-based architecture for the EMS software (cf. [8])

reading relevant information about the vehicle such as the current operation mode and requested system characteristics (omitted here). In addition, special driver components operate as wrappers to the different energy producers and consumers, and can be either located on the central ECU or on the local ECU of the producer resp. consumer.

Between the driver and core component, a standard protocol can be employed which permits reusing the core in many settings, while the driver components have to be adjusted depending on the application-specific interface they can employ to control and monitor the different producers and consumers.

Assuming that all employed interfaces are defined by a related real-time protocol to encode modes and timing constraints,[4] we can formally define a component as follows:

Definition 1. *A component C is a pair $(\mathcal{M}^C, M^C)$ with a set $\mathcal{M}^C$ of automata $M_1^C, \ldots, M_h^C$ denoting a protocol for each port of the component and the overall component behavior in form of a single automaton M^C.[5]*

While usually in models without time the connector behavior is omitted, channel delay and reliability are of crucial importance for real-time systems and thus have to be addressed explicitly in the form of an additional connector automaton:

Definition 2. *A connector N is a pair $(\mathcal{M}^N, M^N)$ with a pair $\mathcal{M}^N$ of automata M_1^N and M_2^N for each connector end and the connector automaton M^N.*

---

[4] See AUTOSAR modes or UML protocol state machines for related modeling concepts. In addition, the exchanged information (the parameters of the exchanged messages/signals) is assumed to be modeled using an appropriate interface description language (e.g., AUTOSAR).

[5] See Appendix A for the basic definition of automata employed here.

Using the definition for components and connectors, we can thus define the formal system model as follows:[6]

Definition 3. *A component-based system S is a triple $(\mathcal{N}, \mathcal{C}, map)$ with a set $\mathcal{N}$ of connector instances $N_1, \ldots N_n$, a set $\mathcal{C}$ of component instances $C_1, \ldots, C_m$, and a bijective mapping map from the set of all connector automata $\{M_i^N \in \mathcal{M}^N | N \in \mathcal{N}\}$ onto all components ports $\{M_i^C \in \mathcal{M}^C | C \in \mathcal{C}\}$.*

For a correctly composed architecture, we assume that the ports conform to the connector automata they are mapped to (in fact it must hold a refinement relation as defined in Definition 12: $M_i^C \sqsubseteq map(M_i^C)$) which ensures that all signals are properly connected and that the interface match w.r.t. their timing protocols.

Given a correctly composed architecture, we can derive its behavior by simply combining all component behaviors M^{C_i} and connector behaviors M^{N_j}:

$$(\|_{C \in \mathcal{C}} M^C) \quad \| \quad (\|_{N \in \mathcal{N}} M^N).$$

3.2   Pattern-Based Architecture

A component-based architecture focuses on the potential for reuse present in the form of the different components. The protocols and interaction between the components are valuable assets for reuse in practice, too. While for the protocols this reuse often occurs in the form of reuse of the interfaces, for the interaction behavior the potential for reuse at the conceptual level has lead to the concept of patterns [11] and pattern-oriented software architectures [12]. A related architecture which extends the one depicted in Figure 1 by employing patterns is presented in Figure 2 using the UML concept of collaborations for the patterns.

The protocol and role behavior for the interaction between the core and its drivers has become a first class entity of the architecture and thus the reuse that was implicit present before is documented explicitly.

A simplified version of the Consume pattern is depicted in Fig. 3 where instead of different service levels only the normal and critical mode of a consumer are supported using UPPAAL timed automata [13]. In Fig. 3(a), the behavior of the consumer role is depicted. The consumer can stay in mode normal as long as it receives ping events each 2 msec. If not, it has to switch in at most 4 msec to the mode critical, which requires that no energy or only minimal energy is consumed. The connector behavior which could result in a delay of at most 2 msec is depicted in Fig. 3(b). Finally, the possible behavior of the coordinator role is outlined in Fig. 3(c). In normal operation it is required that the ping is sent at least after 2 msec. If the critical mode has been reached, the coordinator will not send the ping events any more.

In our approach, a pattern thus extends the notion of a connector and permits multiple and not only two connection points. It comprises of a set of roles that

---

[6] For the different component and connector instances and their automata, we assume an appropriate labeling (cf. [10]).

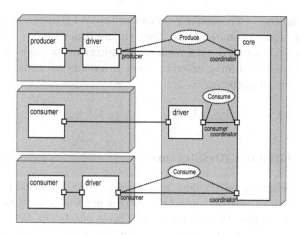

Fig. 2. Pattern-based architecture for the software of the Energy-management system

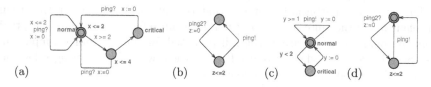

Fig. 3. The Consume pattern with automata for the two roles and the connector

interact only via connectors. The roles will later connect the related component ports in the final system. In addition, the connector behavior which defines the expected channel delays and reliability are also included in the pattern in form of an automaton.

Definition 4. *A pattern P is a pair $(\mathcal{M}^P, M^P)$ with a set $\mathcal{M}^P$ of automata $M_1, \ldots, M_k$ for each role and the connector automaton M^P.*

It is to be noted that the beforehand employed notion of a connector is included in this definition of a pattern. The explicit consideration of a connector further ensures that besides the client and server protocols, the effects of the communication medium are also taken into account. A system with a pattern-based architecture can thus be built by a number of components and patterns which overlap at their ports resp. roles. Using these assumptions, a system can be formally defined as follows:

Definition 5. *A system $\mathcal{S}$ is a triple $(\mathcal{P}, \mathcal{C}, map)$ with a set $\mathcal{P}$ of pattern instances $P_1, \ldots P_n$, a set $\mathcal{C}$ of component instances $C_1, \ldots, C_m$, and a bijective mapping map which maps to each component instance port $\{M_i^C \in \mathcal{M}^C | C \in \mathcal{C}\}$ the related unique pattern instance role $\{M_i^P \in \mathcal{M}^P | P \in \mathcal{P}\}$.*

We further require for a correctly composed pattern-based architecture that the ports conform to the role automata they are mapped to ($M_i^C \sqsubseteq map(M_i^C)$)

which like in the case with connectors ensures that all signals are properly connected and the interface match w.r.t. their timing protocols.

For a correctly composed pattern-based architecture, we can then derive its behavior by simply combining all component behaviors M^{C_i} and the connector behaviors C^{P_j} for all patterns:

$$(\|_{C \in \mathcal{C}} M^C) \quad \| \quad (\|_{P \in \mathcal{P}} M^P).$$

3.3   Service-Oriented Architecture

Following the definition of services in [14], we define a service by "the interaction among entities involved in establishing a particular functionality."[7] The entities are further called the service roles. This general definition includes simple request/response interaction scheme as well as complex coordination patterns between different independent roles [5]. Therefore, this notion of a service can be seen as a generalization of the pattern concept.

The success of patterns has shown that the interaction scheme rather than the elements of that interaction are the right vehicle for reuse at the conceptual level. As depicted in Figure 4, the full potential for reuse in our example can also only be realized when we consider the whole web of interacting roles and embedded components as a reusable asset.

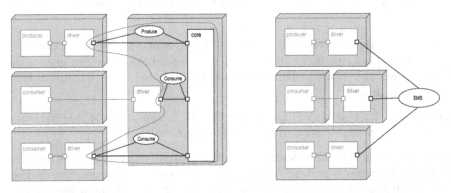

Fig. 4. Service-oriented architecture for the software of the energy management system

While the decomposition of components into a set of subcomponents is simply the standard way how the architectural principle of hierarchical decomposition is employed, applying the same principle to services such that a subset of a system with only unconnected pattern roles results in a *service* is not present in the component- or pattern-based approaches (see Figure 4).

---

[7] It is to be noted that there exist other definitions of the term service which focus more on their run-time composition. However, in the considered domain of automotive software such a restricted view on what constitutes a service is too restrictive.

Definition 6. *A service* W *can thus be defined as a tuple* $(\mathcal{P}, \mathcal{C}, map, \mathcal{R})$ *with* $\mathcal{P}$ *a set of patterns* $P_1, \ldots P_n$, $\mathcal{C}$ *the set of components* $C_1, \ldots, C_m$, *map a injective mapping from the component ports to pattern roles, and* $\mathcal{R}$ *the set of unconnected pattern roles* $M_1^R, \ldots, M_k^R$ *such that a pattern role is either mapped to a port or element of* $\mathcal{R}$.

It is to be noted that like for patterns and connectors the definition of a service includes the one of a pattern as a special case. In addition, it might include components which are essential to achieve the functionality of the service or can contain other services as elements.

The tight relation between the notion of a pattern and the introduced notion of a service can also be seen by the fact that for each service W we can build the related *composed pattern* by $P = (\mathcal{M}^P, M^P)$ as follows:

- $\mathcal{M}^P = \{M_1^R, \ldots, M_h^R\}$ is the set of role protocols and
- M^P is the connector automaton built by $M^{P_1} \| \ldots \| M^{P_n} \| M^{C_1} \| \ldots \| M^{C_m}$.

This mapping permits service definitions which rely on other service definitions and to derive the formalization of a system with services using their related composed pattern.

The producer and consumer components in our example will not only interact with the core of the intelligent energy-management system, but will also interact with other vehicle functions which might also be described as a service. Even though we have the driver components operating as adapters between the specific components and the core, the specific components have to provide sufficient interfaces and internal processing which ensures that a correct coordination with respect to all services it is involved in is guaranteed. This is of course a major hindrance to reuse as the specific components cannot know *a priori* with which services they have to coordinate later on.

In the domain of automotive software, the required integration of the components with all the service roles they realized can be restricted to three cases: (1) the *reading of data* when a given role requires that the component provides some required information to the service, (2) the *writing of data* when the service intents to control a specific parameter of that component, and (3) the *synchronization* of the reactive behavior of the component with the coordination of the service (via the role protocol). The first straightforward solution to avoid this problem is the use of standardized interfaces (e.g., all components are capable of cooperating with a standard interface for energy management). Later in Section 4.2 we will describe our solution which handles this problem by synthesizing the required wrapping behavior to a great extent.

4   Services During the Different Development Phases

The introduced service-oriented description of software makes the overlapping specification of required functionality the rule rather than the exception. In the following, it is outlined how and why this paradigm shift can help in the different development phases to address the problem of many system configurations and reuse across different architectures.

4.1 Requirements Engineering

In requirement engineering for automotive systems, a number of major functions are usually identified and a functional decomposition approach is used to decompose them into smaller functions. At this level, a scenario and service-oriented description is natural, as the requirements do not respect any *a priori* decomposition of the system.

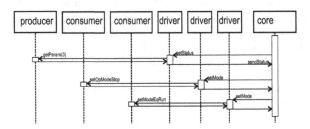

Fig. 5. Service-oriented description of the required behavior by means of scenarios

For our example, a possible scenario of the service is specified in Figure 5. The core is checking the status of the producers and setting the mode for the consumers via the driver components. The driver translates the command to the specific interface of the specific components.

It is to be noted that for the requirements level it might be sufficient to describe the interaction using a number of scenarios. Later, the complete behavior has to be defined using an operational model which, to a certain extent, might be derived using available synthesis approaches (cf. [15,10]).

In addition to the scenarios, required properties of the system might be specified using, for example, temporal logic.

4.2 Architectural Design

When employing the outlined service-oriented approach during the architectural design, complex functions are described as services. Within each service the coordination of the roles by means of command and/or data flow and fully embedded components are specified to make up the service. In this macro view of the architecture, the different roles are mapped on related architectural components or subsystems. How the assigned roles are coordinated is described on the micro architectural level within the components.

Macro Architecture. The assignment of roles to architectural components is described in Figure 6. The producer and consumer component both take over the corresponding role. In the example of Fig. 3, the states of the related role protocols define the permitted energy consumption of the consumer. The states normal and critical imply that the regular amount of memory resp. only a minimal amount of energy or no energy can be consumed (taking only the mechatronic actuators and sensor and not the ECU into account).

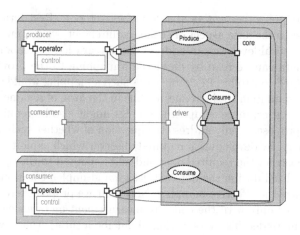

Fig. 6. Service-oriented architecture for the software of the energy-management system with operator and controller micro-architecture

The outlined guarantees for the energy consumption are captured in the approach with So-called *role invariants* (cf. [16,5]). These role invariants capture the constraints which must hold for different operational modes (cf. AUTOSAR). The constraints for the components result from the combination of the different role invariants of its ports. Usually, the simple logical conjunction of the role constraints is sufficient here. In our example, we have to consider for each component which realizes the energy consumer role that its energy consumption in mode critical is minimal denoted by the role invariant (consumer.critical => energy_min).

However, when shared resources are described, also additive constraints are possible. E.g., if one role requires that the energy usage is below a certain threshold and a second role referring to another function of the same component makes a similar constraint, the sum of both thresholds has to be ensured.

Micro Architecture. For the internal architecture of the software components, we propose to distinguish between a *controller* part which provides the permanent service (e.g., a feed-back control algorithm) and an *operator* part which takes care of the mode management of the component, failure management, and the communication with other components (cf. [17]).

In the outlined service-oriented setting, the different roles played by these components via their ports which have their origin in the related system services have to be addressed in the operator part. The controller in contrast realizes the available control strategies and the constraints concerning the switching between them.

Due to the domain-specific restrictions of automotive software concerning the required integration of the reactive behavior of the operator, we thus have to face the following integration problems:

1. A service requires the *reading of data* via a given port. Restricting our attention at first to the data aspect of such a requirement, we can envision that at the architectural level we can address this integration by elaborating which required data can be read by providing a mapping to the provided data of the embedded controller. In simple cases such a mapping would simple relate a provided data item to the requested one in the form of a name mapping. In practice, however, more complex mappings might also be required. In these cases, we propose to only address the question of whether such a mapping is possible (e.g., by developing a required observer which exploits the provided data to construct the required one) and add a method to the operator which is to be realized during the detailed design and implementation stage in order to realize the effective mapping. Note that we propose here to equip the interfaces not only with the concrete measurement units for each value but also with more detailed information about its accuracy (max. value failure, covered frequency spectrum, period, jitter, . . .).

2. A more complicated case is the *writing of data*. A similar mapping of the value including a mapping from the provided must-value of the port to the must-values of the underlying controller can be employed and a corresponding method of the operator must be added. However, if multiple ports want to write a must-value which affects the same provided must-value of the underlying controller, such a straightforward treatment would result in conflicting write requests. Possible strategies to resolve such conflicts are a prioritization of the services. However, this can only resolve the conflict, if the lower priority service includes operation modes which do not result in the conflict. In the next case we will consider such conflicts taking the full reactive behavior related to a port into account.

3. Finally, the reactive behavior of the controller which is responsible for the mode coordination has to resolve all conflicts between the modes of the ports and the controller interface. In addition, the operator has to realize the read and write operations via the ports by mapping them on the available operations of the controller. To address the latter case, the operator has to periodically execute the related mapping methods to propagate the read or written values. If all involved operations are mode-independent, the required propagation can be derived straightforward from the information available in all required interfaces. In contrast, in the latter case – the integration of the remaining reactive behavior which includes the mode-dependent read and writes operations and fulfills the constraints for the modes of the related ports and the controller – is a complicated and error-prone undertaking. We will present our concepts for automatically addressing this issue by an appropriate synthesis algorithm which extends earlier work on the separation

of concerns at the architectural level (cf. [18]). The algorithm at first allows determining whether such integration is possible at all. In addition, the algorithm outputs a synthesis result which is correct by construction.

Existence and Synthesis of the Operator. While the cases 1 and 2 are mainly addressed in the detailed design and implementation (cf. Section 4.3), the existence of a proper realization for the *synchronization* of the ports is of crucial importance and has to be ensured earlier during the architectural design of the system.

Besides the local rules specified for each service role, we may also have more general requirements: e.g., the valid mode combinations for the roles of the multimedia subsystem and the EMS require that the multimedia system is switching to a mode with only minimal energy consumption when the EMS identifies critical conditions. In our example the multimedia component provides an interface and protocol play to start or pause the multimedia presentation which in its core form is depicted in Fig. 7(a).

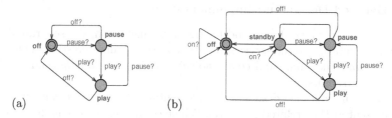

Fig. 7. Two alternative play protocols

Given automata $M_1, \ldots, M_n$ for the ports of a component the algorithm formally defined in [18,19] can be employed to derive an automaton M which refines $M_1 \| \ldots \| M_n$ and fulfills all constraints concerning mode conflicts if such an automaton exists at all (see Appendix A).[8] As such an automaton only describes the *synchronization skeleton* (cf. [20]) of the required operator behavior, the more detailed functional behavior including its functional behavior in the form of the matching methods remains to be integrated also.

The synthesis checks how the main play concern of the multimedia component and the energy management concern (represented by the coordinator role of Fig. 3(a)) can be combined. This combination has to take care that in the case of the critical state of the consumer role the play interface must not be in a state which consumes more than a minimal amount of energy captured by the condition (consumer.critical => energy_min) and ((play.play or play.pause) => not energy_min) (how this condition is derived from the employed pattern roles is

---

[8] For the case without time, we have shown in [18] that due to the construction of an symbolic synthesis algorithm and an appropriate variable ordering for the employed symbolic encoding, an only linear increase for the size of the encoding with respect to the number of involved automata can be guaranteed.

later outlined in Section 4.4). Thus, the states play and pause cannot be combined with the critical mode of the consumer protocol.

In our example, the synthesis reports that there is a conflict. The source of this conflict is that the play protocol is not able to leave the conflicting states play or pause and that even the state off requires that a play request will be granted. In contrast the second variant of the play protocol depicted in Fig. 7(b) can be combined requiring 0.769 sec to run the algorithm. An additional state called standBy which replaces the off state, the modified state off which really covers the idea of an inactive behavior, and transition to this state give the component the degree of freedom to leave the critical states in time. Therefore, the synthesis step is now successful.

In the consider case, the controllers represent reusable assets which can be provided by different suppliers as block-box components. The required integration within the operator in contrast is highly application specific but can be to a great extent automated in such a manner that crucial properties can be guaranteed by construction.

4.3   Detailed Design and Implementation

At the level of detailed design and for the implementation, the separate design and implementation of the services and its roles seems an interesting perspective which supports the often required division of labor between vendors and suppliers resp. subcontractors.

The resulting detailed design and implementation of a service can extend the reuse present at the architectural level. Whole components such as the core may be simply reused.

As outlined for the micro-architecture, the embedded controllers are integrated by the operator which adjusts the interaction in a wrapper-like style. Therefore, the controllers can also be considered reusable assets at the implementation level.

Concerning the operator, the automated synthesis of the reactive synchronization skeletons including the required execution of the mapping methods can be employed. In addition, manual refinement steps can be considered which further restrict the possible behavior while still providing behavioral consistency.

While case 3 is thus more or less covered at the architectural level, the cases 1 and 2 remain to be addressed during the detailed design and implementation. In the case of simple direct mappings, the required code for the methods may be also automatically derived using the mapping tables as input. In the case of more complex functional behavior, either a realization with classical CAE block diagram tools or a programming language are the possible choices.

4.4   Verification

It is important to notice that the verification activities have already been started at the architectural level. Choosing a service-oriented description which decouples the functions and a declarative specification of the constraints concerning that interaction allows us to rule out any other unexpected interference by means of correctness by construction due to the described synthesis step and additional verification steps outlined in the following.

To ensure correctness for a pattern or service, we verify whether the behavioral requirements specified by means of a temporal logic formula ϕ and $\neg\delta$ (denoting deadlock freedom) hold for the related pattern or composed pattern.

Definition 7. *A pattern or composed pattern* $P = (\mathcal{M}^P, M^P)$ *with a set* $\mathcal{M}^P$ *of automata* $M_1^P, \ldots M_k^P$ *is locally correct w.r.t. a constraint* ϕ^P *iff:*

$$M_1^P \| \ldots \| M_k^P \| M^P \models \phi^P \wedge \neg\delta. \tag{1}$$

This can be verified using testing and/or a real-time model checker by building the model $M_1^P \| \ldots \| M_k^P \| M^P$ and then verify whether the constraint $\phi^P \wedge \neg\delta$ holds. For the Consume pattern we can thus verify deadlock freedom as well as the crucial property that a consumer is shutdown after at most 6 msec after this decision has been made by the controller switching into the state critical by checking A[] (coordinator.critical and coordinator.y>6) imply consumer.critical for y the local clock of the coordinator.

While this is rather obvious for a failure-free channel, we can also proof this for a slightly modified connector which also models signal omissions depicted in Fig. 3(d). This allows us to also check whether the protocol is crash resistant and can handle lost messages. A more detailed analysis of the simple pattern would also reveal that the performance of the protocol is not satisfactory as jitter in the channel behavior could result in unnecessary consumer shutdowns.

If for a resulting system $\mathcal{S}$ with behavior $M^{\mathcal{S}}$ holds $M^{\mathcal{S}} \models \phi^P \wedge \neg\delta$ we say that the system *preserves* the correctness of the pattern P.

In addition, the role automata M_i^P may be equipped with role invariants ϕ_i^P which capture the mode specific constraints and guarantees which must hold for any component that realizes that role. In case of the Consume pattern, the consumer role has the invariant consumer.critical => energy_min. In case of the former play protocol the condition will be (play.play or play.pause) => not energy_min.

Besides the patterns, the components also have to be verified. We therefore have to verify that the required constraints ψ^C for the component behavior which results from the invariants of the related roles hold.

$$\psi^C = \bigwedge_{M_j^P = map(M_i^C) \wedge M_i^C \in \mathcal{M}^C} \phi_j^P.$$

In addition, the component must refine each port automaton (cf. $\sqsubseteq_{I/O}$ in Definition 13) denoted by the following notion of a correct component.

Definition 8. *A component* $C = (\mathcal{M}^C, M^C)$ *with a set* $\mathcal{M}^C$ *of automata* $M_1^C, \ldots, M_h^C$ *for the ports is locally correct w.r.t. a condition* ψ^C *iff:*

$$M^C \sqsubseteq_{I/O} M_1^C \| \ldots \| M_h^C \quad and \quad M^C \models \psi^C \wedge \neg\delta \tag{2}$$

We can again use testing and/or a real-time model checker to prove $\psi^C \wedge \neg\delta$ for M^C. To ensure that M^C refines each of the role protocols associated to its ports we can also use available automated refinement checks [21].

If for a resulting system $\mathcal{S}$ with behavior $M^{\mathcal{S}}$ holds $M^{\mathcal{S}} \models \psi^{C_j} \wedge \neg\delta$ we say that the system *preserves* the correctness of the component $\mathcal{C}_j$.

The *correctness* of the wiring can be checked statically if the correct connection of the ports and roles has been verified and is defined as follows:

Definition 9. *A system* $\mathcal{S} = (\mathcal{P}, \mathcal{C}, map)$ *is correctly composed iff map is a partial bijective mapping between the set of all ports of any component instance in* $\mathcal{C}$ *and the set of all pattern instance roles of* $\mathcal{P}$. *The mapping must further ensure that the pattern role are valid refinements of the related port protocols:*

$$\forall M_k^{P_i} = map(M_h^{C_j}) : M_h^{C_j} \sqsubseteq M_k^{P_i}.$$

If map is total we have a closed *system where each component instance port is uniquely mapped to a compatible pattern instance role.*

The *correctness* of a correctly composed system w.r.t. the pattern invariants and the component invariants is defined as follows:

Definition 10. *For a correctly composed system* $\mathcal{S} = (\mathcal{P}, \mathcal{C}, map)$ *with a set* $\mathcal{P}$ *of pattern instances* $P_1, \ldots P_n$, *a set* $\mathcal{C}$ *of component instances* $C_1, \ldots, C_m$, *and a bijective mapping map is* globally correct *iff the pattern constraints* ϕ_i^P *and component invariants* ψ_j^C *also hold for the system itself:*

$$M^{P_1} \| \ldots \| M^{P_n} \| M^{C_1} \| \ldots \| M^{C_m} \models \phi^{P_1} \wedge \cdots \wedge \phi^{P_n} \wedge \neg\delta \text{ and} \qquad (3)$$

$$M^{P_1} \| \ldots \| M^{P_n} \| M^{C_1} \| \ldots \| M^{C_m} \models \psi^{C_1} \wedge \cdots \wedge \psi^{C_m}. \qquad (4)$$

Note that the conditions 3 and 4 are by construction fulfilled by the synthesis considered earlier where $\psi^{C_1} \wedge \cdots \wedge \psi^{C_m}$ equals (consumer.critical => energy_min) and ((play.play or play.pause) => not energy_min).

Due to the compositional nature of our approach, only a verification of the local correctness of the patterns and components as well as the correct composition is required to ensure global correctness.

Theorem 1. *(from [5,22]) A correctly composed closed system* $\mathcal{S} = (\mathcal{P}, \mathcal{C}, map)$ *with a set* $\mathcal{P}$ *of locally correct pattern instances* $P_1, \ldots P_n$ *and a set* $\mathcal{C}$ *of locally correct component instances* $C_1, \ldots, C_m$ *is globally correct.*

This result can be used to compositionally verify required properties. It not only ensures the scalability of the approach (cf. [22]) but also permits restricting the required verification efforts in the case of changes, as only the modified patterns, services and components affected by the changes of its roles have to be verified again.

5   Related Work

The outlined approach employs the concept of port protocols. This concept has already been advocated for embedded real-time systems in the ROOM approach [23] and has also finally found its way in the UML in the form of protocol state machines. A more formal source for such a proceeding are interface automata [24], which provide in combination with compatibility checks a number of advantages similar to the presented approach. However, these approaches remain rooted in the component-based architectural view, while the presented approach supports services.

A number of results concerning the service-oriented development of automotive software targeting the requirement and architecture phases exist (cf. [25,26,27]). In [27] aspect weaving is employed to derive the first behavioral prototypes which can help to guide early architectural decisions. The resulting prototypes are evaluated to detect inconsistencies which result from their overlapping and possibly conflicting behavior. The presented approach in contrast suggests equipping the patterns and services with additional constraints in the form of pattern invariants and role invariants which can then be systematically checked by a compositional verification approach. To ease the integration of a single component into multiple services, in contrast to the validation via prototyping the presented approach presents a synthesis algorithm which helps to identify whether a consistent behavior is possible at all and the correct by construction synthesis result can serve as a starting point for realizing the required coordination within the component in the operator.

6   Conclusion

While the envisioned solution provides a number of conceptual benefits such as support for many variants and reuse across type series, which makes it especially attractive and beneficial for automotive software, the outlined vision for the service-oriented development of automotive software still has to be further elaborated and evaluated. In particular, a tighter integration with approaches which address the earlier phases [25,26,27] is required to enable a seamless development of automotive software with reusable services.

It is to be stressed that the introduced concepts are to some extent already implicitly present in the employed example. We claim here that a service-oriented view of the example is not only the result of the employed concepts but already inherently present in the function-oriented description chosen by the engineers (cf. [8]). Therefore, we are optimistic that switching to a service-oriented view for the architectural descriptions of the system is possible in practice without a great cultural change.

Acknowledgement

I hereby thank Andreas Seibel for developing the employed real-time synthesis tool (cf. [19]) and his support with the application example.

References

1. Grimm, K.: Software technology in an automotive company: major challenges. In: ICSE 2003: Proceedings of the 25th International Conference on Software Engineering, Washington, DC, USA, pp. 498–503. IEEE Computer Society, Los Alamitos (2003)
2. Hardung, B., Kölzow, T., Krüger, A.: Reuse of software in distributed embedded automotive systems. In: EMSOFT 2004: Proceedings of the 4th ACM international conference on Embedded software, pp. 203–210. ACM Press, New York (2004)
3. Weber, M., Weisbrod, J.: Requirements engineering in automotive development: Experiences and challenges. IEEE Software 20, 16–24 (2003)
4. Thiel, S., Hein, A.: Modeling and using product line variability in automotive systems. IEEE Software 19, 66–72 (2002)
5. Giese, H., Tichy, M., Burmester, S., Schäfer, W., Flake, S.: Towards the Compositional Verification of Real-Time UML Designs. In: Proc. of the 9th European software engineering conference held jointly with 11th ACM SIGSOFT international symposium on Foundations of software engineering (ESEC/FSE-11), pp. 38–47. ACM Press, New York (2003)
6. Burmester, S., Giese, H., Oberschelp, O.: Hybrid UML Components for the Design of Complex Self-optimizing Mechatronic Systems. In: Informatics in Control, Automation and Robotics, Springer, Heidelberg (2006)
7. Giese, H., Burmester, S., Schäfer, W., Oberschelp, O.: Modular Design and Verification of Component-Based Mechatronic Systems with Online-Reconfiguration. In: FSE 2004, pp. 179–188. ACM Press, New York (2004)
8. Rosenmayr, M., Schöllmann, M., Schmidt, R.: Intelligentes energiemanagement. In: Internationaler CTI-Automobil-Technologie-Kongress AutoTec. (2005)
9. Szyperski, C.: Component Software, Beyond Object-Oriented Programming. Addison-Wesley, Reading (1998)
10. Giese, H.: Towards Scenario-Based Synthesis for Parametric Timed Automata. In: Proc. of the 2nd International Workshop on Scenarios and State Machines: Models, Algorithms, and Tools (SCESM), Portland, USA (ICSE 2003 Workshop 8) (2003)
11. Gamma, E., Helm, R., Johnson, R., Vlissides, J.: Design Patterns, Elements of Reusable Object-Oriented Software. Addison-Wesley, Reading (1994)
12. Buschmann, F., Meunier, R., Rohnert, H., Somerlad, P., Stal, M.: Pattern-Oriented Software Architecture - A System of Patterns, 1st edn. John Wiley & Sons, Inc, Chichester (1996)
13. Larsen, K., Pettersson, P., Yi, W.: UPPAAL in a Nutshell. Springer International Journal of Software Tools for Technology 1 (1997)
14. Deubler, M., Meisinger, M., Rittmann, S., Krüger, I.: Modeling Crosscutting Services with UML Sequence Diagrams. In: Briand, L.C., Williams, C. (eds.) MoDELS 2005. LNCS, vol. 3713, pp. 522–536. Springer, Heidelberg (2005)
15. Krüger, I.H., Mathew, R.: Component Synthesis from Service Specifications. In: Leue, S., Systä, T.J. (eds.) Scenarios: Models, Transformations and Tools. LNCS, vol. 3466, pp. 255–277. Springer, Heidelberg (2005)
16. Giese, H.: A Formal Calculus for the Compositional Pattern-Based Design of Correct Real-Time Systems. Technical Report tr-ri-03-240, Lehrstuhl für Softwaretechnik, Universität Paderborn, Paderborn, Deutschland (2003)
17. Hestermeyer, T., Oberschelp, O., Giese, H.: Structured Information Processing For Self-optimizing Mechatronic Systems. In: Araujo, H., Vieira, A., Braz, J., Encarnacao, B., Carvalho, M. (eds.) Proc. of 1st International Conference on Informatics in Control, Automation and Robotics (ICINCO 2004), Setubal, Portugal, pp. 230–237. INSTICC Press (2004)

18. Giese, H., Vilbig, A.: Separation of Non-Orthogonal Concerns in Software Architecture and Design. In: Software and System Modeling (SoSyM), pp. 136–169 (2006)
19. Seibel, A.: Behavioral synthesis of potential component real-time behavior. Master's thesis, University of Paderborn, Department of Computer Science, Paderborn, Germany (2007)
20. Emerson, E.A., Clarke, E.M.: Using branching time temporal logic to synthesize synchronization skeletons. Science of Computer Programming 2, 241–266 (1982)
21. Giese, H., Hirsch, M.: Modular Verification of Safe Online-Reconfiguration for Proactive Components in Mechatronic UML. In: Bruel, J.-M. (ed.) MoDELS 2005. LNCS, vol. 3844, pp. 67–78. Springer, Heidelberg (2006)
22. Giese, H., Schilling, D., Tichy, M., Burmester, S., Schäfer, W., Flake, S.: Towards the compositional verification of real-time uml designs. Technical Report tr-ri-03-241, Lehrstuhl für Softwaretechnik, Universität Paderborn, Paderborn, Deutschland (2003)
23. Selic, B., Gullekson, G., Ward, P.: Real-Time Object-Oriented Modeling. John Wiley and Sons, Inc., Chichester (1994)
24. de Alfaro, L., Henzinger, T.A.: Interface automata. In: ESEC/FSE-9: Proceedings of the 8th European software engineering conference held jointly with 9th ACM SIGSOFT international symposium on Foundations of software engineering, pp. 109–120. ACM Press, New York (2001)
25. Krüger, I.H., Nelson, E., Prasad, K.V.: Service-based software development for automotive applications. In: Proceedings of Convergence (2004)
26. Krüger, I.: Service-oriented software and systems engineering - a vision for the automotive domain. In: 3rd ACM & IEEE International Conference on Formal Methods and Models for Co-Design (MEMOCODE 2005). Proceedings, Verona, Italy, July 11-14, 2005, p. 150. IEEE, Los Alamitos (2005)
27. Krüger, I.H., Mathew, R., Meisinger, M.: Efficient exploration of service-oriented architectures using aspects. In: ICSE 2006: Proceeding of the 28th international conference on Software engineering, pp. 62–71. ACM Press, New York (2006)
28. Giese, H., Hirsch, M.: Checking and Automatic Abstraction for Timed and Hybrid Refinement in Mechtronic UML. Technical Report tr-ri-03-266, University of Paderborn, Paderborn, Germany (2005)

A   Appendix

The following notion of a discrete real-time automaton is used to describe the required real-time behavioral of a systems and its elements, the refinement and the basic idea of the synthesis algorithm. For a more detailed formal treatment which includes the dense time case please see [28,19].

Definition 11. *A real-time automaton is a 7-tuple* $M = (S, I, O, T, Q)$ *with a finite set* S *of states, a finite set* I *of input signals, a finite set* O *of output signals, a finite set of transitions* $T \subseteq S \times \wp(I) \times \wp(O) \times S$, *and the initial state set* Q.

Within the presented formal model signals are used to describe the synchronization of a real-time automaton with its environment. A restriction operator can be further used to abstract from signals where required. For an automaton $M = (S, I, O, T, Q)$ we define its *I/O restriction* for I''/O'' denoted by $M|_{I''/O''}$ as the automaton (S', I', O', T', Q') with $S' = S$, $I' = I \cap I''$, $O' = O \cap O''$, $Q' = Q$, and $(s_1, A', B', s_2) \in T'$ iff $(s_1, A, B, s_2) \in T$ exists with $A' = A - I''$ and $B' = B - O''$. Using the restriction operator, we further define the *hiding* $M_i \backslash_{I/O}$ as $M_i|_{I_i - I/O_i - O}$.

An appropriate notion for refinement has to ensure two fundamental properties. (1) We require that each behavior of the refining behavior can be observed in the original one and (2) if the original behavior offers a transition with specific input and output signals the refining behavior must also offer a transition with the same I/O signal sets to ensure that deadlock freedom is preserved. When both requirements are fulfilled, a notion of refinement which is strong enough to preserve deadlock freedom and weak enough to permit further refinements results.

The employed notion of refinement is defined as follows:

Definition 12. *For automata* $M = (S, I, O, T, Q)$ *and* $M' = (S', I', O', T', Q')$ *we call* M *a refinement of* M' *denoted by* $M \sqsubseteq M'$ *iff a relation* $\Omega \subseteq S \times S'$ *exists with* $\forall q \in Q \ \exists q' \in Q' : (q, q') \in \Omega$ *and for all* $(s_1, s_1') \in \Omega$ *holds:*

$$\forall (s_1, A, B, s_2) \in T \quad \exists (s_1', A, B, s_2') \in T' : (s_2, s_2') \in \Omega, \tag{5}$$

$$\forall (s_1', A', B', s_3') \in T' \quad \exists (s_1, A', B', s_3) \in T. \tag{6}$$

The relation Ω initially ensures that for each initial state of the refinement an appropriate interpretation in terms of the initial state of the refined automaton exists. For each transition in the refinement M equation 5 further ensures that a related transition in M' exists that again leads to an appropriate state pair in Ω.

Equation 6 further ensures that for each pair of I/O signal sets offered by a state in M' a corresponding transition offering the same pair of I/O signal sets is provided in its refinement M. However, the condition does not itself require that s_3 and s_3' build a pair contained in Ω.

To have a refinement notion that permits the refined behavior to extend the original one, we have to combine refinement with abstraction using the restriction operator $|$.

Definition 13. *For automata* $M = (S, I, O, T, Q)$ *and* $M' = (S', I', O', T', Q')$ *we name* M *an I/O refinement of automaton* M' *denoted by* $M \sqsubseteq_{I/O} M'$ *iff* $M|_{I'/O'} \sqsubseteq M'$.

The I/O refinement adjusts the considered signals and can be further used to characterize if an automaton is a correct concretization of another one.

The refinement notion results in a partial ordering on the set of all automata. Therefore, w.r.t. a specific invariant ψ we are able to derive the maximal refined automaton M' that satisfies ψ and also refines a given automaton M as follows:

We start the processing simply with $S_0 = \{s \in S \mid M, s \models \psi\}$. Then, we compute the largest fix-point for a property ψ and condition 6 with the following step:

$$S_{i+1} = \{s_1 \in S_i | \forall (s_1, A, B, s_2) \in T \; \exists (s_1, A, B, s_2') \in T : s_2' \in S_i\}$$

When a fix-point with $S_{i+1} = S_i$ is reached, a maximal automaton M' which refines M has been computed. For the automaton M' further holds $M' \models \psi$.

It is to be noted that the proof that the above algorithm does indeed compute the maximal refinement requires that the implicitly defined function $(f_{\sqsubseteq, \psi}(S_i) := \{s_1 \in S_i | \forall (s_1, A, B, s_2) \in T \; \exists (s_1, A, B, s_2') \in T : s_2' \in S_i\})$ on the state set is monotonous and determines uniquely which states have to be erased.

Author Index

Lecture Notes in Computer Science

Sublibrary 3: Information Systems and Application, incl. Internet/Web and HCI

For information about Vols. 1– 4717
please contact your bookseller or Springer

Vol. 4892: A. Popescu-Belis, S. Renals, H. Bourlard (Eds.), Machine Learning for Multimodal Interaction. XI, 308 pages. 2008.

Vol. 4882: T. Janowski, H. Mohanty (Eds.), Distributed Computing and Internet Technology. XIII, 346 pages. 2007.

Vol. 4881: H. Yin, P. Tino, E. Corchado, W. Byrne, X. Yao (Eds.), Intelligent Data Engineering and Automated Learning - IDEAL 2007. XX, 1174 pages. 2007.

Vol. 4877: C. Thanos, F. Borri, L. Candela (Eds.), Digital Libraries: Research and Development. XII, 350 pages. 2007.

Vol. 4872: D. Mery, L. Rueda (Eds.), Advances in Image and Video Technology. XXI, 961 pages. 2007.

Vol. 4871: M. Cavazza, S. Donikian (Eds.), Virtual Storytelling. XIII, 219 pages. 2007.

Vol. 4858: X. Deng, F.C. Graham (Eds.), Internet and Network Economics. XVI, 598 pages. 2007.

Vol. 4857: J.M. Ware, G.E. Taylor (Eds.), Web and Wireless Geographical Information Systems. XI, 293 pages. 2007.

Vol. 4853: F. Fonseca, M.A. Rodríguez, S. Levashkin (Eds.), GeoSpatial Semantics. X, 289 pages. 2007.

Vol. 4836: H. Ichikawa, W.-D. Cho, I. Satoh, H.Y. Youn (Eds.), Ubiquitous Computing Systems. XIII, 307 pages. 2007.

Vol. 4832: M. Weske, M.-S. Hacid, C. Godart (Eds.), Web Information Systems Engineering – WISE 2007 Workshops. XV, 518 pages. 2007.

Vol. 4831: B. Benatallah, F. Casati, D. Georgakopoulos, C. Bartolini, W. Sadiq, C. Godart (Eds.), Web Information Systems Engineering – WISE 2007. XVI, 675 pages. 2007.

Vol. 4825: K. Aberer, K.-S. Choi, N. Noy, D. Allemang, K.-I. Lee, L. Nixon, J. Golbeck, P. Mika, D. Maynard, R. Mizoguchi, G. Schreiber, P. Cudré-Mauroux (Eds.), The Semantic Web. XXVII, 973 pages. 2007.

Vol. 4823: H. Leung, F. Li, R. Lau, Q. Li (Eds.), Advances in Web Based Learning – ICWL 2007. XIV, 654 pages. 2008.

Vol. 4822: D.H.-L. Goh, T.H. Cao, I.T. Sølvberg, E. Rasmussen (Eds.), Asian Digital Libraries. XVII, 519 pages. 2007.

Vol. 4820: T.G. Wyeld, S. Kenderdine, M. Docherty (Eds.), Virtual Systems and Multimedia. XII, 215 pages. 2008.

Vol. 4816: B. Falcidieno, M. Spagnuolo, Y. Avrithis, I. Kompatsiaris, P. Buitelaar (Eds.), Semantic Multimedia. XII, 306 pages. 2007.

Vol. 4813: I. Oakley, S.A. Brewster (Eds.), Haptic and Audio Interaction Design. XIV, 145 pages. 2007.

Vol. 4810: H.H.-S. Ip, O.C. Au, H. Leung, M.-T. Sun, W.-Y. Ma, S.-M. Hu (Eds.), Advances in Multimedia Information Processing – PCM 2007. XXI, 834 pages. 2007.

Vol. 4809: M.K. Denko, C.-s. Shih, K.-C. Li, S.-L. Tsao, Q.-A. Zeng, S.H. Park, Y.-B. Ko, S.-H. Hung, J.-H. Park (Eds.), Emerging Directions in Embedded and Ubiquitous Computing. XXXV, 823 pages. 2007.

Vol. 4808: T.-W. Kuo, E. Sha, M. Guo, L.T. Yang, Z. Shao (Eds.), Embedded and Ubiquitous Computing. XXI, 769 pages. 2007.

Vol. 4806: R. Meersman, Z. Tari, P. Herrero (Eds.), On the Move to Meaningful Internet Systems 2007: OTM 2007 Workshops, Part II. XXXIV, 611 pages. 2007.

Vol. 4805: R. Meersman, Z. Tari, P. Herrero (Eds.), On the Move to Meaningful Internet Systems 2007: OTM 2007 Workshops, Part I. XXXIV, 757 pages. 2007.

Vol. 4804: R. Meersman, Z. Tari (Eds.), On the Move to Meaningful Internet Systems 2007: CoopIS, DOA, ODBASE, GADA, and IS, Part II. XXIX, 683 pages. 2007.

Vol. 4803: R. Meersman, Z. Tari (Eds.), On the Move to Meaningful Internet Systems 2007: CoopIS, DOA, ODBASE, GADA, and IS, Part I. XXIX, 1173 pages. 2007.

Vol. 4802: J.-L. Hainaut, E.A. Rundensteiner, M. Kirchberg, M. Bertolotto, M. Brochhausen, Y.-P.P. Chen, S.S.-S. Cherfi, M. Doerr, H. Han, S. Hartmann, J. Parsons, G. Poels, C. Rolland, J. Trujillo, E. Yu, E. Zimányie (Eds.), Advances in Conceptual Modeling – Foundations and Applications. XIX, 420 pages. 2007.

Vol. 4801: C. Parent, K.-D. Schewe, V.C. Storey, B. Thalheim (Eds.), Conceptual Modeling - ER 2007. XVI, 616 pages. 2007.

Vol. 4797: M. Arenas, M.I. Schwartzbach (Eds.), Database Programming Languages. VIII, 261 pages. 2007.

Vol. 4796: M. Lew, N. Sebe, T.S. Huang, E.M. Bakker (Eds.), Human–Computer Interaction. X, 157 pages. 2007.

Vol. 4794: B. Schiele, A.K. Dey, H. Gellersen, B. de Ruyter, M. Tscheligi, R. Wichert, E. Aarts, A. Buchmann (Eds.), Ambient Intelligence. XV, 375 pages. 2007.

Vol. 4777: S. Bhalla (Ed.), Databases in Networked Information Systems. X, 329 pages. 2007.

Vol. 4761: R. Obermaisser, Y. Nah, P. Puschner, F.J. Rammig (Eds.), Software Technologies for Embedded and Ubiquitous Systems. XIV, 563 pages. 2007.

Vol. 4747: S. Džeroski, J. Struyf (Eds.), Knowledge Discovery in Inductive Databases. X, 301 pages. 2007.

Vol. 4744: Y. de Kort, W. IJsselsteijn, C. Midden, B. Eggen, B.J. Fogg (Eds.), Persuasive Technology. XIV, 316 pages. 2007.

Vol. 4740: L. Ma, M. Rauterberg, R. Nakatsu (Eds.), Entertainment Computing – ICEC 2007. XXX, 480 pages. 2007.

Vol. 4730: C. Peters, P. Clough, F.C. Gey, J. Karlgren, B. Magnini, D.W. Oard, M. de Rijke, M. Stempfhuber (Eds.), Evaluation of Multilingual and Multi-modal Information Retrieval. XXIV, 998 pages. 2007.

Vol. 4723: M. R. Berthold, J. Shawe-Taylor, N. Lavrač (Eds.), Advances in Intelligent Data Analysis VII. XIV, 380 pages. 2007.

Vol. 4721: W. Jonker, M. Petković (Eds.), Secure Data Management. X, 213 pages. 2007.

Vol. 4718: J. Hightower, B. Schiele, T. Strang (Eds.), Location- and Context-Awareness. X, 297 pages. 2007.